Duncan Petersen's

CHARMING SMALL HOTEL GUIDES

AUSTRIA, SWITZERLAND & THE ALPS

Duncan Petersen's

CHARMING SMALL HOTEL GUIDES

AUSTRIA, SWITZERLAND & THE ALPS

Fiona Duncan

Duncan Petersen

1st edition

Conceived, designed and produced by
Duncan Petersen Publishing Ltd,
Studio 6, 82 Silverthorne Road, Battersea, SW3 8HE

Editorial director Andrew Duncan
Series editor Fiona Duncan
Contributing editor Claire Rogers
Production editor Claire Rogers
Designer Lizzie Ballantyne
Cover design Nicky Collings
Maps Map Creation Ltd
Photo credits see below for individual credits

A CIP catalogue record for this book is available
from the British Library

ISBN 978-0-9575759-0-5

DTP by Duncan Petersen Publishing Ltd
Printed by Imprint Academic Ltd

Loos Haus credit: www.redtenbacher.net
Cover photos: LeCrans Hotel & Spa (front), Hotel Zistelalm (back),
Grafenast (spine)

Contents

Introduction

In this introductory section:

Welcome to this first edition of *Charming Small Hotel Guides Austria, Switzerland & the Alps*. It combines (and replaces) two previously published *Charming Small Hotel Guides*, one covering Austria and one covering Switzerland. It is the only English-language guide to charming places to stay in those two countries, and to the Alps in their own right. To complete the coverage of the mountains, we have included places to stay in the French, Italian and German Alps.

Of course, Austria and Switzerland are not all Alpine, and you'll find here many recommendations in the lowland areas, including the cities – Vienna, Geneva, Lausanne, and so on.

However, the Alps as a tourist destination – the summer and winter playground of Europe regardless of national borders – are now so well established that they deserve a guide that brings together their most interesting accommodation for the independent traveller. Alpine holidays are easy with internet booking of flights and accommodation – especially with regular bus links between airports and major resorts.

Though innovative in its content, this guide remains true to the values of the other five in the series (Britain & Ireland, France, Germany, Italy and Spain), which have won them many followers. The first *Charming Small Hotel Guides* were published in 1986, so the series has an exceptional record, selling hundreds of thousands in the UK, the USA and in five European languages. The guides are now reaching a new market as ebooks for different devices, including smartphones.

This title covers our usual range of charming places to stay, plus a sprinkling of self-catering chalets and apartment houses. These are for families and individuals staying a week or more on a winter sports or summer walking holiday, who often prefer the independence, privacy and economy that self-catering offers.

Why are we unique?

This is the only independent (no hotel pays for an entry) UK-originated accommodation guide that:

• concentrates on places that have real charm and character;

• is fussy about size and highly selective. Most hotels have fewer than 30 bedrooms; if there are more, for example in cities and ski resorts, the hotel must have the feel of a much smaller place. Time and again we find that a genuinely warm welcome is *much* more likely to be found in a small hotel;

• gives proper emphasis to description – doesn't use irritating symbols;

• is produced by a small company with like-minded reporters.

Above all, the text doesn't read as if it's an advert, paid for by the hotel, which is the case with most other guides. Our reviews are honest: objective, distanced and they mention negatives *and* positives.

So what exactly do we look for?
Our selection criteria

• A peaceful, attractive setting. Obviously, if the entry is in an urban area, we make allowances.

• A building that is handsome, interesting, historic or characterful.

• Adequate space, but on a human scale. We don't go for places that rely too much on grandeur.

• Good taste and imagination in the interior decoration. We reject standardized, chain hotel fixtures, fittings and decorations.

• Bedrooms that look like real bedrooms, not hotel rooms, individually decorated.

• Furnishings and other facilities that are comfortable and well maintained. We like to see interesting antique furniture that is there to be used, not simply revered.

• Proprietors and staff who are dedicated and thoughtful, offering a personal welcome, but who aren't intrusive or overly effusive.

• A sympathetic atmosphere; an absence of loud people showing off their money; or the 'corporate feel'.

• If it's self-catering, added value.

Introduction

No fear or favour

To us, taking a payment for appearing in a guide seems to defeat the object of producing a guide. If money has changed hands, you can't write the whole truth about a hotel, and the selection cannot be nearly so interesting. This seems to us to be proved at least in part by the fact that pay guides are so keen to present the illusion of independence: most only admit taking payment in small print inside.

Types of accommodation in this guide

Despite its title, the guide does not confine itself to hotels or places that behave like hotels. On the contrary, we actively look for places that offer a home-from-home. We include small and medium-size hotels; traditional guesthouses (*gästehaus*) – some offering just bed and breakfast, some offering food at other times of the day, too; restaurants with rooms; and self-catering apartments.

The Austrian and Swiss hotel scene

There is a long and impressive tradition of family-run accommodation of all sorts in the lowlands and mountains of Austria and Switzerland, and indeed in the mountains of France, Italy and Germany. Naturally, these old inns and hotels, in the same family for generations, perhaps with their origins in farm buildings, play a big part in our selections. In the best, standards of welcome and service remain as high as ever – hosts can't do enough for their guests. Of course, for many of us, an exceptional place to stay combined with the clean air and beauty of the mountains makes for the most magical experience of all.

Perhaps the most dominant (relatively) new theme in Alpine hotels is spa and 'wellness' facilities, together with 'bio' or organic food. Some places, as elsewhere in Europe, feel they can't compete without them. This guide is not over-impressed with such add-ons: we are more interested in the essentials described on page 7.

Self-catering is mixed in quality all over the Alps. There are too many ill-equipped, dirty, cramped flats charging too much money because they're close to ski lifts. Exceptional charm and added value is hard to find – but we've tried. Let us know if you find anywhere exceptional – we would like to build up our collection.

In ski resorts, many hotels and guesthouses of all types are generally pleasant enough, but formulaic. Once again, our aim has been to single out places offering something out of the ordinary.

Introduction

Check the price first

In this guide we have used price bands, rather than giving actual prices. This is because prices are often subject to change. The price bands refer to the approximate price of a standard double room (high season rates) with breakfast for two people. They are as follows:

€	under €110	F	under 100 CHF
€€	€110-180	FF	100-200 CHF
€€€	€180-260	FFF	200-300 CHF
€€€€	€260-350	FFFF	300-400 CHF
€€€€€	more than €350	FFFFF	more than 400 CHF

To avoid unpleasant surprises, always check what is included in the price (for example, VAT and service, breakfast, wi-fi) when booking.

How to find an entry

In this guide, the entries are arranged by geographical and regional groups. At the top right of the page is the country e.g. Austria, Switzerland, or French, Italian & German Alps; on the left is the region e.g. Vorarlberg, Kärnten, Suisse Romande, Graubünden, French Alps, Italian Alps, German Alps.

Using the guide

We use three different hotel entry formats in order to give you the richest content. Always begin with the maps on pages 13-18 – they show the locations of all the hotels in the guide. **Whole pages** are the cream of our selection – mainstream charming small hotels that tick all or most of our boxes. **Half pages** shouldn't be overlooked or under-rated. They are also true charming small hotels, all of them good, some excellent. Usually, but by no means always, because of their larger size, they don't conform to our main criteria so closely as the whole page hotels. They are grouped at the end of each regional section, after the whole page entries. **Section opener entries** are some useful back-up addresses with a small photo and very brief description on the introductory page to each section. Again, don't overlook these. They are all great places, but just not quite as faithful to our criteria as whole- and half-page entries.

So remember, within each regional section you need to look in three different places to get the whole range of recommendations in that region, not forgetting that the entire contents are made easily accessible by the maps – and the indexes on pages 249-260.

Introduction

If you're looking for a hotel near a certain place, as well as the maps you can use the index of hotel locations on pages 255-260.

Telephoning from abroad

To call a hotel from the UK, dial 00 (from the US, dial 011), then the international dialling code (see below), then dial the number. When dialling Italy only, include the initial 0.

Austria	43
Switzerland	41
Liechtenstein	423
France	33
Italy	39
Germany	49

Travel to Europe from the UK

By road: we enjoy crossing the English Channel by the Eurotunnel because it is so flexible and comfortable. The UK terminal is just outside Folkestone and the French terminal just outside Calais. If you miss a shuttle, you have a fair chance of getting on the next one half an hour later. The crossing time is 35 minutes. **By boat:** almost as fast from Dover to Calais, is P&O Ferries with a crossing time of 1.5 hours. They carry eight million passengers, one million cars and one million trucks a year with a fleet of six ships sailing on the Dover-Calais service. On board there are restaurants, shops, bars, children's play areas and a *bureau de change* with commission-free foreign exchange services. **By air:** plenty of low-budget airlines fly from the UK to Austria and Switzerland, as well as Lyon for access to the French Alps; Milan for the Italian Alps; or Munich for the German Alps. It is worth bearing in mind, however, that with some airlines you definitely get what you pay for in terms of service and quality.

Visit charmingsmallhotels.co.uk

This printed guide has a successful companion website that includes entries from all over Europe and selected worldwide destinations, all with independent reviews and up to five photographs for each entry. It's the best research tool on the web for finding our kind of hotel.

Exchange rates

As we went to press, $1 bought 0.73 euros or 0.90 CHF, and £1 bought 1.18 euros or 1.45 CHF.

HOW TO READ AN ENTRY

City, town or village, and region, in which the hotel is located.

SALZBURGERLAND   AUSTRIA

Salzburg

Postal address and other key information.

Places of interest within reach of the hotel.

This sets the hotel in its geographical context and should not be taken as precise instructions as to how to get there; always ask the hotel for directions.

Rooms described as having a bath usually also have a shower; rooms described as having a shower only have a shower.

Name of hotel.

Type of establishment.

Description – never vetted by the hotel.

Breakfast is normally included in the price of the room. Other meals, such as afternoon tea, may also be available.

Mönchsberg Park 26, 5020 Salzburg

Tel 066/ 8485550
e-mail salzburg@monchstein.at
website www.monchstein.at

Nearby Mönchsberg lift/elevator;
Salzburg Museum (1 km).
Location above Salzburg, car park-
ing outside
Food breakfast, lunch, dinner,
snacks
Prices €€€€-€€€€
Rooms 24; 11 double, 13 suites, all
with bath or shower; all rooms have
central heating, phone, Sky TV,
DVD player, air conditioning, mini-
bar, hairdryer, safe, wi-fi; some suites
have terrace
Facilities 2 dining rooms, restau-
rant, sitting room, spa, bar, terraces
Credit cards AE, DC, MC, V
Children welcome
Disabled lift/elevator
Pets accepted, not in restaurant
Closed never
Manager Samantha Kaidel

Hotel Schloss
Mönchstein Castle hotel

We half expected to see Rapunzel leaning out of the 14thC tower of this imposing, award-winning hotel, built on a crag above the heart of Salzburg. Instead, we found guests in shorts and open-neck shirts ordering coffee and cake on the ter-race. Inside, highly polished tables and gold plush sofas are reflected in large, gilt mir-rors. It all looks very stiff and formal, yet the uniformed staff are young and friendly and can't do enough to help. The two old dining rooms have been converted into a suite, and now you can choose from the Orangerie Apollo terrace bar, or the classy gourmet Restaurant Schloss Mönchstein. You can also rent the Gothic Salon with its heavy wooden furnishings, or 'the smallest restaurant in the world' in the tower, which only seats four people – 'crazy and romantic', said a recent visitor.

Bedrooms are grand without being over-decorated. Number 32, high up under the eaves, is decorated in garden greens; number 11 has a tapestry on the wall. Many have antiques, and all have modern bathrooms. Half look over the city, the other half over the gardens and extensive park. Used by businessmen and touring North Americans and Japanese, it also has guests who settle in for a week at a time. Weddings take place in the small chapel and there are weekend harp concerts.

63

This information is only an indication for wheelchair users and the infirm. Always check on suitability with the hotel.

Always let the hotel know in advance if you want to bring a pet. Even where pets are accepted, certain restrictions may apply, and a small charge may be levied.

We list the following credit cards:

AE   American Express
DC   Diners Club
MC   Mastercard
V   Visa

Most hotels accept many other credit cards.

Reporting to the guide

Please write and tell us about your experiences of small hotels, guesthouses and inns, whether good or bad, whether listed in this edition or not. As well as hotels in Austria, Switzerland and the Alps, we are interested in hotels in Britain, France, Italy, Germany, Spain and the USA.

Readers whose reports prove particularly helpful may be invited to join our Travellers' Panel. Members give us notice of their own travel plans; we suggest hotels that they might inspect, and help with the cost of accommodation.

The address to write to us is:

Editor, *Charming Small Hotel Guides*
Studio 6, 82 Silverthorne Road, Battersea, SW8 3HE.

Checklist

Please use a separate sheet of paper for each report; include your name, address and telephone number on each report.

Your reports will be received with particular pleasure if they are typed, and if they are organized under the following headings:

Name of establishment
Town or village it is in, or nearest
Full address, including postcode
Telephone number
Website address
Time and duration of visit
The building and setting
The public rooms
The bedrooms and bathrooms
Physical comfort (chairs, beds, heat, light, hot water)
Standards of maintenance and housekeeping
Atmosphere, welcome and service
Food
Value for money

We assume that in writing you have no objections to your views being published unpaid, either verbatim or in an edited version. Names of major outside contributors are acknowledged, at the editor's discretion, in the guide.

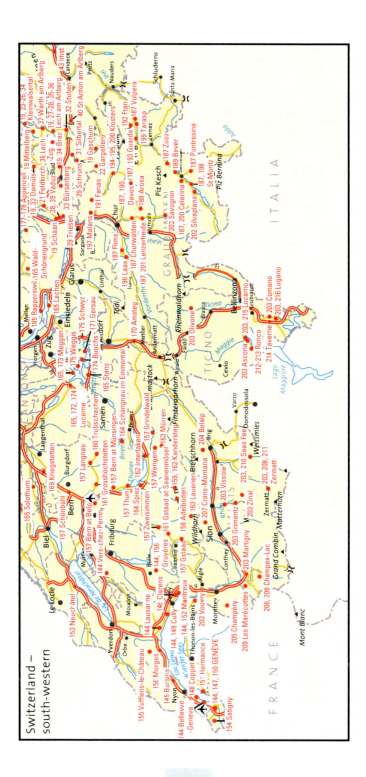

Switzerland –
south-western

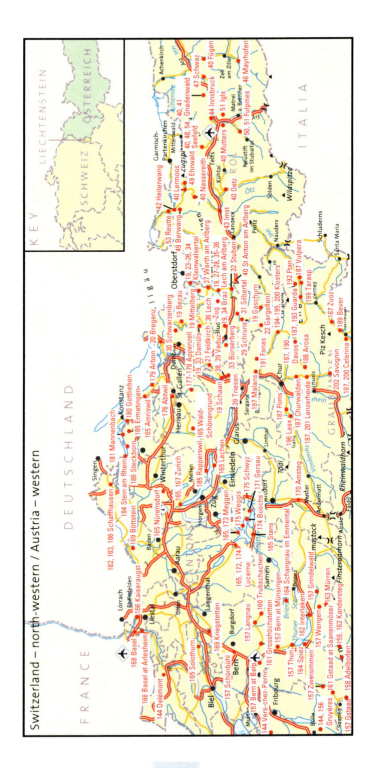

Switzerland – north-western / Austria – western

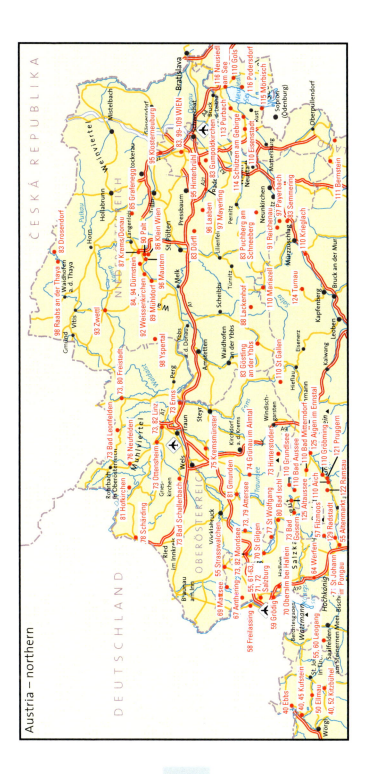

Austria – northern

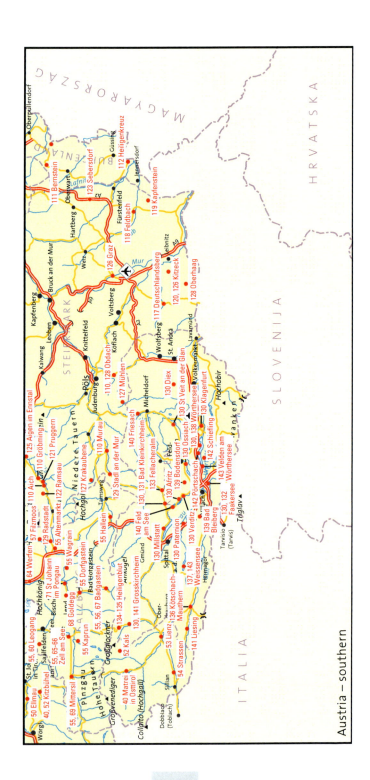

Austria – southern

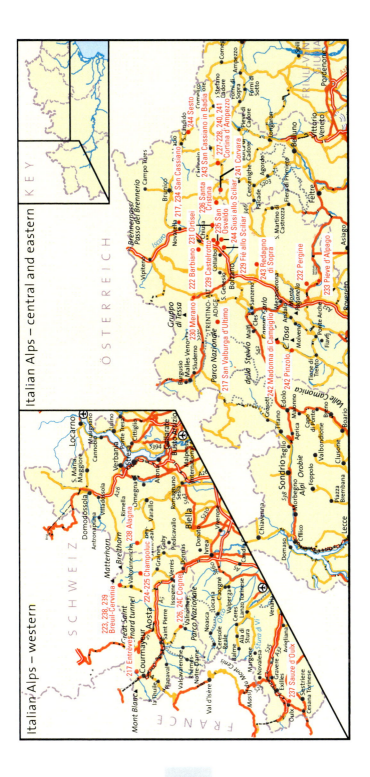

Italian Alps – western

Italian Alps – central and eastern

KEY

SCHWEIZ

ÖSTERREICH

FRANCE

Mont Blanc

Matterhorn

Breithorn

Monte Rosa

S. Maria Maggiore

Locarno

Verbania

Stresa

Brissago

Omegna

Domodossola

Antronapiana

Rimella

Villadossola

Varallo

Alagna

Gressoney

Gaby

Issogne

Verrés

Donnas

Ivrea

Romagnano Sesia

Vercelli

Biella

S. Donato

Candia

Courmayeur

Aosta

Saint Pierre

La Thuile

Pré-Saint-Didier

Cogne

Valnontey

Parco Nazionale

Valsavarenche

Rhèmes-Notre-Dame

Val d'Isère

Mont Cenis

Bardonecchia

Oulx

Cesana Torinese

Sestriere

Exilles

Gravere

Susa

Avigliana

Ala di Stura

Lanzo Torinese

Ceres

Balme

Ceresole Reale

Valprato

Noasca

Locana

Ciaorgiè

Turin

Chivasso

Brusasco

Casale Monferrato

Chivasso

Vinovo

Pinerolo

Saluzzo

223, 238, 239 Breuil-Cervinia

217 Entrèves/Mont-Blanc tunnel

Great-Saint Bernard tunnel

224-225 Champoluc

238 Alagna

226, 24C Cogne

237 Sauze d'Oulx

SCHWEIZ

Chiavenna

Domaso

Chiasso

Lecco

Lugano

Como

Sondrio

Teglio

Morbegno

Tirano

Edolo

Aprica

Alpi Orobie

Foppolo

Piazza Brembana

Clusone

Boario

Breno

Capo di Ponte

Valbondione

Valbondione

Malonno

Vallecamonica

Ponte di Legno

Brennerpass/Passo del Brennero

Vipiteno

Brunico

Campo Tures

S. Candido

Sesto

Dobbiaco

Cortina d'Ampezzo

Pieve di Cadore

S. Stefano di Cadore

Comelico

Forni di Sotto

Longarone

Belluno

Feltre

Asiago

Rovereto

Trento

Pergine

Borgo

Mezzocorona

Cles

Malè

Madonna di Campiglio

Andalo

Molveno

Fai

Fiavé

Tione di Trento

Storo

Mori

Merano

Bolzano

Ortisei

Chiusa

Collalbo

S. Genesio

Sarnonico

Novacella

Bressanone

Fié allo Sciliar

Siusi allo Sciliar

Sluderno

Malles Venosta

Burgusio

Glorenza

Parco Nazionale dello Stelvio

Gruppo di Tessa

TRENTINO-ALTO ADIGE

Parco Naturale

217, 234 San Cassiano

243 San Cassiano in Badia

227-228, 240, 241 Cortina d'Ampezzo

241 Corvara

244 Sesto

236 Santa Cristina

235 San Oswaldo

244 Siusi allo Sciliar

229 Fié allo Sciliar

222 Barbiano

231 Ortisei

239 Castelrotto

243 Redagno di Sopra

232 Pergine

242 Pinzolo, C. Tosa

242 Madonna di Campiglio

230 Merano

217 San Valburga d'Ultimo

233 Pieve d'Alpago

FRIULI-VENEZIA GIULIA

Pordenone

Vittorio Veneto

Iscaro

Adige

Agordo

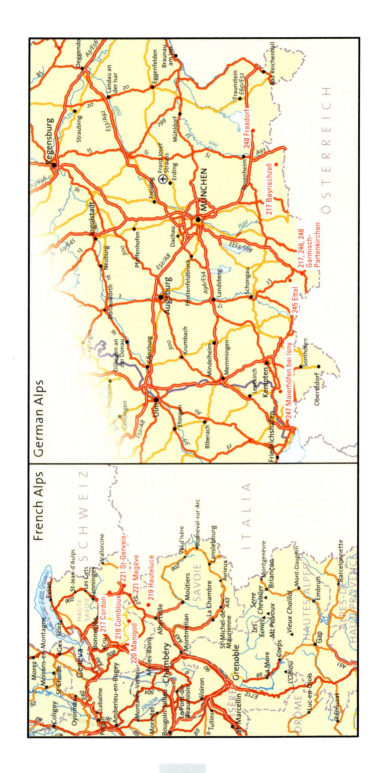

French Alps

German Alps

Area introduction

The westernmost of Austria's Federal States, Vorarlberg is, apart from Vienna, the smallest. It's cut off from the rest of the country by the Arlberg mountains. Bordering Germany, Switzerland and Liechtenstein, it's an international playground with excellent tourist facilities. One unique area is Kleinwalsertal, itself cut off from Vorarlberg by high mountains. The only road in is from Germany via Oberstdorf, and though politically part of Austria, this valley is economically part of Germany – homes have German and Austrian dialling codes and postcodes. The skiing in Vorarlberg is famous worldwide, and ranges from resorts such as Lech to villages such as Gargellen.

Liechtenstein is a country in its own right, but we include it in our Austria section. It's so tiny – 25 km by 6 km – that we only found four charming, small hotels here. It's mountainous, with well-marked hiking trails.

Below are some useful Vorarlberg and Liechtenstein back-ups if other places are booked:

Gasthof Sonne
Old inn and apartments,
Bezau Tel 05514 2262
www.diesonnigen.at
Cleverly blends old and new;
local cheese; free travel pass.

Traube Braz
Valley spa hotel, Braz bei
Bludenz Tel 05552 28103
www.traubebraz.at
Spa and golf hotel with
award-winning food.

Berghotel Madlener
Village hotel, Damüls
Tel 05510 2210
www.berghotel-madlener.at
Chalet high in the Bregen-
zerwald with wood panelling.

Landhotel Älpili
Mountain hotel, Gaschurn
Tel 05558 873371
www.aelpili.at
Modern hotel with striking
furnishings in large rooms.

Hotel Saladina
Mountain hotel, Gaschurn
Tel 05558 82042
www.saladina.com
One minute from gondola
station; sauna; pool.

Hotel Jagdhof
Town hotel, Kleinwalsertal
Tel 05517 5603
www.hotel-jagdhof.de
Quiet bedrooms with bal-
conies; across from casino.

Hotel Bergkristall
Mountain hotel, Lech am
Arlberg Tel 05583 2678
www.bergkristall-lech.at
Modern, stylish fitness-
focussed hotel; great views.

Brunnenhof
Mountain hotel, Lech am
Arlberg Tel 05583 2349
www.brunnenhof.com
Fashionable hotel with mas-
ter chef; open in winter only.

Hotel Haldenhof
Mountain hotel, Lech am
Arlberg Tel 05583 24440
www.haldenhof.at
Recently refurbished hotel
near ski school; new spa.

Hotel Madlochblick
Mountain chalet, Lech am
Arlberg Tel 05583 2220
www.madlochblick.at
Deep chairs in cosy *Stuben*;
swimming pool in spa.

Hotel Garni Ingeborg
Mountain hotel, Mittelberg
Tel 05517 57580
www.hotel-garni-ingeborg.at
Traditional family-run hotel;
good for budget ski trips.

Hotel Sylva Suburban
hotel, Schaan, Liechtenstein
Tel 042323 23942
www.hotel-sylva.com
Plush furnishings; ask for
room overlooking garden.

Ehre-Guta-Platz 4, 6900 Bregenz

Tel 05574 47800
e-mail rezeption@deuring-schloessle.at
website www.deuring-schloessle.at

Nearby Lake Constance (600 m);
Pfänder mountain (2.5 km); old
Upper Town.
Location on medieval square in old
town; own car parking
Food breakfast, lunch (during
summer Bregenz Festival), dinner
Prices €€-€€€
Rooms 13 suites, all with bath or
shower; all suites have central
heating, phone, TV
Facilities dining room, sitting room,
conference room; terrace
Credit cards AE, DC, MC, V
Children accepted
Disabled not suitable
Pets accepted; not in restaurant
Closed Feb to Mar
Proprietors Heino Huber

Deuring Schlössle
Castle hotel

'Dramatic' was our reaction to this 17thC castle, up in the old part of Bregenz, overlooking Lake Constance. The scale is huge. The breakfast room looks like a medieval hall with a ceiling over 6 metres high, ancient beams, and walls over 1 metre thick. We expected to see the lord and lady with their retinue instead of just tables and chairs beneath the swords, pikes and minstrel gallery. The bedrooms are more like suites, furnished with silk fabrics and antiques. Some are large enough for a dozen people to waltz in, others are cosier; each is special. In 2011 the hotel was given four stars, making it the smallest four star on Lake Constance.

The food matches the surroundings. In 1989, along with his late father, talented chef Heino Huber, took over this castle. Dishes use the best of local produce and seasonal ingredients including pike caught in the lake. The dungeon-like wine cellar has an impressive international collection.

Rosengasse 6, 6800 Feldkirch

Tel 05522 72175
e-mail hotel@gutwinski.cc
website www.gutwinski.cc

Nearby Schattenburg castle (100 m); cathedral (200 m); Katzenturm (200 m).
Location in pedestrian area in old town but access for guests allowed; own car parking
Food breakfast, snacks
Price €€
Rooms 27; 21 double, 5 single, 1 suite, all with bath or shower; all rooms have central heating, phone, TV, minibar, hairdryer, most have air conditioning
Facilities sitting room, 2 breakfast rooms, restaurant
Credit cards AE, DC, MC, V
Children welcome
Disabled easy access to one room; lift/elevator
Pets accepted
Closed never
Proprietors Gutwinski family

Gutwinski Hotel
Bed-and-breakfast hotel

This is just the sort of hotel we always hope to find in a pretty old town but seldom do. Located in the pedestrian zone, at the end of a tiny cobbled passageway, roses climb along the front of the building which has been in the same family for generations. The current owner, who took over from her grandmother several years ago, is always making improvements and the latest renovation was in early 2013.

Despite these changes, the traditional atmosphere is not lost in the bedrooms: paintings or prints hang above the beds, and each room has a little writing desk and carved chairs (though there is a flat-screen TV mounted to the wall directly above). Bathrooms are on the small side but well thought-out and modern, with large mirrors and adequate shelf space. Even the corridors are pleasant, with 19thC portraits and furniture

Reservations must be made well in advance of the Schubertiade festival in June, when many rooms are taken by artists, and you may even hear singers and musicians practising.

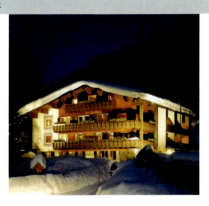

No. 53, 6787 Gargellen

Tel 05557 6319
e-mail hotel@heimspitze.com
website www.heimspitze.com

Nearby Gaschurn (8 km); Schruns
(12 km).
Location across bridge, on east side
of valley; covered car parking outside
Food breakfast, lunch, dinner,
snacks
Prices €€-€€€€
Rooms 10; 9 suites, 1 double/twin,
all with bath or shower; all rooms
have central heating, phone, TV,
hairdryer, safe, wi-fi
Facilities 2 dining rooms, sitting
room, bar, sauna; terrace,
playground, garden, animal pens;
winter sports, hiking nearby
Credit cards AE, DC, MC, V
Children very welcome
Disabled not suitable
Pets by arrangement
Closed mid-Apr to mid-Jun; mid-
Oct to mid-Dec
Proprietors Thöny family

Alpenhotel Heimspitze
Resort hotel

Set across the river from the village, the
hotel has an atmosphere of seclusion,
with a large garden and nothing but mountains behind. Originally a simple *pension*, it
was rebuilt in 1969 in a traditional style
but with modern spaciousness. The Thöny
family like to collect, and they have examples from all over the world: plenty of
china, some pewter, and hundreds of
ducks. There are even ducks in the sauna.

The bedrooms have oatmeal-coloured
carpeting, either a panel of fabric on a wall
to match the curtains, or a black-and-
white photograph, and crisp white bed
linen. Bathrooms are modern with slate
and large, well-lit mirrors.

There are two dining rooms and a basement bar but the most popular room is
the century-old, candle-lit *Montafonerstube*
with tiny wildflower pictures and inlaid-
wood tables. The award-winning kitchen
produces home-made jams, *Stollen* and a
choice of five or six different cakes, plus a
menu that changes daily. In summer, children climb on the adventure playground
and look for frogs in the nearby pond.

A recent visitor praised the staff's helpfulness with children, but said that families
with active children may not want to visit,
because of the large number of fragile
ornaments about the place.

Eggstr 14, 6991 Riezlern,
Kleinwalsertal

Tel 05517 6266
e-mail info@breitachhus.com
website www.breitachhus.com

Nearby Parsenn ski lift.
Location on hillside above Riezlern;
ample car parking
Food breakfast, dinner, snacks
Price €€
Rooms 10 double, all with bath or
shower; all rooms have central
heating, phone, TV, hairdryer
Facilities dining room, sitting room,
TV room, whirlpool in cellar;
terrace; winter sports, hiking nearby
Credit cards not accepted
Children very welcome
Disabled not suitable
Pets not accepted
Closed 2-4 weeks after Easter, Nov
to early Dec (snow)
Proprietors Riezler family

Breitachhus
Mountain farmhouse

In winter, this looks like an iced ginger-bread house; in summer clematis, roses, and geraniums cover the front. Bought by Harald and Christl Riezler 30 years ago, the building dates back more than 300 years and has the darkened wood to prove it. Step across the deep porch, bend your head through the tiny doorway and you are inside a private home. It is furnished with an eclectic mixture of old and new and there are pictures of children everywhere.

Bedrooms come in all shapes and sizes and are prettily, if simply, decorated. Two have four-poster beds; all have balconies and modern bathrooms. Harald's menu is good, home-style cooking with vegetarian choices and, at breakfast, jams and whole-meal rolls are home-made. Breitachhus has recently become a member of a group of Austrian restaurants awarded for 'home-made culinary expertise'.

Guests get to know one another, talking in the little sitting room with its warming oven and eating in the honey-coloured, wood-panelled dining room. In summer, Christl leads guided walks and guests can use several of the mountain railways and all bus services for free; in winter, there is skiing a few minutes away.

Am Berg 26, 6992 Hirschegg,
Kleinwalsertal

Tel 05517 5433
e-mail info@kleinwalsertal-sonnenberg.de
website www.kleinwalsertal-sonnenberg.de

Nearby Mittelberg (2.5 km);
Fellhorn/German border (4 km).
Location W side of valley above
Hirschegg; car parking across street
Food breakfast, dinner, snacks
Prices €-€€
Rooms 15 double, 1 single,
2 suites, all with bath or shower; all
rooms have central heating, phone,
TV, radio, hairdryer
Facilities dining room, sitting room,
indoor swimming pool; terrace,
garden
Credit cards not accepted
Children accepted
Disabled not suitable
Pets small dogs only
Closed Apr to mid-May, Nov to
mid-Dec
Proprietor Harald Zepper

Der Sonnenberg
Traditional chalet

Every now and then we like a place so much we are tempted to keep it just for ourselves. This is it. Set high above the village of Hirschegg, the approach is up one of the steepest hills we have ever driven, or walked. When we arrived in summer, the garden was abloom with daisies, poppies, and iris. New owner Harald Zepper took over from Kurt and Martine Krieger a few years ago, and takes just as much delight in showing off this 1530s house as they did.

Ceilings are low and the ancient wood creaks with every step up to the bedrooms; each has a different colour scheme, but all have canopied four-poster beds plus bathrobes and walking sticks. Some hotel bedrooms are just for sleeping; these are comfortable enough to spend time in, though guests also relax in the basement sitting room, where picture windows look straight across the valley. A small, indoor swimming pool is like a grotto, built into a wall of rock.

Tables in the two snug dining rooms are shared, so guests get to know one another over leisurely evening meals. Once a week there are gourmet suppers where the chef cooks six courses of French, Italian or regional specialities.

Kleinwalsertal

Bödmerstr 46, A - 6993, D - 87569
Mittelberg, Kleinwalsertal

Tel 05517 20311
e-mail info@hotel-steinbock.at
website www.hotel-steinbock.at

Nearby Mittelberg; Baad (3 km);
Bregenzerwald (10 km); Allgäu (10
km).
Location in southernmost village of
valley; ample car parking
Food breakfast, lunch, dinner,
snacks
Price €€ (half board)
Rooms 29 double and suites, all with
bath or shower; all rooms have
central heating, phone, satellite TV,
minibar, safe, wi-fi, most have
balcony/terrace
Facilities 2 dining rooms, sitting
room, bar, sauna; terrace, garden
Credit cards MC, V
Children very welcome
Disabled not suitable
Pets accepted (not in restaurant)
Closed 2 weeks after Easter, Nov to
mid-Dec
Proprietors Haller family

Steinbock
Mountain resort hotel

Hans Vogler believed in having 'a good life as well as a good business,' and new owners, the Haller family, do too. Expansion and improvements have been made carefully; for example, the lower-level bar is so well insulated that guests in the restaurant above cannot hear the music. The bedrooms are all different shapes and layouts, but all have a sitting area and blue, beige, red or green carpet patterned with flowers. Furnishings throughout are solid and comfortable.

The focus is on outdoor activities: the ski lifts are just a short walk from the hotel and in summer there are guided tours, mountain bike trails, and golf courses in neighbouring towns. Children are also well catered for, with a childcare and activity program in the summer (hiking, treasure hunts and an adventure playground) and a ski school in winter. There's also a playroom next to the restaurant to entertain restless children at dinner time. After dinner, guests can head next door to the Steinbock's sister hotel for bowling, or visit the bar downstairs for a cocktail.

Eggstraße 2, 6991 Riezlern,
Kleinwalsertal

Tel (05517) 53460
e-mail info@walserstuba.at
website www.walserstuba.at

Nearby Parsenn ski lift.
Location on hillside above village of
Riezlern; car parking outside
Food breakfast, lunch, dinner,
snacks
Prices €
Rooms 24; 20 double, 4 single, all
with bath or shower; all rooms have
central heating, phone, TV, radio,
hairdryer, safe
Facilities 3 dining rooms, sitting
room, bar, terrace, baby-sitting,
winter sports nearby
Credit cards MC, V
Children very welcome
Disabled some access
Pets accepted
Closed Nov to mid-Dec; restaurant
only, Mon, Tues
Proprietors Riezler family

Walserstuba
Country inn

The village of Riezlern is named for this family, one of the original Walsers who left Switzerland some 600 years ago. The owners of the Breitachhus just up the hill (page 23) are cousins. Not surprisingly, this is a traditional household.

In the Walser Marriage Gallery, the family tree on the wall dates back to the 16th century. A glass case displays the wedding crown, handed down through seven generations, along with the bridal dress.

Furnishings are exactly what is expected of a traditional country inn, with decorative carved wood and bench seating. Yet it was built in 1985, so most rooms are larger than in most old buildings. Local game features on the menu, but a vegetarian dish is also offered and those with smaller appetites can ask for reduced portions. Colouring pencils are provided so children can draw on their special menus. The resident 'babysitter' is Laura, a noisy, yellow and blue parrot who does acrobatic tricks on her swing and shows off constantly.

Lech am Arlberg

No. 62, 6764 Lech am Arlberg

Tel 05583 2407
e-mail contact@hotel-angela.at
website www.hotel-angela.at

Nearby Schlegelkopf lift.
Location up twisting road on
hillside above town; ample car
parking; indoor garage
Food breakfast, lunch, dinner
Prices €€€€-€€€€€
Rooms 30; 28 double and suites, 2
single, all with bath or shower; all
rooms have phone, TV, central
heating, minibar, radio, safe
Facilities restaurant, dining room,
reception with open fireplace, bar,
library, meeting room, spa; terrace,
winter sports nearby
Credit cards AE, MC, V
Children very welcome
Disabled not suitable
Pets not accepted
Closed May to June, Oct to Nov
Proprietors Walch Fernandez
family

Hotel Angela
Village resort hotel

Many hotels promise great comfort
and a home-from-home ambience;
few achieve both. This one does. 'My mother has taught me to anticipate our guests'
every wish', says Elisabeth Walch Fernandez
who runs the Angela (third generation).

Over the last 50 years, the former farmhouse has been transformed into a hotel,
without losing its traditional roots. The old
back door, cracked with age, with a trum-
peting angel, still welcomes guests in the
reception area, next to an open fireplace.
The decoration is warm with cream walls
and soft red fabrics: the key tags, rooms
numbers and guest welcome packs are all
made of felt.

Rooms have mountain views and different fabrics, from tartans to Austrian *loden*
and linen. The 'small' ones are far from
cramped, while the Landhaus suites are
handsome, with bold patterns standing out
against a white and cream background. The
penthouse has a kitchen and a maid will
come in to cook breakfast. Dinner in the
elegant dining room runs to six courses;
the *Hubertusstube* restaurant is à la carte.

Just above the village, the hotel is surrounded by meadows full of gentian and
cows in summer, and ski slopes in winter.
Herr Walch senior, as a former head of the
ski school, can advise on the best places to
ski, starting right from the door.

6764 Lech am Arlberg

Tel 05583 2330
e-mail info@hotelelisabeth.com
website www.hotelelisabeth.com

Nearby Lech ski lifts; Zürs (5 km);
St Anton (13 km); Stuben (10 km);
St Christoph (10 km).
Location up small lane from Lech's
main thorough fare; ski lifts less than
5 minutes on foot; ample private car
parking
Food breakfast, lunch, dinner
Price €€€
Rooms 26 double, single and suites,
all with bath or shower; all rooms
have phone, TV, hairdryer, safe, wi-fi
Facilities dining room, sitting room,
bar, restaurant, spa; sun terrace,
swimming pool
Credit cards MC, V
Children welcome
Disabled lift/elevator
Pets by arrangement
Closed May to June, Oct to Nov
Proprietors Gafgo family

Hotel Elisabeth
Village hotel

Marion Gafgo, likely as not in tradition-al Austrian dress, is one of those
hosts who always seems to be around –
even when she's not present, she's there in
spirit. She is one of the most naturally gift-
ed hoteliers we've met, exuding good
cheer and humorous intelligence. She's
backed up by exceptionally well-trained,
friendly young staff, who all seem to work
in effortless synchronisation.

The hotel is named after Marion's
mother Elisabeth, who began the business
with her husband Ortwin Gafgo (the sur-
name is Czech) in the 1960s as the first
self-service restaurant in Arlberg, later
adding rooms. Marion took over in 2004
when they retired. Since then it's been redesigned and overhauled to keep pace
with the times, but the genuine charming
small hotel experience remains.

Comfortable bedrooms, all modestly individual with stencilled decorations, range
from smallish singles to generously-sized
doubles and suites. As well as the priceless
service and atmosphere, there's a spa and
a small swimming pool. It was recommended to us by one of our most hard-to-
please reporters, who has been coming
here for 20 years – indeed, much of the
Elisabeth's business is repeat. We visited
recently and found everything as he said.

Kronengasse 1, 6780 Schruns

Tel 05556 72255
e-mail info@kroneschruns.at
website www.kroneschruns.at

Nearby old town; Montafon ski
area; bus station (3 mins).
Location near middle of town, next
to river; car parking across the street
Food breakfast, lunch, dinner,
snacks
Prices €€–€€€
Rooms 15; 10 double, 2 single, 3
suites, all with bath or shower; all
rooms have central heating, phone,
TV, DVD player, hairdryer, safe,
wi-fi
Facilities dining room, sitting room,
spa area; terrace; winter sports and
hiking nearby
Credit cards AE, DC, MC, V
Children welcome
Disabled accessible (lift/elevator)
Pets accepted
Closed 1 week after Easter to mid-
Jun, early Nov to early Dec;
restaurant only, Wed
Proprietor Max Gebhardt

Hotel Restaurant Krone
Restaurant-with-rooms

Though the Mayers no longer run this
200-year-old hotel, the restaurant is
still one of the finest in the Montafon valley, serving traditional Vorarlberg dishes,
such as *Käspätzl* (egg noodles with
cheese), *Gröstl* (pork and potatoes with
fried egg), *Kalbsleber* (calves' liver) and
wiener schnitzel (breaded, fried veal). The
Montafonerstube, with its caramel-
coloured, heavily-knotted pine panelling is
a must for visitors. The windows are leaded and the octagonal tables are inlaid with
slates, which was used both as a stand for
hot pans and as a chalk board for farmers
doing business on market-day.

Upstairs, the ceiling of the *Kronestube* is
painted with signs of the zodiac. The bedrooms have been renovated since we last
visited, with new bathrooms and modern
comforts. Recent visitors have declared the
refurbished bedrooms excellent value for
money – particularly the spacious suites.

The terrace garden is a plus, as is the
location – in the village centre, just a few
steps from the middle of the lovely old
part of Schruns, and just three minutes'
walk from the train and bus stations.

Schwarzenberg

6867 Schwarzenberg

Tel (05512) 29440
e-mail
info@hirschenschwarzenberg.at
website
www.hirschenschwarzenberg.at

Nearby Dornbirn (8 km); Bregenz
(13 km); Lake Constance (13 km);
skiing at Arlberg (40 km).
Location in middle of old village;
ample car parking, garage
Food breakfast, lunch, dinner,
snacks
Price €€
Rooms 33; 24 double, 5 single, 4
suites, all with bath or shower; all
rooms have central heating, phone,
TV, minibar, hairdryer
Facilities 3 dining rooms, sitting
room, *Stube*, seminar rooms, spa
area; terrace, garden
Credit cards AE, MC, V
Children welcome
Disabled not suitable
Pets accepted **Closed** never;
restaurant only, Wed, Thurs (except
summer) **Proprietors** Fetz family

Romantik Hotel Hirschen **Village inn**

You can't miss this 18thC inn, opposite
the church on the main crossroads in
the village. The whole of Schwarzenberg is
a national treasure, with its wood-shingled
houses so typical of the Bregenzerwald
valley. Few hotels succeed in being all
things to all people but the Fetz family,
who have been here for more than 100
years, manage to do just that. Locals pop in
for a drink in the low-ceilinged *Jägerstube*,
but for special occasions book into the
restaurant, rated one of the best in the
area. There is also a function room with an
original 19thC wood ceiling.

Families arrive in winter for ski holidays,
but during the summer the hotel is filled
with couples and lovers of art and good
food. There is even a choice of style in
bedrooms, each decorated individually and
dedicated to an artist. The old house is traditional and romantic, either with Louis
Philippe-style furniture or Laura Ashley
prints. Rooms are larger in the modern
annexe, with more of a country look.
Colours here are delicate shades of purple, blue and green, with touches of bright
pink or yellow. This is also where small
business seminars are held, away from
other guests.

Behind the village, the Hochälpelekopf is
covered with ski runs; cross-country trails
loop round the valley.

Silbertal im Montafon

Kristberg 240, 6782 Silbertal im Montafon

Tel 05556 72290
e-mail info@kristberg.at
website kristberg.at

Nearby Kristbergbahn (600 m).
Location above Silbertal valley; phone ahead for access by car; otherwise 5 minutes' walk from cable car
Food breakfast, lunch, dinner, snacks
Price €€
Rooms 16; 12 double, 3 single, 1 cabin, most with bath or shower; all rooms have phone TV, central heating, wi-fi
Facilities dining room, sitting room, bar, gymnasium; terrace; mountain bikes, winter sports equipment
Credit cards MC, V
Children very welcome
Disabled not suitable
Pets accepted
Closed 1 week after Easter, 3 weeks May, Nov to mid-Dec
Proprietors Zudrell family

Panoramagasthof Kristberg **Mountain lodge**

When everyone else has gone down to the valley and the cable car has stopped for the night, guests at this simple inn have the mountain to themselves. There are few other buildings on this slope high above Silbertal and just 250 m from the top of the Kristbergbahn. The Zudrell family welcome guests and run the kitchen. Everything from eggs to meat comes from local farms. At the entrance, a display case overflows with their children's ski trophies. The atmosphere is more 'home' than 'hotel'. Bedrooms in the new wing are cheerful, with a teddy bear pattern on children's duvets; the few old rooms with shared bath and lavatory facilities are ideal for groups of friends or families who appreciate a bargain.

'You have to want to be with other people,' one of the daughters, told us in her excellent English. Guests spend time talking after dinner, there are games for children, and sometimes a torch-lit evening walk in winter. In summer, farmers in green boots congregate at the Stammtisch and walkers stop for cold drinks. Informality is the rule; this is not for anyone wearing designer clothes and expecting five-star service.

Stuben am Arlberg

6762 Stuben am Arlberg

Tel 0664 3858266
e-mail info@berghaus-stuben.com
website www.berghaus-stuben.com

Nearby Zürs (4 km); Lech (8 km); St
Anton (9 km).
Location from S16 motorway, take
Arlberg Pass exit, then follow
Arlbergstr. 197 to Stuben
Food breakfast, lunch, dinner
Price €
Rooms 10; 6 double, 2 twin, 2 triple,
all rooms have bath or shower
Facilities dining room, spa
Credit cards MC, V
Children accepted
Disabled not suitable
Pets not accepted
Closed Jun to Nov
Proprietors Christine and Gert
Bregant

Berghaus Stuben
Mountain hotel

This conveniently placed hotel, just 1 km
from Langen railway station on the
Zurich to Vienna main line, was recommended by a much-travelled reporter. It's
just over the hill from Lech and Zürs, but at
1,900 m it is about the same height as Lech
(1,450-2,450 m). Plus, skiers can take the lift
behind the hotel, then get off half-way up
the Stuben mountain system and ski
straight down into the St Anton ski system.

Though the pretty village of Stuben is
downmarket from the more popular Lech
and Zürs ski area – and the prices reflect
this – Berghaus Stuben has all the facilities
of a modern ski hotel, except a swimming
pool. The ten bedrooms are standardized,
bright and crisp. 'The food is hearty, whole-
some and tasty', and even when they are
fully-booked – which they often are – the
service is swift and friendly.

The owners claim that staying here has
several health benefits, including reducing
blood pressure. We don't know about this,
but people do seem more relaxed here.
Perhaps it's the elevation, or the free use
of the sauna, or maybe just getting a good
night's sleep on the quiet mountain.

Bürserberg

Tschengla 1, 6707 Bürserberg

Tel 05552 63104
e-mail office@schillerkopf.at
website www.schillerkopf.at
Food breakfast, lunch, dinner,
snacks
Prices €€-€€€€
Closed after Easter to mid-June,
Oct to mid-Dec
Proprietors Bosek family

Alpinresort Schillerkopf
Mountain hotel

Our reporter felt at home instantly. It's the sort of place to settle into and relax, where attention to detail ranges from hand-carved ceiling panels to bright rugs. All this and a terrific view over Bludenz some 6 km away. The Bosek family have been here, at the base of the Schillerkopf mountain, since 1899, opening their house as a hotel in 1927.

Sporty types are kept happy with guided walks, parcour and mountain biking; in winter, guests ski out and ski back, or spend the day in one of the other resorts around Bludenz. The Schillerkopf is sustainably run and the Boseks serve regional dishes made from locally-sourced produce.

Book a bedroom with a view over the valley or straight up the mountain.

Damüls

Kirchdorf 131, 6884 Damüls,
Bregenzerwald

Tel 05510 211
e-mail info@alpenhotel-mittagspitze.at **website** www.alpenhotel-mittagspitze.at
Food breakfast, lunch, dinner
Prices €€-€€€
Closed 1 week after Easter, Nov to
early Dec
Proprietor Ingo Madlener

Alpenhotel Mittagspitze
Mountain resort hotel

Despite several changes of ownership over the years, readers still rate this the best small hotel in town. Our impression on entering the restaurant and bar was 'strikingly modern, Italian influence'. Glasses glitter against a mirror, reflecting light on to the white walls. In one room, chairs are in patterns of deep purple, black and red; in another, chair cushions and table-cloths are bright orange. Only the white stove looks typically Austrian. The bedrooms are modern and standardized, though some have a little character.

Guests include families who now bring their grandchildren. No doubt they approve of the changes. What remains the same is the two-minute run down through the woods to the Uga ski lift.

Innerbraz

Arlbergstrasse 61, 6751 Innerbraz

Tel 05552 281050
e-mail office@roesslebraz.at
website www.roesslebraz.at
Food breakfast, lunch, dinner,
snacks
Price €
Closed 4 weeks Jun/Jul, 1 week Dec;
restaurant only, Mon, Tue
Proprietors Bargehr family

Gasthof Rössle
Village inn

The Bargehr family's imaginative menu is locally renowned. Head chef and owner Valentin Bargehr sources his ingredients locally wherever possible. There are four cosy dining rooms in the restaurant, each decorated differently, and in summer food can be served in the shady garden. On Monday and Tuesday guests have the restaurant to themselves: reservation is recommended on other days.

The family has run the inn, located next to the church, since 1919. There are ten attractive, rustic-style bedrooms inside. In summer, there is golf and hiking; in winter, it's a good base for Klostertal skiers.

Kleinwalstertal

Walserstraße 83, 6991 Riezlern,
Kleinwalsertal

Tel 05517 5004
e-mail info@almhof-rupp.at
website www.almhof-rupp.at
Food breakfast, dinner, snacks
Prices €-€€€
Closed after Easter to mid-May;
Nov to mid-Dec
Proprietor Friedhelm Rupp

Almhof Rupp
Restaurant-with-rooms

Friedhelm Rupp has won acclaim and two toques from Gault Millau for his cuisine. As well as the superb à la carte menu, the half-board menu is impressive with dishes such as asparagus with smoked salmon strips, calves' liver with Madeira sauce, and rhubarb strudel.

Rooms are decorated with panels of natural linen, white paint on the wood, and a carpet of cream and blue. In the bar, bench seats surround the circular open fireplace and look right into the old-fashioned, rustic restaurant, with brown wood and orange curtains. It's just off the main road, but the back overlooks a mountain stream and the Kanzelwandbahn lift. Herr Rupp enjoys leading hiking tours in the summer and guides skiing tours in winter.

Lech am Arlberg

6764 Lech am Arlberg

Tel 05583 3410
e-mail info@lechapollonia.at
website www.lechapollonia.at
Food breakfast, self-catering
Prices €€-€€€€€
Closed never
Proprietor Norbert Moosbrugger

Apollonia Apartments
Mountain apartments

Apartments with a little more than the average – above all a great location in Oberlech, the car-free settlement on gentle slopes above the main village of Lech. It's also child friendly, and has a play area and a sauna (nudity a must).

Decoration is neutral. Not all the nine apartments are as spacious as each other, and there are occasional reports of haphazard housekeeping – and a manager who can be abrasive – so on arrival, check that your flat is 100 per cent clean and that the equipment is in good order. If it isn't, don't move in until you're satisfied. Feedback welcome.

Lech am Arlberg

Tannberg 130, 6764 Lech am Arlberg

Tel 05583 2214
e-mail reservation@aureliolech.com
website www.aureliolech.com
Food breakfast, lunch, dinner
Price €€€€€
Closed never
Proprietor Axel Pfefferkorn

Hotel Aurelio
Mountain hotel

Your wallet will take a hit at Hotel Aurelio, but if you're looking for luxury, you're at the right place. We immediately noticed the quietness of the hotel, and liked the top-quality spa, the comfortable beds and the Licca lounge. The emphasis here is on relaxation. In this vein, rooms are decorated with a simplistic elegance. Walls are dark, 'flash-roasted' pine, contrasting with the white beds. Technophiles will appreciate the latest multimedia equipment, but we missed a kettle for a quick cup of tea.

The restaurant's cuisine has been recommended, but we're not sure that hearty appetites would appreciate the smaller-than-normal Alpine portions. In winter, the hotel responds to skiers' needs; in summer, don't miss their llama treks.

Lech am Arlberg

6764 Lech am Arlberg

Tel 05583 2311 0
e-mail eldorado@hotelolympia.at
website www.eldorado-appartements.at
Food self-catering
Prices €€-€€€
Closed never
Proprietor Alfred Jochum

Eldorado Apartments
Hotel and apartments

These well-managed two- three-, four- and five-room apartments in the centre of Lech opposite the Schlosskopf lift caught our attention because they have reasonable space and are decorated to a high standard.

More to the point, they're owned by the nearby Hotel Olympia (€200 a night in skiing season): apartment tenants can use its restaurant and spa (steam room, sauna).

There's free parking and bread is delivered to the door. Enhanced self-catering.

Lech-Zug

Zug 5, 6764 Lech-Zug am Arlberg

Tel 05583 34350
e-mail gasthof@rotewand.com
website www.rotewand.com
Food breakfast, lunch, dinner, snacks
Price €€€€
Closed mid-April to early June, Nov to early Dec
Proprietors Walch family

Rote Wand
Mountain resort hotel

The à la carte restaurant is as traditional as you can get and famous for fondues, but the tradition ends there. The rest of the hotel is fresh and sleek: bright sofas in the bar, plush neutral fabrics in the restaurant, sheepskin covered metal chairs on the terrace, and clinically white furnishings in the spa treatment rooms. Bedrooms are furnished with lots of wood, grey sofas and colourful cushions.

The emphasis is on health and fitness: climbing courses, hiking, tennis and golf in summer; guided snow-shoe walks, skiing, tobogganing, snowboarding and sleigh rides in winter. There's even a sports shop on site. Children, too, are well-catered for with a swimming pool, an outdoor playground and a superb indoor playroom.

Warth am Arlberg

6767 Warth am Arlberg

Tel 05583 2677
e-mail info@lechtalerhof.at
website www.lechtalerhof.at
Food breakfast, lunch, dinner,
snacks
Prices €€-€€€€
Closed after Easter to early May,
Oct to early Dec
Proprietors Brenner family

Hotel Lechtalerhof
Mountain chalet hotel

This family-run hotel is right next to what now claims to be the biggest skiing area in Austria – the Arlberg region has 340 slopes and the whole area (comprising Warth, Lech, Zurs and St. Anton) will be interconnected with the opening in 2013-14 of the Auenfeldjet lift between Warth and Lech.

Inside, the Lechtalerhof is cosy, with a relaxed atmosphere and a first-class restaurant. The rooms and suites may be standardized, but they are certainly comfortable. The spa is ideal after a day hiking or skiing, cooling down in the panoramic pool, or relaxing in the new sauna garden.

Special adventure holidays for skiers, walkers, mountain bikers. Ski school next to the hotel.

Warth am Arlberg

Dorf 37, 6767 Warth am Arlberg

Tel 05583 35020
e-mail hotel@walserberg.at
website www.walserberg.at
Food breakfast, lunch, dinner,
snacks
Prices €€-€€€
Closed end Apr to early Dec
Proprietors Walch family

Hotel Walserberg
Mountain village hotel

Warth is a remote village high in the mountains, so the Walch family provide a lot for guests, from a pizzeria to a bakery. In winter there's a ski run straight to the hotel; Irene and Thomas Walch can organize an area ski pass for your arrival. It gives access to 94 ski lifts and 340 km of slopes in the Arlberg *skigebiet* (ski resort), suitable for all standards.

The spacious rooms are decorated in green, blue or red. Some have four-poster beds. The seven suites are modern and open plan, most with the bathroom area separated by a curtain. The wellness suite has its own sauna. In the spa area there are three more saunas and a gym.

Modern and comfortable, a good mountain hideaway for families.

Herrengasse 35, 9490 Vaduz

Tel (+423) 238 11 44
e-mail office@hotel-loewen.li
website www.hotel-loewen.li

Nearby national museum (500 m);
Vaduz castle (600 m).
Location on main road on edge of
Vaduz; ample car parking
Food breakfast, lunch, dinner,
snacks
Price FFFF
Rooms 7; 6 double, 1 single, all with
bath or shower; all rooms have cen-
tral heating, phone, satellite TV,
minibar, wi-fi
Facilities 2 dining rooms, bar; ter-
race, garden, winter sports nearby
Credit cards AE, DC, MC, V
Children welcome
Disabled not suitable
Pets accepted
Closed Christmas, New Year
Manager Adele Gantenbein

Hotel-Gasthof Löwen
Wayside inn

A century ago, travellers agreed that 'if
you stop in Liechtenstein, you have to
stay at the Löwen.' Thanks to careful and
expensive restoration, that advice holds
true again. This is, perhaps, the oldest inn in
the country, having stood on the main
road between Germany and Italy since
1380. Now it is almost a living museum:
there is a 400-year-old fresco in the dining
room, where Goethe once ate; an intri-
cately painted ceiling that renovations
uncovered many years ago in the elegant
Johannes-Stube; and the tale of the
Niebelungen is carved into the panelling of
the *Lucretia-Stube*.

White walls and parquet floors provide
a simple backdrop for antiques and oriental carpets. Many have matching massive,
carved wooden beds and armoires.
Bathrooms are modern with thick towels
and excellent lighting, decorated all in
white with tiled walls and mirror frames.
Some doubles have 'his and hers' wash-
basins. Rooms overlooking the road can
be noisy in summer if windows are open;
those at the back face the garden and vineyards – the Gantenbein family's wine is
highly recommended by recent visitors.

The centre of Vaduz and the museum
are walking distance, or there is a bus stop
50 m down the road.

Triesen

Landstrasse 80, 9495 Triesen

Tel (+423) 399 12 12
e-mail info@schatzmann.li
website www.schatzmann.li
Food breakfast, lunch, dinner,
snacks
Prices FF-FFF
Closed Christmas Day to early Jan;
restaurant only, 3 weeks July to Aug
Proprietors Klaus and Inge
Schatzmann

Schatzmann
Restaurant-with-rooms

Klaus Schatzmann has built up a reputation for fine cooking, and delights in adapting traditional recipes to suit modern tastes. He was awarded a Michelin star in 1996 and several recent visitors have commented that they could taste every flavour in each dish. There is a good choice at the breakfast buffet: eggs, omelettes, smoked salmon, cooked meats, cheeses, cakes and more.

The ten original bedrooms are plain and simple; the bedrooms and suites in the annexe, which was added in 1994, are very quiet, modern and more spacious.

Vaduz

9490 Vaduz

Tel (+423) 232 02 02
e-mail real@sonnenhof.li
website www.sonnenhof.li
Food breakfast, lunch, dinner,
snacks
Prices FF-FFFFF
Closed mid-Dec to early Jan
Proprietors Real family

Sonnenhof
Suburban hotel

'Total seclusion and a perfect view of Vaduz Castle' wrote our reporter. There are cosy corners in this Relais & Châteaux hotel, such as the *Stübli*, a glassed-in former terrace, and the *Kaminzimmer*, with its fireplace, books and squashy leather sofas and armchairs. The dining room is the showcase for Michelin-starred head chef Hubertus Real's culinary talents and is reserved for those staying at the hotel.

The large bedrooms are individually designed in styles that vary from smart luxury to colonial to Parisian chic. Most have a view of the Rhine valley, the Alps and Vaduz Castle; suites also have a large sitting area. Our reporter thought the trapeze suspended above the swimming pool looked like fun. 'Very comfortable, away from it all.'

Area introduction

Tyrol (Tirol in German) must be Austria's most famous state, thanks to spectacular scenery, great skiing and photogenic villages. It has a turbulent history: the name of Andreas Hofer, an early 19thC resistance fighter, crops up everywhere. Tyrol's riches have always attracted its neighbours. After the First World War, a large chunk of Tyrol was ceded to Italy, and is today known as South Tyrol – see pages 222-244. Statistics show that this much-visited region is also the least-populated of Austria – so there are still peaceful corners to be discovered.

Many Tyrol hotels rely on tour groups, but we still find hoteliers who ignore the fast buck, preferring the high standards set by their families for decades. One or two are in the very heart of Innsbruck or Igls, others are at the end of remote valleys or on picturesque lakes: all offer quality that is hard to match.

Below are some useful back-up places to try if our main selections are fully booked:

Hotel Unterwirt
Old inn, Ebbs
Tel 05373 42288
gourmethotel-unterwirt.at
Village known for summer
concerts; light, regional food.

Hotel Haidachhof
Resort hotel, Fügen
Tel 05288 62380
www.haidachhof.com
Surprisingly luxurious with
warm welcome; near ski lift.

Speckbacher Hof
Country hotel, Gnadenwald
Tel 05223 52511
www.speckbacherhof.at
Good food and informality;
Stube serves hearty dishes.

Hotel Resch
Village resort hotel, Kitzbühel
Tel 05356 62294
www.hotel-resch.at
Suited to the limited skier's
budget; pretty restaurant.

Lanthalerhof
City hotel, Kufstein
Tel 05372 64105
www.lanthalerhof.at
Near Riedel glass factory;
own ski bus; peaceful garden.

Zugspitze
Resort hotel, Lermoos
Tel 05673 2630
www.hotel-zugspitze.at
Tyrolean style hotel; torch-lit
tobogganing; cycling tours.

Hotel Panzlwirt
Village inn, Matrei in Osttirol
Tel 04875 6518
Hotel in Goldreid ski area;
good for families; few
English speakers.

Hotel Sonnhof
Resort hotel, Mutters
Tel 0512 548470
www.sonnhof-mutters.at
Ideal for families with small
children; large garden; skiing

Hotel Schloss
Fernsteinsee Old inn,
Nassereith Tel 05265 5210
fernsteinsee.at
Eccentric hotel with outrageous marble and gilt fittings.

Gasthof Zum Stern
Village inn, Oetz
Tel 05252 6323
www.gasthof-zum-stern.at
Family-run well-priced inn
with unusual oriel window.

Garni Almhof
Suburban apartments,
Seefeld Tel 05212 3066
www.wildmoosalm.at
Functional apartments on
edge of Seefeld; spa.

At Antoner Hof Hotel and
apartments, St Anton am
Arlberg Tel 05446 2910
www.antonerhof.at
Fun, Tyrolean style, with pool
and modern Austrian cooking

Gnadenwald

6060 Gnadenwald

Tel 05223 48128
e-mail michaelerhof@aon.at
website www.michaelerhof.at

Nearby Innsbruck (13 km); Seefeld (30 km).
Location on plateau near Innsbruck; own car parking
Food breakfast, lunch, dinner, snacks
Prices €-€€
Rooms 20; 13 double, 5 single, 2 suites, all with bath or shower; all rooms have central heating, phone, satellite TV, internet, some have balcony
Facilities 4 restaurants (2 non-smoking), sitting room, bar; winter sports, riding nearby
Credit cards AE, DC, MC, V
Children very welcome
Disabled not suitable
Pets accepted
Closed 2 weeks before Easter, early Nov to early Dec; restaurant only, Mon, Tue
Proprietors Schiestl family

Gasthof Michaelerhof
Country inn

Even from the road we reckoned this would make a good place to stay and closer inspection proved us right. The Schiestls took over this farmhouse in 1965, turning it first into a restaurant, then a hotel. Herr Schiestl worked as a chef all over the world, in Istanbul and Nairobi, Japan and Sweden before settling in this tiny hamlet and marrying a local woman.

Proof of the family's confidence is their open kitchen, visible through windows in the bar and the doorway opposite reception. Menus are international, with dishes such as Indonesian *Nasi goreng*, curry from India and Scandinavian smoked fish alongside the familiar schnitzel and *Tafelspitz*.

Similarly, animal skins from Africa lend an exotic touch to the traditional Austrian interior. Instead of one main restaurant, there are four little *Stuben*: one has a collection of wooden bowls, another French windows that open to the patio in summer, two are non-smoking. Only a ten-minute drive from the middle of Innsbruck, this is as popular for Sunday lunch as it is for business visitors during the week. Bedrooms are comfortable if unexceptional. There are tennis courts, a playground and trails in the forest.

Heiterwang

6611 Heiterwang

Tel 05674 5116
e-mail hotel@fischeramsee.at
website www.fischeramsee.at

Nearby Ehrenberg (4 km);
Oberammergau (30 km); Innsbruck
(55 km); castles.
Location at end of lane, facing lake;
ample car parking
Food breakfast, lunch, dinner,
snacks
Prices €€-€€€
Rooms 20; 18 double and single, 2
suites, all with bath or shower; all
rooms have central heating, phone,
satellite TV, safe
Facilities 3 dining rooms, sitting
room, library, bar, spa, fishing and
winter sports nearby
Credit cards not accepted
Children very welcome
Disabled not suitable
Pets accepted
Closed last 2 weeks Jan, mid-Oct to
mid-Dec
Manager Marina Colorful

Fischer Am See
Lakeside hotel

Our hearts sank when we saw a camping and caravan site near this hotel.
Fortunately, it proved to be less intrusive
than we feared. Apparently, some children
like to sleep in a tent while their parents
take bedrooms in the hotel. These are
above average in size, with comfortable
beds, large windows and small but adequate bathrooms. The hotel has recently
been redesigned and refurbished, with a
modern whitewash and brick exterior and
adding more bedrooms and two two-floor
suites with private rooftop terraces.

Like the bedrooms, the dining rooms
are practical rather than pretty. The food is
prepared from local ingredients and fresh
herbs from the kitchen garden. Views of
trees, mountains and water fill the modern
picture windows. The spa also has lovely
views from the floor-to-ceiling windows.

Below the terrace is a landing stage for
launches that shuttle up and down the
interconnecting lakes of Heiterwangsee
and Plansee. There's fishing, canoeing and
rowing on the lake, but at this altitude
(1,000 m) the water is only warm enough
for swimming in July and August. In winter,
moon-lit cross-country skiing excursions
on the lake finish with steaming *Glühwein*
(mulled wine) at the bar.

Eduard-Wallnöferplatz 3, 6460 Imst

Tel 05412 66555
e-mail info@post–imst.at
website www.post–imst.at

Nearby SOS Children's Village,
Garmisch-Partenkirchen (40 km).
Location in heart of village in own
grounds; ample car parking
Food breakfast
Price €
Rooms 26; 13 double, 3 single, 10
suites, all with bath or shower; all
rooms have central heating, phone,
TV, some have minibar, hairdryer
Facilities 2 dining rooms, sitting
room, conference room, terrace; gar-
den, indoor swimming pool, skiing
nearby
Credit cards AE, DC, MC, V
Children very welcome
Disabled not suitable
Pets accepted
Closed Jan to Apr
Proprietors Raggl-Pfeifer family

Hotel Post
Town coaching inn

Thomas Raggl is the driving force
behind the success of what was once
Sprengenstein Castle. The old building,
with its red and white chevrons on the
shutters, seems steeped in history.
Reception is at the top of the stairs, where
the long, white corridor has a decorated
ceiling and a gilded, wrought-iron gate.
Antique chests of drawers, tables with
huge vases of flowers, armchairs and mirrors create an ambience that is grand
without being imposing.

Photographs do not do justice to the
main dining room. Not only are the wood
panels dense with hand-carved trees and
leaves, there is also a collection of the
hideous masks for which the town is
famous. The *Schemenlauf* (parade of spirits)
takes place at Shrovetide every four years
right outside the hotel. Every summer,
however, guests sit out on the extraordinary covered terrace, decked with vines
and flowers.

Bedrooms are handsome, with highly
polished wood and plush, Edwardian-style
fabrics; bathrooms, however, are right up-
to-date. Breakfast is served on the covered terrace. A large garden and an enormous indoor swimming pool are added
bonuses.

Kiebachgasse 8 in der Altstadt, 6020 Innsbruck

Tel 05125 83057
e-mail weisses@roessl.at
website www.roessl.at

Nearby Goldenes Dachl (200 m); Hofburg (50 m); Olympic Museum.
Location in heart of old town, semi-pedestrian zone; public car parking nearby
Food breakfast, lunch, dinner, snacks
Price €€
Rooms 14 double, all with bath or shower; all rooms have central heating, phone, radio, TV, hairdryer
Facilities 3 dining rooms, terrace
Credit cards AE, MC, V
Children welcome
Disabled reasonable access; lift/elevator
Pets accepted
Closed 2 weeks after Easter, 2 weeks Nov
Proprietors Plank family

Weisses Rössl
Town guesthouse

Popular tourist spots are all too often short of hotels that are right for this guide. This one is all but perfect, and right in the middle of the medieval old town. It was originally owned by current owner Klaus Plank's great-grandfather, but hard times forced the family to sell the 600-year-old inn. Klaus's late father Werner then worked his way around the world, saving up to re-install the Planks at the sign of the White Horse. That was 30 years ago, then in 2011 Klaus took over the business – the fourth generation.

The medieval building was completely renovated ten years ago: rewiring, replumbing and exposing the 16thC beams. The decoration, with modern colours and furniture, is sympathetic. The comfortable bedrooms have high ceilings, plain walls in shades of grey with bare wood, and soft blue curtains at the large windows. The restaurant is a meeting place for locals, who pop in for a chat and a game of cards. They don't look at the menu, just order the special of the day, whether it is home-made pasta, potato pancakes or *strudel*. Breakfast is served in the old *Stuben*, hung with Tyrolean paintings, or on the quiet terrace.

Kufstein

Weissachstr 47, 6330 Kufstein

Tel 05372 62122
e-mail hotel@alpenrose-kufstein.at
website www.alpenrose-kufstein.at

Nearby Riedel glass factory.
Location in quiet back street on
edge of town; car parking, garage
Food breakfast, lunch, dinner,
snacks
Prices €€-€€€
Rooms 27; 21 double, 5 single, 1
suite, all with bath or shower; all
rooms have central heating, phone,
TV, safe, minibar, internet, some
have air conditioning
Facilities 3 dining rooms, 2 sitting
rooms, TV room, 2 conference
rooms, sauna, spa; garden; winter
sports nearby
Credit cards AE, MC, V
Children welcome
Disabled lift/elevator, specially
adapted room
Pets accepted
Closed Palm Sunday to Easter
Proprietors Dr Simone Telser and
Johann Telser

Alpenrose
Restaurant-with-rooms

Kufstein is famous for its Riedel glass
factory and, guests would say, the
nearby Alpenrose restaurant. The Telser
brothers took over their parents' modest
guest-house 40 years ago and built an
international reputation for food. The current guardians of this reputation are
Johann Telser and his daughter Simone,

The award-winning restaurant is still
considered 'the best place in town'. There
are several major companies nearby and
this is where the executives come to do
business, so the sober, masculine atmosphere of the main dining room is no surprise. Dark wood and brass are softened
by warm fabrics and flowered curtains;
candles gleam against Riedel glassware.
Tables in secluded corners are, no doubt,
reserved for private conversations. The
impressive wine list catalogues some 200
wines from France and Italy as well as
Austria itself.

Thankfully, Johann and Simone have not
rested on their laurels. The last refurbishment was in 2011 when all of the bathrooms and bedrooms were renovated. The
conference, fitness and spa facilities have
also been upgraded. At breakfast, the Bio-
Ecke, the healthy corner, encourages
guests to start the day with muesli, natural
yoghurt and juices.

Mayrhofen

Dursterstrasse 250b, 6290
Mayrhofen, Zillertal

Tel 05285 63347
e-mail info@apparthotel.com
website www.apparthotel.com

Nearby Penkenbahn cable car.
Location on edge of village; ample
car parking
Food breakfast, self-catering
Prices €€€-€€€€€
Rooms 9 apartments, all with bath;
all apartments have central heating,
phone, TV, minibar, wi-fi, kitchen
with *Kachelofen*, microwave, some
have dishwasher, most have balcony
Facilities breakfast room, bar, gym,
spa with sauna, whirlpool, swimming
pool; terrace, garden, bicycle hire,
winter sports nearby
Credit cards not accepted
Children welcome
Disabled not suitable
Pets dogs welcome (€11 per day)
Closed Nov; chalet only, mid-Apr to
early Jun, early Oct to early Dec
Managers Huber family

Apparthotel Veronika
Village apartment hotel

Readers confirm that the Hubers were right to choose quality rather than quantity when they built their hotel with just nine apartments back in 1984. Only two minutes' walk from the middle of this popular resort village, yet surrounded by fields, the Veronika is 'somewhere between a castle and a farmhouse', according to son Bernhard: you have the luxury of the first combined with the cosiness of the second. Family treasures – old pictures on the walls, carved figures in niches – are dotted around.

On one floor, green is the theme colour; on another it is red, but every apartment is different and all reflect Frau Huber's taste. 'The advantage we have is that when the weather is poor, guests can use their rooms without feeling cramped.' The *Kellerbar* is used for breakfast, though some like to have breakfast in their apartments, with fresh rolls delivered to their doors. No other meals are served: apartments have well-equipped kitchens and Mayrhofen has plenty of good restaurants, so the Hubers decided not to compete.

They also rent out a chalet on top of the Penkenjoch mountain (2,100 m), which is accessible by the gondola in Finkenberg. Breakfast isn't served here, but fresh bread can be bought at the restaurant next door.

Am Hochpillberg, 6130 Schwaz

Tel 05242 63209
e-mail sehnsucht@grafenast.at
website www.grafenast.at

Nearby Schwaz (3.5 km); Innsbruck
(24 km).
Location on the Hochpillberg
mountain; ample car parking
Food breakfast, lunch, dinner,
snacks
Price €€
Rooms 28; 17 double, 11 single, all
with bath or shower; all rooms have
phone, internet
Facilities 2 dining rooms, 3 sitting
rooms, sauna, solarium, fitness and
health centre, garden, swimming
pool, fishing and winter sports near-
by
Credit cards DC
Children very welcome
Disabled not suitable
Pets accepted
Closed after Easter to early June,
Nov to mid-Dec
Proprietors Waltraud and Peter
Unterlechner

Hotel Grafenast
Mountain hotel

'**Y**ou reach it by taking the steepest
chairlift I have ever been on,' one
reader reports. Equally nerve-jangling is
the 10-km drive up from the valley to the
hotel, which is at 1330 m, but everyone
agrees that it is well worth it for the views.
It was back in 1907 that the great-grandfather of the present owners built a hut for
toboggan enthusiasts. This is now the
Grafenast's popular *Stube*. With its dark-
brown wood and green *Kachelofen*, this is
the heart what has grown into a comfortable health and beauty eco-resort.

The Unterlechners provide all the fun
and games you'd expect when staying half
way up an Austrian mountain, from musical
evenings to walks in the woods with flam-
ing torches. The chef has awards for his
health-conscious cooking, and all the food
and drinks served are organic.

The bedrooms are pretty and snug, with
floral pink carpets and plenty of plain
wood, but few guests spend much time in
them, especially in winter. The ski school
is one minute away, while the chair lift conveniently stops outside the door on its
way to the Kellerjoch ski area (2030 m).
Best of all, the hotel's lone television set is
almost impossible to find.

Haspingerstrasse 475/555, 6100
Seefeld

Tel 05212 2652
e-mail info@hotel-charlotte.com
website www.hotel-charlotte.com

Nearby Zirl (7 km); Innsbruck (17 km).
Location 0.5 km from centre of Seefeld, in own garden; private car parking
Food breakfast, dinner
Prices €-€€ (rooms); €-€€€€ (apartments)
Rooms 7; 5 doubles, 2 singles, all with bath; all rooms have TV, central heating; 8 two-room studios, 19 apartments for 2-8, all with kitchen
Facilities 3 dining rooms, bar, spa, swimming pool, Jacuzzi, table tennis room, playroom, internet; garden
Credit cards MC, V
Children welcome
Disabled no special facilities
Pets accepted (extra charge)
Closed Apr to May, end Oct to mid-Dec
Proprietors Köstinger family

Hotel Charlotte
Chalet hotel and apartments

This has been a family-run hotel for 50 years, known for its comfort and character. The Köstinger family (the youngest daughter, Carola, is the manager) run it as a team, aiming for an informal, friendly atmosphere. The Tyrolean-style interior means, of course, wood everywhere; including some lovely panelling. There's an original wood-burning stove in the corner of one dining room; and a pleasant bar in the hall provides a relaxed focus.

The Köstinger family have two other enterprises: Altes Wirtshaus, a delightful, rustic restaurant in a beautifully restored Alpine farmhouse, ten minutes' walk away; and Appart Charlotte Exclusiv, a newly-built (2008) apartment house across the street, with 11 apartments for 2-8 people. Like the Hotel Charlotte, the apartments are decorated with wood; some have dark, knotted panelling and low beams; others have pine and colourful rugs and carpets.

With families in mind, the Köstingers provide table tennis, a children's playroom, and a laundry room for guest use. In fact, out of 34 living units here, only 15 are hotel bedrooms – the rest are apartments (some in the Appart Charlotte), giving it a different atmosphere to a conventional hotel. The Köstingers keep llamas, which apparently make good walking companions for the hotel guests.

Berwang

6622 Berwang

Tel 05674 84230
e-mail hotel.edelweiss@berwang.at
website www.edelweiss-berwang.at
Food breakfast, lunch, dinner, snacks
Price €
Closed after Easter to early June, Oct to mid-Dec
Proprietor Sprenger family

Edelweiss
Town hotel

By building on a semi-circular dining room, the Sprengers have made their Tyrolean-style hotel bright and welcoming. The 20 single, double and family rooms are modern and comfortable. Dinner is served in the cosy restaurant or on the terrace, and includes typical Tyrolean dishes as well as vegetarian options.

They have recently added a spa with sauna, steam bath, infrared cabin, Kneipp bath (herbal and mineral bath) and a hammam. Massages are also available. There's a gym, though in winter you'll probably want to spend most days on the slopes; the ten nearby ski lifts are within walking distance. Slopes are ideal for beginners and low intermediates.

Ehrwald

6632 Ehrwald

Tel 05673 22250
e-mail info@hotel-spielmann.com
website www.hotel-spielmann.com
Food breakfast, lunch, dinner, snacks
Prices €€€-€€€€
Closed mid-Oct to mid-Dec
Proprietors Spielmann family

Hotel Spielmann
Mountain chalet and apartment

Staying here is like staying with Austrian friends. Herr Christian Spielmann is a well-known mountain climber as well as a first-rate chef. The restaurant has a sound reputation and the five-course evening meal (with vegetarian option and a good choice of wine) features ingredients such as lamb and bread from the village.

Bedrooms are decorated in traditional Tyrol style and all, even the singles, have a balcony. There is an apartment for families: children love the spotlessly clean barns, playground and indoor and outdoor swimming pools; parents are thankful for the washing machine. Best of all are the weekly hikes with Herr Spielmann in summer and the choice of slopes in winter, finishing the day at the spa.

Ellmau

Village 29, 6352 Ellmau

Tel 05358 2210
e-mail info@steinbacher-ellmau.at
website www.steinbacher-ellmau.at
Food breakfast
Prices €-€€€
Closed never
Proprietor Hannes Stingl

Steinbacher
Bed-and-breakfast & apartments

Steinbacher's mountain backdrop is a nat-ural stage for film and television crews and attracts holidaymakers all year round. This apartment hotel is a functional base for activities in the Wilder Kaiser region (the first Alpine area to receive the Austrian hiking seal of approval). The apartments are clean and the kitchens are well equipped, but space is limited. The decoration (save some jazzily-striped fabric) is reminiscent of a standardized Travelodge. Even the spa is only open for three hours a day.

Yet the organization is efficient. An ample breakfast is served daily, or guests can pre-order from the local bakery (breakfast service from 7 a.m.). Reasonably priced hik-ing equipment rental and guided mountain tours for all abilities.

Fulpmes

Medrazerstrasse 10, 6166 Fulpmes

Tel 05225 62294
e-mail hotel@hubertus-fulpmes.at
website www.hubertus-fulpmes.at
Food breakfast, dinner (100 m)
Price €
Closed end Apr to end May, 3 weeks Oct
Proprietor Carmen Jenny-Wurzer

Hotel-Garni Hubertus
Town bed-and-breakfast

Skiers from as far afield as the USA are repeat visitors in this informal, turn-of-the-century bed-and-breakfast that over-looks the bandstand. At up to 112 euros for a double room in winter, and only 72 euros in summer, this is sound value.

A breakfast buffet is served at the hotel and dinner can be eaten at the Restaurant Pavillion, which is a 100-m walk away and serves traditional Tyrolean dishes. There is a small spa area with an indoor swimming pool, a sauna and an infrared cabin.

The big local winter sports attraction is the Stubai Glacier: the owners can organ-ize basic glacier training. Guests can also enjoy tours of the local area, schnapps tast-ing, riding and hiking.

Fulpmes

Sonnegg 22, 6166 Fulpmes

Tel 05225 63135
e-mail info@family-resort-stubai.at
website www.family-resort-stubai.at
Food breakfast, dinner, snacks
Price €€
Closed 4 weeks after Easter, Nov to mid-Dec
Proprietors Family Atzinger

Family Resort Stubai
Village hotel and apartments

On the edge of Fulpmes, this hotel offers both good value and a range of activities for family holidays. For the children there is riding at the Reitarena Stubai and for parents there is hiking or skiing. The facilities are right up-to-date, including a spa area with swimming pool and saunas, a supervised children's playroom with qualified carers and an outdoor play area.

Bedrooms in the hotel are decorated with pine and red fabric – some may prefer the young family apartment, 50 m from the hotel, with a well-equipped kitchenette. The dining room is colourfully decorated and there is an original Tyrolean *Stube*. The Atzinger family make a point of using local products – eggs, milk, butter and cheese.

Igls

6080 Igls

Tel 0512 377217
e-mail hotel@schlosshotel-igls.com
website www.schlosshotel-igls.com
Food breakfast, lunch, afternoon tea, dinner, snacks
Price €€€€€
Closed 4 weeks after Easter, Nov to mid-Dec
Proprietors Beck family

Schloss Igls
Castle apartment

Once a hotel, the Schloss Igls is now only available for large groups. Why do we keep it in the guide? Despite its prices, this remains a special treat.

The Owner's Residence, a private apartment in the castle with its own entrance, is decorated in an elegant country style and has a large sitting room, two bedrooms and a study with a view of the Nordkette.

The swimming pool is luxurious and, at the push of a button, a wall of glass disappears into the ground so swimmers can walk out into the garden.

The rest of the castle can be rented by parties of 15 to 33 guests. All inclusive board (€160 per guest per night) includes Champagne, wines, digestifs, soft drinks, afternoon tea and a four-course dinner.

Kals

9981 Kals am Grossglockner

Tel 04876 8226
e-mail info@taurerwirt.at
website www.taurerwirt.at
Food breakfast, lunch, dinner, snacks
Price €€€
Closed after Easter to end May, early Oct to mid-Dec
Proprietors Rogl family

Taurerwirt
Mountain hotel

The location is stunning, at the head of a valley on the southern slopes of the Grossglockner, approached by a twisting road, past gushing waterfalls (providing the hotel's electricity), isolated chapels and the meadow where *Heidi* was filmed. When we first visited, we were impressed by the enthusiasm of the Rogls, who are justifiably proud of their environmentally-friendly improvements. The restaurant serves up hearty portions and, because of chef Sigi Rogl's hunting skills, the menu is never short of local game.

Children have an adventure playground in the pine trees while adults hike in the mountains and fish the rivers. Winter brings skiers, since the ski school, ski kindergarten and lifts are right outside the door.

Kitzbühel

Schulgasse 3, 6370 Kitzbühel

Tel 05356 64311
e-mail info@hotel-goldener-greif.at
website www.hotel-goldener-greif.at
Food breakfast, lunch, dinner
Prices €€–€€€€
Closed never
Proprietor Josef Harisch

Hotel Goldener Greif
Mountain hotel

The Baroque exterior of Goldener Greif belies an interesting mix of old and new, where wood decoration is used to great effect. Our reporter noted 'pleasant carved features' (chairs in the wine cellar, animals on cupboard doors), which blend with renovated bathrooms, bar and dining areas and an up-to-date spa. The owner's unusual collection of religious artefacts features in the corridors, but his eclectic zeal doesn't penetrate the spacious rooms. These are individually decorated, but not overstated – the woodwork and pretty escutcheons pack the greatest punch – and most have a balcony overlooking the mountains.

Many visitors report excellent service, and this is matched by hearty Austrian fare in the dining room. Short walk to ski lifts.

Lienz

9907 Lienz, Tristachersee

Tel 04852 67666
e-mail parkhotel@tristachersee.at
website www.parkhotel-tristach-ersee.at
Food breakfast, lunch, dinner, snacks
Prices €€-€€€
Closed mid-Oct to mid-Dec; restaurant, never
Proprietors Kreuzer family

Parkhotel Tristachersee
Lakeside hotel

Rules are made to be broken. We include the Tristachersee because it is definitely charming and the atmosphere is of a small hotel despite the 42 bedrooms. We would happily spend our holiday watching the colours of the lake change a hundred times a day, from brilliant blue in sunshine to soft green in the rain.

Bedrooms, all facing the water or the woods, are expensively furnished, paintings are chosen with care and even the indoor swimming pool has a mural. Public rooms are large, especially the conservatory right on the water. The award-winning restaurant reflects Josef 'Pepi' Kreuzer's passion for food, especially local fish, such as trout, zander and pike. This is a sophisticated retreat where luxury is tempered by informality.

Reutte

Holz 1, 6600 Wängle bei Reutte

Tel 05672 64234
e-mail hotel@fuerstenhof.at
website www.fuerstenhof.at
Food breakfast, dinner, snacks
Prices €€-€€€€
Closed never
Proprietor Hartmann Weirather

Hotel Fürstenhof
Modern town hotel

Although this hotel has changed hands recently, reports from German and Italian readers insist that it deserves to stay in the book. New owner Hartmann 'Harti' Weirather is a 1982 downhill skiing champion and his passion for outdoor activities shows. As well as skiing (a five-minute walk to lifts) there is Nordic walking, swimming, climbing, rafting and archery nearby.

Bedrooms are modern and practical, but box-like. The bar, however, is designed for socializing, with squashy leather chairs. The dining room has themed nights, but the *à la carte* menu is traditional Austrian, with some international dishes.

With its big terrace, broad lawns and tennis courts, the Fürstenhof has the feel of an American country club.

Seefeld

Hohe Munde Str. 589, 6100 Seefeld

Tel 05212 4441
e-mail hotel@viktoria.at
website www.viktoria.at
Food breakfast, lunch, dinner, snacks
Prices €€ €€€€
Closed 4 weeks after Easter
Proprietors Hans Hell and Anita Kaltschmid

Viktoria Residenzen
Town apartment hotel

Owner Hans Hell created this new apartment house out of the old Hotel Viktoria. There are nine stylish apartments on a quiet, sunny little hill near the pedestrian zone in the centre of Seefeld.

The modern apartments are all made of natural woods and materials, and decorated in beiges and greys with hints of purple, red, green or yellow, except for number nine on the top floor, with its bright orange sofa and splashes of gold.

Service (daily towel change and weekly bed linen) is extra, unless you choose the suite option, which also includes breakfast. All rentals include use of the spa, which has a sauna and an infrared cabin.

Strassen

Dorfstraße 28, 9918 Strassen

Tel 04846 6354
e-mail hotel@strasserwirt.com
website www.strasserwirt.com
Food breakfast, lunch, dinner
Price €
Closed Easter to Mothering Sunday, Nov
Proprietors Bachmann family

Strasserwirt
Village manor house

East Tirol is a backwater by Austrian standards: quiet, with few tourists and even fewer hotels. What was the village meeting point for over 350 years is now a hotel run by the Bachmann family, who host concerts and plays in the old barn.

Four of the bedrooms have four-poster beds and the owners recently refurbished four of the suites with wood and *Loden*, a Tyrolean fabric. They also added a spa with four saunas. Downstairs, there are reading and television rooms. Chef Werner Gander has a fine reputation for his traditional Tyrolean dishes as well as more health-conscious organic products.

Come here for the unspoiled Dolomite hikes and climbs in summer, and the downhill at the Hochpustertal in winter.

Area introduction

Salzburg the city and Salzburg the state have rich landscape and a rich history. Mozart is virtually synonymous with the old city, which celebrates its love of music during the annual festival. All around are mountains and lakes for skiing and sailing.

The city is dominated by the Hohensalzburg fortress, at its foot magnificent buildings such as the Baroque cathedral, St Peter's Abbey and, of course, Mozart's birthplace. Salzburg also boasts great chefs and restaurants, some of which have elegant bedrooms. The Province's southern extremity is blocked by Austria's highest mountain, the Grossglockner. A little to the north, the smaller but significant Honigkogel, near Zell am See, claims to be the geographic centre of Europe. Towns such as Hallein grew rich on the salt from the nearby mines. We like the cluster of lakes to the north of the city, where hotels can be the base for a short commute into Salzburg.

Below are some useful back-up places to try if our main selections are fully booked:

Hotel Lebzelter
Town inn, Altenmarkt
Tel 06452 6911
www.lebzelter.com
Modern and traditional base
for skiing in Zauchensee.

Hotel Der Lindenhof
Town hotel, Badgastein
Tel 06434 26140
www.lindenhof-vital.com
In middle of resort; restaurant
has good reputation.

Unterbergerwirt
Country hotel, Dorfgastein
Tel 06433 7077
www.unterbergerwirt.com
Child-friendly, excellent
food; views to Gastein valley.

Gasthof Hohlwegwirt
Restaurant-with-rooms,
Hallein Tel 06245 824150
www.hohlwegwirt.at
Family-run; ambitious dishes
– reservation recommended.

Der Kaprunerhof
Resort-village hotel, Kaprun
Tel 06547 7234
www.kaprunerhof.at
Quiet hotel good for walks,
cycling and golf (discounts).

Hotel Rupertus
Village hotel, Leogang
Tel 06583 84660
www.rupertus.at
Busy, jolly hotel with lake and
health and fitness floor.

Hotel Wieser
Country hotel, Mittersill
Tel 06562 4270
www.hotel-wieser.at
Family-oriented hotel; skiing
at Kitzbühel Pass (15 mins).

Romantik Hotel Gmachl
Country inn, Salzburg (at
Elixhausen) Tel 0662 480212
www.gmachl.com
Greatly expanded hotel with
pleasant atmosphere.

D'Amici Restaurant-with-
rooms, Strasswalchen
Tel 06215 82060
www.damici.at
Overnight stop; highly rated
for traditional dishes.

Hotel Alpina
Village hotel, Wagrain
Tel 06413 8337
www.hotelalpina.at
Sports hotel with light and
traditional food; ski from door.

Gasthof Grafenwirt
Village inn, Wagrain
Tel 06413 8230
www.grafenwirt.com
Good base for exploring Enns
Valley; local lamb.

Romantikhotel Zell am
See Spa hotel, Zell am See
Tel 06542 72520
www.romantik-hotel.at
520-year-old timbered hotel;
useful for families.

Kaiser-Franz Joseph Str 16, 5640
Badgastein

Tel 06434 51010
e-mail info@villasolitude.com
website www.villasolitude.com

Nearby Casino.
Location in middle of Badgastein,
overlooking falls; car parking out-
side, garage on request
Food breakfast, dinner (next door)
Price €
Rooms 8; 7 double, 1 suite, all with
bath or shower; all rooms have cen-
tral heating, phone, TV, DVD play-
er, minibar, hairdryer, some have safe
Facilities terrace, wi-fi in lobby, golf
(at partner hotel)
Credit cards MC, V
Children accepted
Disabled not suitable
Pets accepted
Closed May, Nov
Proprietor Josef Laggner

Villa Solitude
Converted town villa

Back in 1838, this idyllic villa was the
only building overlooking the famous
Gastein Falls. Surprisingly, it still offers
peace and quiet, despite being on the main
road and next door to the casino, since
most of the bedrooms are at the back,
looking over the valley. In 1990, the
Blumschein family rescued this minor
treasure and recreated its original 19thC
style with antiques and silk fabrics. Then in
2005 a new owner took over and restored
the villa once more, adding three rooms in
the eaves.

Each room reflects a previous owner or
visitor. The Kaiserin Sissy Suite has a double bed tucked into a panelled alcove; the
Kaiser Wilhelm Suite retains the original
large, square, wooden floor tiles, but now
sunshine-yellow curtains frame the tall
French windows. In summer, breakfast is
served on a large terrace with a view of
the mountains and waterfall. In winter
guests relax by the fireplace in the lobby.

Bedrooms and bathrooms are regal,
with a ribbon-and-tassel motif repeated
on thick dressing gowns. Guests are
encouraged to use the excellent Lutter &
Wegner restaurant next door, which
receives good reviews and has a vast wine
list. Readers have singled out the Villa as a
'special spot' for romantic breaks.

Am Dorfplatz 1, 5532 Filzmoos

Tel 06453 8204
e-mail info@hotelhubertus.at
website www.hotelhubertus.at

Nearby Salzburg (55 km);
Grossglockner (75 km).
Location in middle of village; car
parking, garage
Food breakfast, lunch, dinner,
snacks
Prices €€€-€€€€
Rooms 15; 12 double, 3 junior
suites, all with bath or shower; all
rooms have central heating, phone,
TV, wi-fi, balcony
Facilities 2 dining rooms, bar,
sauna, solarium, steam bath; terrace,
garden, cooking courses, winter
sports nearby
Credit cards AE, MC, V
Children very welcome
Disabled lift/elevator
Pets dogs accepted
Closed early Apr to early May; end
Oct to mid-Dec
Proprietors Maier family

Hotel Hubertus
Mountain village hotel

On our first visit, we were impressed by the quality and imagination of Johanna Maier's cooking. Since then, she has served dinner for the King of Thailand, written a cookbook, opened a cooking school and won several awards, including the Goldener Tafelspitz lifetime achievement award. No wonder bookings must be made in advance to eat in the Art Deco-influenced purple and white formal restaurant. Despite this reputation for gourmet dining, we are pleased that Austrian traditions of hospitality continue. Throughout the day, walkers and skiers drop by for light meals as well as coffee and cake in the café or on the terrace.

This is very much a family enterprise. Husband Dietmar manages the excellent wine list and also teaches fly-fishing on the nearby lakes and rivers, while their sons are up early to bake breakfast rolls. The gourmet dinner package is excellent value, as are the winter ski breaks, which include lift passes.

'Better than ever' is our verdict on this modern, angular hotel, where the ground floor is open plan, with big windows, while above, bedrooms are a fresh-looking combination of pale pine, white walls and polished wood floors, with balconies.

Wasserburger Str 52, 83395
Freilassing, Germany

Tel 08654 63060
e-mail info@moosleitner.com
website www.moosleitner.com

Nearby Salzburg (6 km); castles;
churches.
Location W side of town; autobahn
A1/E60 (Freilassing/Bad Reichenhall
exit) 5 km via B20; free car parking
Food breakfast, lunch, dinner,
snacks
Price €€
Rooms 50; 25 double, 25 single, all
with bath or shower; all rooms have
phone, TV, hairdryer, safe, minibar
Facilities 2 dining rooms, sitting
room, bar, meeting room, children's
play room, spa, gym, wi-fi; garden
Credit cards AE, DC, MC, V
Children welcome
Disabled lift/elevator
Pets accepted (extra charge)
Closed restaurant only, Sun
Proprietors Toni & Beate
Niederbuchner

Gasthof Moosleitner
Country inn

Though this hotel is in Germany, it's just
over the border and very close to
Salzburg (5 km), so we include it with our
Austrian hotels. During the 1300s it was a
rest house for traders carrying salt to
Munich from the mines of Salzburg ('Salt
Town'). Now, travellers heading for
Salzburg often stay here instead.

The Niederbuchner family has cared for
this delightful inn for generations, updated
the old bedrooms with great taste, and
acquired an 1800s guesthouse across the
road for extra rooms, and a small annexe
next door for families.

The room rates are lower than over the
border, and the hotel has a Finnish sauna, a
steam room, a gym and a big garden. The
kitchen brings an Austrian lightness to
Bavarian cooking, with a modern twist in
dishes such as spinach dumplings with
sauerkraut and garlic butter, and game
stew with a cheese and nut omelette and
cranberries. The restaurant is visually com-
pelling, all pillars, arches and alcoves, but
white and light, with antlers discreetly
positioned to hint at tradition.

The old salt route is now the main road
into Salzburg, so the quieter rooms are in
the annexe and at the back of the inn
overlooking the garden; the guesthouse
rooms have the best mountain views.

Hauptstrasse 9, 5082 Grödig near
Salzburg

Tel 06246 72521
e-mail info@sallerhof.com
website www.sallerhof.com

Nearby Salzburg (7 km).
Location at foot of Untersberg
mountain, 1 km from the Salzburg-
Sued motorway exit; car parking
Food breakfast
Prices €-€€
Rooms 24 double, all with shower;
all rooms have TV, safe, hairdryer,
internet, balcony
Facilities breakfast room; garden
Credit cards AE, MC, V
Children accepted
Disabled not suitable
Pets not accepted
Closed never
Proprietors Barbara and Klaus
Schnöll-Reichl

Hotel Sallerhof
Village guesthouse

This place goes back 600 years, when
the estate was owned by (and named
after) the Saller family. In 1961 it was
bought by the Schnöll-Reichl family, who
turned it into a small *pension*. Klaus Schnöll
and his wife Barbara took over from his
parents 15 years ago and, under their
watch, the guesthouse has moved on
impressively, becoming more and more
popular with international guests.

The 24 bedrooms are standardized and
modern, but have balconies with a view of
the Untersberg mountain, or the garden.
'Regular guests are drawn back by the individual atmosphere and the personal attention we pay to them,' says Klaus, and we
can see why. Breakfast is served in the
large breakfast room, with cheeses and
yoghurts made by local farmers, Austrian
meats (strictly AMA quality only) and
home-made marmalade and pastries. For
dinner, Barbara and Klaus are eager to give
personal restaurant recommendations.

The house is in a pretty little village
right next to the Untersberg, so there's
walking and hiking right on the doorstep.
Plus, just 7 km south of Salzburg city centre, it's a quiet place to return to after a
day in the city. The garden is a calming spot
in the evening for a glass of wine surrounded by greenery.

No. 3, 5771 Leogang

Tel 06583 8216
e-mail info@K1326.com
website www.K1326.com

Nearby Zell am See (13 km);
Kitzbühel (28 km); Salzburg (45 km).
Location in village; ample car park-
ing
Food breakfast, lunch, dinner,
snacks
Price €€
Rooms 17 double, all with bath or
shower; all rooms have central heat-
ing, phone, TV, hairdryer, wi-fi; 5
apartments for 2 to 5 people, all with
kitchenette
Facilities dining room, sitting room,
bar, wine cellar, Jacuzzi, sauna; gar-
den, winter sports nearby
Credit cards MC, V
Children welcome
Disabled limited access
Pets not accepted
Closed after Easter to May, Nov
Proprietors Unterrainer family

Kirchenwirt
Village hotel and apartments

The Kirchenwirt comes highly recommended by both families and skiers, as
well as food-lovers. The building, dating
from 1326, is the oldest in the valley. Many
of the medieval features are still visible:
thick walls, low vaulted ceilings and carved
wood. By comparison, the Unterrainer
family are newcomers with only 130 years
of ownership behind them. Sepia-coloured
photographs of ancestors line the bright,
white walls; the next generation are
already involved.

Despite its age, this is a light, airy hotel
where 'people, rather than history, come
first', according to one regular. The restaurant has a fine reputation for its traditional Austrian dishes. Bedrooms have been
completely renovated and are individually
furnished with antiques. Bathrooms have
plenty of space for shaving kits and make-
up bags, and some have interesting features such as free-standing bathtubs.

In the meadows at the edge of Leogang,
an annexe, the Ansitz Wirtsgut, has five
striking, modern apartments for longer
stays, which include use of the sauna and
Jacuzzi from Monday to Thursday. A ski lift
and cross-country trails are at the door,
while a free shuttle bus connects with the
extensive Saalbach-Hinterglemm-Leogang
ski area.

Goldgasse 10, 5020 Salzburg

Tel 0662 84 56 22
e-mail hotel@ente.at
website www.ente.at

Nearby Hohensalzburg castle (500 m).
Location Salzburg old town; garage, car parking
Food breakfast, lunch, dinner, snacks
Price €€
Rooms 17; 13 double, 2 twin, 2 single, all with bath or shower; all rooms have phone, TV, hairdryer, safe
Facilities restaurant, lift/elevator; garden
Credit cards AE, DC, MC, V
Children accepted
Disabled not accessible
Pets not accepted
Closed never
Proprietor Mr Nlederleater

Hotel Goldenen Ente

City hotel

We hope that the new owners continue to preserve the best of this hotel's traditional features, as it is clearly loved by many of our readers. The building itself is more than 500 years old, and nestles comfortably in one of Salzburg's most beautiful pedestrianized streets, close to Mozartplatz in the centre of the old town. Warning: the street is very narrow, but you just might be able to drive up to the door, and allow the hotel staff to park for you.

The restaurant could be cosier, but the food is wonderful Austrian fare (they recommend the veal schnitzel as a speciality of the house, and are renowned for their fish dishes) and they like to keep the wine and beer flowing. Breakfasts are worth lingering over. Be sure to enjoy the little touches that make this place so homely and welcoming, such as the chance to griddle your own bacon and eggs at the table.

The bedrooms have been recently refurbished and are decorated in colourful country style, some with antiques. We like the ones with the tiny windows that overlook the streets below – and the eponymous ducks of the hotel's name are hidden in some interesting places. In January 2014, the owner plans to close the hotel to convert all rooms into suites. When it opens it will be renamed Amadeus Suites. Reports on these changes would be welcome.

Höfelgasse 4, 5020 Salzburg

Tel 0662 621765
e-mail hotel@rosenvilla.com
website www.rosenvilla.com

Nearby Hohensalzburg castle (1.5 km); Mirabell Palace (2 km).
Location 15 minutes' walk from centre of Salzburg; ample car parking
Food breakfast, snacks
Price €€
Rooms 15; 8 double, 4 single, 3 suites, all with bath or shower; all rooms have central heating, safe, hairdryer, wi-fi, some have balcony, one has terrace, suites have TV
Facilities breakfast room; terrace, garden
Credit cards MC, V
Children welcome
Disabled not suitable
Pets accepted
Closed never
Proprietors Fleischhaker family

Rosenvilla Hotel Garni
Suburban villa

The Fleischhakers are well known as the chefs of the award-winning Pfefferschiff restaurant in Salzburg, said to be the best in the city. Petra and Klaus travelled the world, cooking on cruise ships, then settled in Salzburg and opened this small B & B hotel early in 1996. Stephanie, their daughter, manages the hotel with pride: she and her team try their best to make guests feel as welcome as possible.

The bedrooms have handmade furniture from Mittersill and pale, restful colours. The rooms are 'a remarkable harmony of split levels, glass, greyish wood, abstract painting and flower petals', said a recent reporter. Breakfast (local and home-made food) on the terrace in summer is idyllic, overlooking a large park with mature trees: even without ordering cooked options, it was a 'varied, extensively and beautifully presented breakfast'. In the evenings, guests are offered appetisers such as *carpaccio* or local cheeses, with wines from the Pfefferschiff restaurant's extensive list. Most guests go out for dinner – there is a bus to the city centre every ten minutes – or Stephanie can arrange a cold supper.

Our reporter said that the attitude and ambience here reminded him of a top oriental hotel.

Mönchsberg Park 26, 5020 Salzburg

Tel 0662 8485550
e-mail salzburg@monchstein.at
website www.monchstein.at

Nearby Mönchsberg lift/elevator; Salzburg Museum (1 km).
Location above Salzburg; car parking outside
Food breakfast, lunch, dinner, snacks
Prices €€€€–€€€€
Rooms 24; 11 double, 13 suites, all with bath or shower; all rooms have central heating, phone, Sky TV, DVD player, air conditioning, minibar, hairdryer, safe, wi-fi, some suites have terrace
Facilities 2 dining rooms, restaurant, sitting room, spa, bar; terraces
Credit cards AE, DC, MC, V
Children welcome
Disabled lift/elevator
Pets accepted; not in restaurant
Closed never
Manager Samantha Teufel

Hotel Schloss Mönchstein **Castle hotel**

We half expected to see Rapunzel leaning out of the 14thC tower of this imposing, award-winning hotel, built on a crag above the heart of Salzburg. Instead, we found guests in shorts and open-neck shirts ordering coffee and cake on the terrace. Inside, highly polished tables and gold plush sofas are reflected in large, gilt mirrors. It all looks very stiff and formal, yet the uniformed staff are young and friendly and can't do enough to help. The two old dining rooms have been converted into a suite, and now you can choose from the Orangerie Apollo terrace bar, or the classy gourmet Restaurant Schloss Mönchstein. You can also rent the Gothic Salon with its heavy wooden furnishings, or 'the smallest restaurant in the world' in the tower, which only seats four people – 'crazy and romantic', said a recent visitor.

Bedrooms are grand without being over-decorated. Number 32, high up under the eaves, is decorated in garden greens; number 11 has a tapestry on the wall. Many have antiques, and all have modern bathrooms. Half look over the city, the other half over the gardens and extensive park. Used by businessmen and touring North Americans and Japanese, it also has guests who settle in for a week at a time. Weddings take place in the small chapel and there are weekend harp concerts.

Markt 46, 5450 Werfen

Tel 06468 5212 0
e-mail ok@obauer.com
website www.obauer.com

Nearby Eisriesenwelt ice caves (2 km); Schloss Hohenwerfen (3.5 km); Salzburg (38 km).
Location on main street of village; own car parking
Food breakfast, lunch, dinner; snacks in café
Price €€€
Rooms 15; 8 double, 3 single, 4 suite, all with bath or shower; all rooms have central heating, phone, TV, radio, minibar, hairdryer, safe
Facilities 2 dining rooms; garden, skiing nearby
Credit cards AE, MC, V
Children welcome
Disabled not suitable
Pets accepted (extra charge)
Closed variable, always phone ahead
Proprietors Karl and Rudolf Obauer

Restaurant-Hotel
Obauer **Restaurant-with-rooms**

Restaurant-with-rooms does scant justice to this converted guesthouse set among the medieval houses of Werfen. The Obauer brothers were voted Chefs of the Year in 1989 and reservations must be made well in advance. After several years working abroad, Karl and Rudolf came home to take on the family business that stretches back 150 years. Signature dishes include a trout strudel with white wine sauce, calves' liver with truffles and chestnuts, and sumptuous desserts like blackberry and chocolate parfait, all with the light inventiveness of contemporary French chefs. The decoration is as sophisticated as the food. The two small dining rooms retain the old, low, beamed ceilings, but tables are set formally with fine linen and fresh flowers.

This contemporary feel continues upstairs where an architect friend designed dramatic, geometric headboards for the grey and white minimalist bedrooms. The white bathrooms are as antiseptic as the Obauers' kitchens. For breakfast, brioches and home-made breads are served to order, perhaps in the garden under gold and white umbrellas.

Erlhofweg 11, Thumersbach, 5700
Zell am See

Tel 06542 566 37
e-mail erlhof@aon.at
website www.erlhof.at

Nearby Zeller Lake (100 m);
Schmittenhöhe mountain (6 km);
Kitsteinhorn mountain (17 km).
Location in own grounds by lake;
car parking outside hotel
Food breakfast, lunch, dinner,
snacks
Price €€
Rooms 14; 8 double, 1 single, 1 fam-
ily, 4 suites, all with bath or shower;
all rooms have phone, TV, minibar,
internet
Facilities 2 dining rooms, sitting
room, bar, sauna, solarium, fitness
room; terrace, garden
Credit cards AE, MC, V
Children accepted
Disabled not suitable
Pets accepted
Closed Nov; restaurant only, Wed
Managers Brüggler family

Landhotel Erlhof
Country inn

The Brügglers follow a line of successful
chefs at Landhotel Erlhof and visitors'
reports of their food are all positive. They
have made few changes to the old farmhouse set on the sunny, quiet side of the
Zeller Lake.

Josef Brüggler's cooking is hearty with
Austrian and Italian influences. Lunch and
dinner are served in the snug dining rooms
with an open fire under the centuries-old,
arched ceiling. In warm weather food can
also be eaten on the terrace, overlooking
the lake. Menus feature local lake fish and
game from the nearby forests.

As well as eating and drinking, guests
chat in the wood-panelled sitting room,
admire the view across the lake to the
snow-frosted peaks of the Hohe Tauern,
and sleep in plain, straightforward bedrooms. Set in spacious grounds, with lawns
running down to the shore, this is a place
to relax. That does not mean there is nothing to do. Some guests work off calories
with golf, tennis, cycling or swimming from
the Erlhof's own beach. When the lake is
frozen, some diners even walk across from
Zell, and the Kitzteinhorn glacier means
there is skiing all year.

5700 Zell am See

Tel 06542 726090
e-mail info@schloss-prielau.at
website www.schloss-prielau.at /
www.mayers-restaurant.at

Nearby Zeller lake (300 m); Zell am
See (2 km); Kaprun (8 km).
Location north end of Zeller lake, in
own park; ample car parking
Food breakfast, lunch, dinner
Prices €€€-€€€€€
Rooms 9; 7 double, 2 suites, all with
bath or shower; all rooms have cen-
tral heating, phone, TV, minibar; 1
apartment
Facilities 2 dining rooms, sitting
room with bar, terrace, sauna, steam
bath, massage, private beach, skiing,
watersports and golf nearby
Credit cards AE, DC, MC, V
Children welcome
Disabled not suitable
Pets welcome
Closed 3 weeks after Easter, end-
Oct to early Dec
Managers Andreas and Anette
Mayer

Schloss Prielau
Castle hotel and apartment

We were impressed by this fortified manor house on our first visit; since Andreas Mayer and his wife Anette took over management in 2004, we are even more enthusiastic. Anette manages the hotel and wedding service; Andreas works his two-Michelin-star magic in the kitchen, where he cooks regional food – served in the restaurant or on the terrace.

The castle, which has stood at the northern end of the Zeller lake for 600 years, was rescued from dilapidation in the mid-1980s. Paintings and carvings by local artists and craftsmen were restored, while Persian carpets were added to give warmth to tile and wood floors. When the Mayers took over, they refurbished all the bedrooms and bathrooms. The result is 'stylish informality', according to one visitor, who relished the intimacy of this hotel.

Bedrooms are large, with curtains and chairs providing colour against white walls, and each has a pretty view. Weekenders come from Munich, businessmen for seminars during the week, and families for skiing in winter and golf in summer. There's a private beach, while the Prielau Kirche, a tiny chapel, is used for services and weddings.

Those who know busy Zell am See will be pleased to find such a secluded retreat only minutes away.

Anthering near Salzburg

Hotel Hammerschmiede
Converted country farm

This pretty 18thC building was once a blacksmith's home and his forge is now a museum. It's secluded (2 km to nearest train station), and the feel is of a homestead, with open fireplaces, peacocks running around outside and the odd deer to spot. Though there are 24 bedrooms, it doesn't feel big – eight of the rooms are in the Villa Loretta annexe next door. They are furnished in pine with a simple pink or blue theme. Most have balconies overlooking the surrounding countryside.

All ingredients are sourced locally – curd cheese, eggs, bread and seasonal vegetables from Anthering; beef, veal, pork and turkey from Ablinger – and breakfast is all organic. At €29 a head for a three-course dinner, it's well-priced for the quality.

Acharting 22, 5102 Anthering near Salzburg

Tel 06223 2503
e-mail info@hammerschmiede.at
website www.hammerschmiede.at
Food breakfast, dinner
Price €€
Closed never
Proprietor Ernestine Stadler

Badgastein

Haus Hirt
Mountain hotel

Any misgivings about this dour 80-year-old building, wedged high above the town, are dispelled immediately by big vases of fresh flowers, Persian carpets on parquet floors, inviting armchairs and views northwest over the Gastein Valley. With 29 rooms it's now too big for a whole page, but it's run by a family who are truly professional hoteliers. Under daughter Evelyn, and her husband Ike's management, the whole house has been refurbished.

Bedrooms have all been modernized, but traditional still blends with modern in some public areas, such as the terrace and some of the balconies. The food is all local, fresh and organic; the breakfast buffet is particularly impressive, with 14 herbal teas, half a dozen home-made jams.

5640 Badgastein, Kaiserpromenade

Tel 06434 2797
e-mail info@haus-hirt.com
website www.haus-hirt.com
Food breakfast, dinner, snacks
Prices €€-€€€€
Closed mid-April to mid-May; mid-Oct to mid-Dec
Proprietors Evelyn and Ike Ikrath

Goldegg

5622 Goldegg

Tel (06415) 81030
e-mail hotel@hotelpost-goldegg.at
website www.hotelpost-goldegg.at
Food breakfast, lunch, dinner, snacks
Prices €-€€
Closed mid-Mar to early May, mid-Oct to mid-Dec
Proprietor Gesinger family

Hotel Gasthof zur Post
Country inn

Set in a pretty, unspoilt village with an old castle and church, the Gasthof zur Post is known for its warm, cosy atmosphere. This family-run inn is surrounded by beautiful skiing areas and there are plenty of opportunities for winter sports as well as golf, hiking, swimming, and fishing in summer. Salzburg is only an hour's drive away.

The best bedrooms are the 16 overlooking the lake, which is right in front of the inn. Those with hearty appetites will appreciate the cooking, which is well above average, and made with fresh local produce. There is a small spa with a sauna and massages, and golf packages are available.

Goldegg

5622 Goldegg am See

Tel 06415 81370
e-mail office@derseehof.at
website www.derseehof.at
Food breakfast, lunch, dinner, snacks
Prices €-€€
Closed mid-Mar to April; Nov and some days Dec
Proprietors Schellhorn family

Hotel Seehof
Country inn

Goldegg is a village of preserved old houses, restored cobbled streets and no modern development. This large white inn is 500 years old. Watercolours line the walls and a battle flag hangs above the stairs.

The 28 bedrooms are individually decorated, with a choice of budget, themed, or the unusual Come and See rooms and suites with glass-walled bathrooms. 'It has been an inn since 1727 and we're the fourth generation of Schellhorns to run it,' said Karola, who was the chef until 15 years ago when her son, Sepp, took charge, producing, among other delights, gossamer-thin strudel pastry to envelope apple or rhubarb. In winter, guests can go on ski safaris, or go ice-skating and curling on the lake; in summer there is golf and swimming.

Mattsee

Schlossbergweg 4, 5163 Mattsee

Tel 06217 5205
e-mail schlosshotel@iglhauser.at
website www.schlosshotel-igl.at
Food breakfast, lunch, dinner, snacks
Price €€
Closed Christmas
Proprietors Iglhauser family

Schlosshotel Iglhauser
Converted lakeside brewery

The current owner of this imposing guesthouse is the sixth Jakob Iglhauser. It's an old brewery, which has been offering guest rooms since 1398, and the bustle of activity hasn't changed. Waiters hurry from the kitchen past the reception desk and into the dining rooms: one with murals and a collection of pewterware; another, less formal, with mis-matched chairs. Frau Iglhauser cooks old Salzburg recipes with fish from the lake and homegrown herbs.

Pastel colours in bedrooms set off frescoed or vaulted ceilings and old beams. The Iglhausers encourage guests to use the hotel's sailing dinghies and windsurfing boards. Not the place for complete relaxation, perhaps, but fun for children and handy for visits to Salzburg (15 km).

Mittersill

5730 Mittersill

Tel 06562 4407
e-mail homepage@felben.at
website www.felben.at
Food breakfast, lunch, dinner, snacks
Price €€-€€€
Closed after Easter to Ascension, Nov to mid-Dec
Proprietors Christoph and Petra Scharler

Kinderhotel Felben
Suburban farm hotel

Surrounded on three sides by fields but close enough to walk into the city, the Scharler family's 1989-vintage hotel is next to the cleanest farmyard we have ever seen. Cows, chickens and horses delight the children of parents who, understandably, book up early to stay here.

Bedrooms are big enough for boisterous families. The owners deserve recognition for making this place truly child friendly: there are seven children's playrooms, youth rooms and a movie theatre. The emphasis is on childcare and health and fitness, with all non-smoking rooms. There is a spa with saunas, a steam bath and a heated swimming pool with a slide. Riding, skiing and swimming courses; activity programme for children and adults, summer and winter.

Oberalm bei Hallein

Oberalm 32, 5411 Oberalm/Hallein

Tel 06245 80662
e-mail info@schlosshaunsperg.com
website www.schlosshaunsperg.com
Food breakfast
Prices €€-€€€
Closed never
Proprietors Gernerth family

Schloss Haunsperg
Manor house hotel

Filled with antiques and heirlooms, this 600-year-old manor house is almost a museum – but to the von Gernerth family it is home. Among the portraits of ancestors is great-grandfather, who wrote the words to *The Blue Danube Waltz*.

The eight bedrooms and suites sleep two to five people and, like the rest of the manor, are furnished with period pieces. In the grounds there are a Baroque chapel and private clay tennis courts. Golf, riding, squash and more tennis nearby.

St Gilgen

Mozartplatz 8, 5340 St Gilgen

Tel 06227 2157
e-mail office@gasthofzurpost.at
website www.gasthofzurpost.at
Food breakfast, lunch, dinner, snacks
Prices €€-€€€
Closed 3-4 weeks in winter
Proprietors Leitner family

Gasthof Zur Post
Village inn

Most visitors to this popular resort on the Wolfgangsee are interested in its Mozart connections. Our reporter was more interested in this inn, built in 1415 and a protected building: all along the front is a lively painted frieze depicting a medieval boar hunt.

Norbert and Katharina Leitner, who took over 14 years ago, renovated in 2013. Upstairs, peasant-style floral patterns still decorate the doors, but the 34 bedrooms are now decorated in a modern interpretation of traditional style: deer antlers on white walls, copper fittings reused as lamps, deerskin rugs on polished wood floors. They have succeeded in meeting modern guests' expectations while preserving the feeling that the inn has been lived in for centuries.

St Johann im Pongau

Bundesstrasse 1, 5600 St Johann/Pg

Tel 06412 6012
e-mail info@hirschenwirt.com
website www.hirschenwirt.com
Food breakfast, lunch, dinner
Price €
Closed Nov to beginning of ski season; dining room only, lunch and dinner, end of ski season to mid-May
Proprietors Gerhard Viehhauser and Madeleine Storm

Hirschenwirt
Village hotel

If you need a simple but pleasant base offering good value in a skiing area suitable for beginners, this is a useful address. Gerhard Viehhauser, a local man involved in several sports organizations, runs the inn with Swedish-born Madeleine Storm. Both speak fluent English, Swedish, Danish and Norwegian, and they offer good value, with a competitive price of 55 euros (as we went to press) for half board in high season.

The main hotel has 12 double and family rooms as well as the breakfast/dining room. The building behind it is mainly used by groups in winter. Don't expect designer-chic bedrooms: they are standard Austrian hotel fare and not particularly spacious. But it's well kept, clean, and friendly – and the main thing here is the surroundings.

Salzburg

Linzergasse 20, 5020 Salzburg

Tel 0662 873545
e-mail welcome@stadtkrug.at
website www.stadtkrug.at
Food breakfast, lunch, dinner, snacks
Price €€
Closed early Feb to mid-March; restaurant only, Tues except during Festival
Proprietors Lucian family

Hotel Stadtkrug
City hotel

Even on a chill, rainy afternoon, the Stadtkrug made a favourable impression on our reporter. Set in the 800-year-old new town, the hotel has ancient beams exposed above the bar and stone arches set off white walls. A lump of granite protrudes behind reception, showing where the hotel is built into the Kapuzinerberg.

Most of the bedrooms have the same deep pink carpet, printed curtains, and no-nonsense furnishings, but room 102 boasts a four-poster bed. Its bathroom looks right out of Hollywood but even ordinary bathrooms have two basins and large, well-lit mirrors. The restaurant is one of the most popular in town, staying open late during the Festival. The four terrace gardens offer <u>fine</u> views of church domes and spires.

Salzburg

5020 Salzburg, Gaisberg

Tel 0662 641067
e-mail mail@zistelalm.at
website www.zistelalm.at
Food breakfast, lunch, dinner,
snacks
Price €
Closed mid-Oct to mid-Dec
Manager Michael Huber

Hotel Zistelalm
Mountain inn

The look of a hunting lodge or mountain hut with heavy beams and walls covered in antlers makes quite a contrast to the city down below. This hideaway, high on the Gaisberg, is especially romantic in winter, with its log fires and deep armchairs.

The 11 double rooms are comfortable, with dark wood, plain walls and floor-to-ceiling windows. The restaurant serves regional, home-cooked meals and there is an open fireplace in the bar.

Gaisberg is a popular retreat for families. At 1,290 m it's high enough to get glimpses of the Grossglockner and views from Salzkammergut to the Chiemgau.

Salzburg (at Anif)

5081 Anif bei Salzburg

Tel 06246 72175
e-mail info@schlosswirt-anif.com
website www.schlosswirt-anif.com
Food breakfast, lunch, dinner,
snacks
Prices €€-€€€
Closed never
Managers Gassner family

Romantik Hotel Schlosswirt **Country inn**

This guesthouse of the nearby castle has changed hands several times in the past 50 years, and when the current owners took over in 2008, they were determined to 'put the soul back in the building'. They renovated rooms to a four-star standard, but kept the traditional atmosphere of the hotel. Wooden benches in the *Gaststube* date from 1607; the dining rooms look turn-of-the-century. Upstairs, pages of 19thC hunting and mountaineering magazines hang on the walls. Each bedroom is different: 17 boasts a large sleigh bed and overlooks the stream and garden at the back.

The kitchen is traditional, and the quality of its food has greatly improved over the last 25 years. Opposite, the Kramerbauer annexe (15thC) has comfortable rooms.

Area introduction

Upper Austria (German, Oberösterreich) has a variety of landscape, including mountains such as the Höllengebirge and the northern slopes of the Totes Gebirge; the broad valley of the Danube; a large part of the Salzkammergut and its lakes.

Linz, the state capital and the home of the *Linzertorte* cake, mixes ancient and modern successfully. The 8thC church of St Martin and the castle contrast with modern industry. Thousands are attracted each year to the Brucknerfest.

We like the province's small towns, where impressive efforts have been made to restore and revive their centres. Hikers and bikers head for the peace and quiet of the Mühlviertel, the Innviertel and Hausruck areas. The Salzkammergut, studded with over 70 small lakes, is particularly popular for water sports. Everywhere we've discovered small inns and rural retreats that are just right for this guide.

Below are some useful back-up places to try if our main selections are fully booked:

Seegasthof Oberndorfer
Lakeside hotel, Attersee
Tel 07666 78640
www.oberndorfer.info
Well-known restaurant with mountain views; private dock.

Hotel Georgshof
Country hotel, Attersee at Unterach Tel 07665 8501
www.georgshof.cc
Hotel at S end of the Attersee; views of surrounding woods.

Landhotel Agathawirt
Country guesthouse, Bad Goisern Tel 06135 8341
www.agathawirt.at
16thC guesthouse; good base for exploring Salzkammergut.

Berggasthof Waldschenke am Sternstein
Country hotel, Bad Leonfeld
Tel 07213 6279
www.waldschenke.at
Secluded woodland house.

Grünes Türl Restaurantwith-rooms, Bad Schallerbach
Tel 07249 481630
www.gruenes-tuerl.at
Basic rooms, popular restaurant: try the trout/venison.

Hotel Lauriacum
Town hotel, Enns
Tel 07223 823150
www.lauriacum.at
Modern rooms, country-style *Stüberl*; secluded garden.

Hotel Goldener Adler
Old inn, Freistadt
Tel 07942 72112
www.hotels-freistadt.at
Former brewery, specializes in beer dishes; pretty courtyard.

Dietlgut Country hotel and apartments, Hinterstoder
Tel 07564 52480
www.dietlgut.at
Health-focussed hotel; hiking, rafting; dogs welcome.

Gasthof Goldener Adler
Bed-and-breakfast, Linz
Tel 07327 31147
http://goldeneradler.at
Family-run; modern rooms; locally popular restaurant.

Seehotel Lackner
Lakeside hotel, Mondsee
Tel 06232 2359
www.seehotel-lackner.at
Visit for the lakeside restaurant with mountain views.

Donauhof
Riverside hotel, Ottensheim
Tel 07234 838180
www.donauhof.cc
Sophisticated hotel-restaurant-café; gourmet evening.

Grünau im Almtal

Almeggstraße 1, 4645 Grünau im Almtal

Tel 07616 6004
e-mail romantikhotel@almtalhof.at
website www.almtalhof.at

Nearby Almsee (10 km).
Location valley of River Alm; ample car parking
Food breakfast, lunch, dinner, snacks
Prices €€-€€€
Rooms 9; 4 double, 2 single, 3 suites, all with bath or shower; all rooms have central heating, phone, some have balcony, fireplace
Facilities 2 dining rooms, bar, indoor swimming pool, massages; terrace; winter sports, golf nearby
Credit cards AE, MC, V
Children very welcome
Disabled 1 specially adapted room
Pets accepted
Closed after Easter to end April, mid-Oct to mid-Dec
Proprietors Leithner family

Romantik Hotel Almtalhof **Mountain inn**

This is more of an experience than a hotel. Stand on the balcony on a spring evening and breathe in the fresh, alpine air of the Alm valley. Lilac bloom in the garden below; further on is the rushing river, between birch, chestnut and sycamore trees. Our reporter responded to the 'wonderfully rambling, seemingly endless *Stuben* and connecting corridors.' Everywhere are cushions embroidered in red and white folk designs by Ulrike Leithner, who runs the hotel with her husband, Karl.

They continually improve the 1911 building, built by a Leithner grandfather. Bedrooms have been enlarged recently, making the most of their pine furniture. Bathrooms show similar care and are fitted with power showers and gilded taps. The food is Austrian with a light touch, using produce from local farms and plenty of game. A typical meal could include a venison ravioli starter, wild boar main and Salzburg dumplings for dessert. Our reporter liked the detailed wine list, which includes bottles from Austria's finest vineyards. The hotel also hosts fondue evenings. An indoor swimming pool, a garden for children, and a new golf course nearby complete the picture. However: we've had some mixed reports of the Almtalhof recently – so more feedback would be welcome.

Kremsmünster

Franz-Hönig Str 16, 4550
Kremsmünster

Tel 07583 5258
e-mail schlair@hotelschlair.at
website www.hotelschlair.at

Nearby Kremsmünster monastery;
Schloss Kremsegg music museum.
Location in town; own car parking
Food breakfast, dinner
Price €
Rooms 39; 25 double, 10 single, 4
family, all with bath or shower; all
rooms have phone, cable TV, central
heating, minibar, wi-fi; apartments
with kitchen available from 2016
Facilities dining room, sitting room,
swimming pool nearby
Credit cards AE, MC, V
Children not suitable
Disabled not suitable
Pets welcome
Closed Christmas to early Jan
Proprietors Maria and Erik Kux

Hotel Schlair
Town hotel

Eric Kux, an American with a huge
chuckle, is also an impressive chef, who
trained in France and Italy. In the dining
room, which is restricted to house guests
only, he serves 'Austrian dishes with a
twist'. There is no set menu, since dishes
are prepared from the best produce available each day in the market. If you do
decide to eat out, there are several decent
restaurants in town, which serve typical
Austrian fare.

The hotel was originally discovered by a
reader from Munich and we were delighted to agree with his enthusiastic report. It
consists of two buildings: the Hotel Schlair,
big and square, in the newer part of
Kremsmünster, and the quiet, 800-year old
Zur Alte Mühle annexe, two minutes' walk
away, up the hill near the former market
place. Breakfast is worth the walk: 'I can't
name the many different kinds of bread
that are served ... the sweet smell of coffee and sugar early in the morning is just
fantastic.' Since the breads come from the
bakery next door, run by Erik's brother-in-
law, this really is a family business. Although
bedrooms are stylish, with the conven-
iences demanded by both tourists and
business visitors, it is the Kux family's 'individual attention' that our reader remem-
bers. A solo traveller, he 'never had the
feeling of being ignored.'

Unternberg 6, 4120 Neufelden

Tel 07282 62 58
e-mail reception@muehltalhof.at
website www.muehltalhof.at

Nearby Danube River (7 km);
Mühlviertel.
Location on a minor road,
overlooking old mill-pond; ample
car parking
Food breakfast, lunch, dinner,
snacks
Prices €€–€€€
Rooms 22; 12 double, 2 single, 1
family, 7 suites, all with bath or
shower; all rooms have central
heating, phone, TV, minibar,
hairdryer, safe, two share roof
terrace
Facilities 3 dining rooms, sitting
room, bar, TV room, spa; terrace;
winter sports, golf nearby
Credit cards DC, V
Children welcome
Disabled not suitable
Pets accepted
Closed Nov
Proprietors Rachinger-Eckl family

Mühltalhof
Waterside hotel

The Rachinger-Eckls are continuing an inn-keeping tradition going back six generations. The atmosphere in their 17thC hotel is very personal: there are family photographs on the walls, and more in an album near the entrance.

Johanna runs the administrative side, brother Helmut does the cooking, which is much praised, and his wife Ira takes care of beauty treatments. Fish and game appear on the ever-changing menu, which could include duck with red cabbage followed by *profesen* (French toast with plums) and home-made cinnamon ice cream, complimented by well-chosen Austrian wines.

The old mill-pond provides swimming and rowing, in summer, and ice skating and curling in winter. Nearby, there are summer walks and cycle routes in the forest and winter skiing. Afterwards, guests can relax in the new spa, with a view of the river. The new covered terrace and all but three of the rooms have river and forest views. When we first visited, those at the top of the building had small windows and low beams, which guests found either 'cosy' or 'dim'; we're glad to say that after the hotel's recent refurbishment bedrooms are more modern, light and airy.

Across the river, Joachim Eckl displays his artwork in his own gallery.

5360 St Wolfgang

Tel 06138 2209
e-mail office@appesbach.com
website www.appesbach.com

Nearby Bad Ischl (14 km); Mondsee (15 km).
Location in parkland; ample car parking
Food breakfast, lunch, dinner, snacks
Prices €€-€€€
Rooms 26 double, all with bath or shower; all rooms have central heating, phone, TV
Facilities dining room, reading room, bar, health and fitness area; terrace, garden, dock, tennis court; golf, hiking, water sports nearby
Credit cards DC, MC, V
Children welcome
Disabled not suitable
Pets accepted; not in restaurant
Closed Nov to Easter; open during advent
Proprietor Johann Frank Schütten

Landhaus zu Appesbach
Lakeside hotel

This elegant country home remains as popular as ever. Readers point out that, despite the popularity of St Wolfgang itself, a large leafy park and private access to the lake ensure total privacy and peace. Now well over a century old, the cream and green villa has neatly trimmed lawns stretching down to the clear, clean waters of the Wolfgangsee.

Back in 1937, the Duke of Windsor, complete with houndstooth suit, stayed here following his abdication of the British throne. Though the hotel has changed hands since then, much of what he enjoyed is still visible today.

The Windsor Suite, with its handsome twin beds sharing one ornate headboard, has the same glorious views over the lake; the reading room still looks as if a dropped pin would cause consternation, while the bar, with its high stools, would be a fine set for a Noel Coward play.

Heritage is preserved here, but you also get the best of today with saunas, a tennis court and a landing stage for sailing and windsurfing.

Schärding

Unterer Stadtplatz 3, 4780
Schärding am Inn

Tel 07712 23020
e-mail info@hotelforstinger.at
website www.hotelforstinger.at

Nearby Danube River (150 m);
Passau (12 km).
Location on main square; own
unattended car parking area
Food breakfast, lunch, dinner,
snacks
Prices €–€€
Rooms 16; 14 double, 2 single, all
with bath or shower; all rooms have
central heating, phone, TV, minibar,
hairdryer, safe, internet
Facilities 2 dining rooms
Credit cards AE, DC, MC, V
Children welcome
Disabled not suitable
Pets accepted
Closed never
Proprietors Förstinger family

Hotel Forstinger
Town inn

Those readers who have stopped in
Schärding have confirmed that the
locals are right: their main square could
well be the 'prettiest in Austria'. The look
is pure storybook, with baroque houses
painted ochre, red or light blue. They followed our reporter's advice to turn off the
main street, under medieval arches to the
bank of the fast-flowing Inn where swans
breast the stream, mallard croak and teal
fall out of the darkness and into the water
like stones.

The tavern dates back to 1606 and its
interior continues the rustic traditions of
days-gone-by, with old beams, vaulted ceilings and intricate carving. In the dining
room, formality rules, with pink linens,
long-stemmed glasses and candle-light giving a glow to the elaborate pine panelling.
The cooking is impressive, with the
emphasis on fish, such as carp, char and
trout from nearby mountain streams. No
doubt fly-fishermen flushed with success
can have their catch cooked for dinner.

Take care when choosing a bedroom.
The older, atmospheric ones, furnished
with antiques, overlook the square where
the Saturday market sets up at 6 a.m. The
newer rooms at the back are quieter but
have less character. All beds and carpets
were replaced in 2008 and flat screen TVs
added. Bathrooms are modern.

Attersee

Seefeld 14, 4853 Steinbach am
Attersee

Tel 07663 8100
e-mail
hotel.foettinger@salzkammergut.at
website www.hotel-attersee.at
Food breakfast, lunch, dinner,
snacks
Price €€
Closed Jan
Proprietors Föttinger family

Activ-Hotel Föttinger
Lakeside hotel and apartment

'Do what Gustav Mahler did' is the motto here. Inside, the large, open-plan lobby is a display case of Mahler memorabilia including a copy of his Symphony No. 3, written in a small summer cabin by the lake, between 1893-96. The garden is still used for concerts and musical evenings.

There is a drawback to staying here. The hotel is right on the lake, but views from the green-shuttered windows are blotted by a caravan park at its busiest in July and August. Otherwise, the bedrooms are all large, with white walls and pine furniture. The restaurant is similarly expansive, with a rustic look thanks to antlers and brown colours.

There's also a self-catering cabin right on the lakefront, with an open fireplace and a terrace, which sleeps up to four people

Attersee

Hauptstr 20, 4863 Seewalchen am
Attersee

Tel 07662 298 60
e-mail welcome@hotel-haeupl.at
website www.hotel-haeupl.at
Food breakfast, lunch, dinner,
snacks
Price €€
Closed never
Proprietors Häupl family

Hotel-Restaurant Häupl **Lakeside hotel**

This is still a winning combination: cooking by top chef Klaus Kobald and views across the largest lake in the Austrian Alps. Gourmets come for regional specialities such as fish from the lake, accompanied by one of six wines available daily by the glass, or beer from the barrel. Book early.

The Häupl family have run this 300-year-old inn for seven generations, during which they have collected some intriguing antiques including a confessional, topped with a statue of St Florian, and an ancient wine press. As for bedrooms, there are two different styles. Lake view rooms are simple, some with painted wood furniture; lifestyle rooms – some with disabled access – are modern with dark, striped wood and lime-green curtains; bathrooms are modern.

Bad Ischl

Steinbruch 43, 4820 Bad Ischl

Tel 06132 23535
e-mail kontakt@villa-schratt.at
website villaschratt.at
Food breakfast
Price €€
Closed never
Proprietor Linda Plech

Villa Schratt
Town hotel

Villa Schratt is proud of its history, but there's little that is old-fashioned about this hotel. Only the Katharina Schratt suite boasts Biedermeier furniture and dark-red walls; the other rooms are bright and filled with rustic, light wood furniture. A terrace connecting the Schratt Suite and the neighbouring Johann Nestroy Room make the pair ideal for a family visit to the Salzkammergut region. Choose from outdoor activities (hiking, golf, fishing nearby) or culture: Bad Ischl is a spa town and hosts seasonal festivals, including the *Glöcklerlauf* at Christmas and, in summer, an Operetta festival.

Villa Schratt only offers breakfast, but a handful of rooms have kitchenettes. A short drive or bus ride away, central Bad Ischl overflows with eateries.

Freistadt

Böhmergasse 8-10, 4240 Freistadt

Tel 07942 722580
e-mail goldener.hirsch@hotels-freistadt.at
website www.hotels-freistadt.at
Food breakfast, lunch, dinner, snacks
Price €
Closed never
Proprietors Jäger family

Hotel Zum Goldenen Hirschen **Town guesthouse**

Our reporter was delighted by the swallows in the arched passage where old wine presses and a hay cutter lend an aura of rusticity. This guesthouse is just inside Freistadt's solid Bohemian Gate and the garden backs on to the old walls.

The cooking is imaginative, with traditional dishes matched by, for example, a pumpernickel soufflé with cheese sauce. Bedrooms are large and some have a separate sitting area; the best offer a view across town towards the Gothic church.

Our reporter liked the two pretty *Stüberl*, the terrace at the back, and the cheerful owners who have expanded into the house next door, and also own the Hotel Goldener Adler, just a few streets away (page 73).

Gmunden

Traunsteinstr 87, 4810 Gmunden

Tel 07612 64905
e-mail info@freisitzroith.at
website www.freisitzroith.at
Food breakfast, lunch, dinner, snacks
Price €€
Closed never; restaurant only, Wed
Proprietor Manfred Asamer

Schlosshotel 'Freisitz Roith' Castle hotel

Most towns would be happy to have one castle; Gmunden has several. Most famous is the 17thC Seeschloss; Freisitz Roith is older by some 100 years and sits grandly on a hill on the Traunsee lake shore.

The entrance is impressive: decorative wrought-iron gates open to the reception area where Renaissance chairs in carved oak look ready for a duke. Do not expect the luxury of some castle hotels. Most bedrooms look over the water, but vary in size and style and are priced accordingly; more if they have baroque-style beds, much less for those with plainer, modern furniture.

The romantic location means this is a popular place for weddings – ask before booking, as the restaurant usually closes for receptions and the hotel is fairly remote.

Hofkirchen im Mühlkreis

Marsbach 2 , 4142 Hofkirchen im Mühlkreis

Tel 07285 223
e-mail info@landhotel-falkner.at
website www.landhotel-falkner.at
Food breakfast, dinner, snacks
Prices €€-€€€
Closed mid-Jan to March, end Oct to mid-Dec
Proprietors Falkner family

Hotel Falkner
Cliff-top hotel

A spectacular setting, perched on a steep hill above the Danube, makes the Falkner family hotel special. Both the open terrace and conservatory have giddy views of the Danube. The 12 bedrooms are decorated with wood, some with patterned fabrics, some with plainer colours.

The restaurant and two sitting rooms, with a piano and library, are traditionally decorated, and feel like a cosy home with plenty of books and photographs on the walls. Maximilian Falkner is in charge of the kitchen, preparing fresh and light regional and international dishes, while Julia manages the wine cellar which specializes in local wines.

The garden has a swimming pool and there is a sauna and fitness area.

Linz

Hauptplatz 19, 4020 Linz

Tel 07327 732910
e-mail office@hotelwolfinger.at
website www.hotelwolfinger.at
Food breakfast
Prices €€–€€€
Closed never
Proprietors Dangl family

Hotel Wolfinger
Bed-and-breakfast hotel

Although this hotel is larger than our norm, readers confirm that the Dangl family maintain the standards expected in this guide. The Wolfinger's 19thC façade hides a history dating back 500 years, originally as a monastery. There is little of the monks' austerity nowadays about the comfortable rooms and tasteful furnishings. Old mirrors, photographs and Biedermeier and art nouveau furniture continue the sense of the old, but bathrooms are modern, with huge mirrors. Most of the bedrooms overlook the quiet, inner courtyard; a few have a view over the Hauptplatz. The comings and goings on the square can also be seen from the breakfast room, if you are lucky enough to get a seat at the window. Popular with cyclists.

Mondsee

5310 Mondsee, Steinerbachstr 6

Tel 06232 6500
e-mail hotel@leitnerbraeu.at
website www.leitnerbraeu.at
Food breakfast, lunch, dinner, snacks
Prices €–€€€
Closed Nov
Proprietors Marschallinger family

Leitnerbräu
Converted brewery

Ever since Leitnerbräu's expansion and redecoration 20 years ago, we've had good feedback about this luxury hotel. Though it now has 30 bedrooms, we keep it in the guide because it scores for location: right in the old part of this attractive town, ten minutes from the lake.

The wrought-iron sign, with lions rampant, hop leaves and barrel, reflects the brewhouse origins of the 18thC building. The bedrooms are decorated with Italian-style furniture, and some have a balcony or terrace. The restaurant, Da Michele, is also Italian-style. The occasional Biedermeier chest of drawers, oil painting and stained-glass window have been preserved, but the overall look is now cool and sophisticated.

Area introduction

Here we cover the neighbouring states of Niederösterreich and Vienna. Niederösterreich is the biggest of the nine states, engulfing the newest, separate state of Vienna. The Danube splits the state in two. On the north bank is the Wachau, famous for its wines. Further north near the Czech border is off-the-beaten track Waldviertel, the wooded quarter. Don't miss the Wachau and Gumpoldskirchen taverns: they are perfect places to try local wines which rarely get exported.

Vienna is crammed with hotels, all used year-round, so staff and furnishings are tested to the limit. Most of the tourist hotspots are within the inner city or along the Ringstrasse. On the fringe of the city are the *Heurigen*, wine taverns among the vineyards on the edge of the Vienna Woods. If you want to stay outside the capital, consider the hotels on pages 90, 93 and 113-116, all within one hour's drive of Vienna.

Below are some useful back-up places to try if our main selections are fully booked:

Pedro's Landhaus
Country mansion, Dörfl
Tel 02744 7387
www.pedros.at
Palatial, plush, pricey country club in Vienna Woods.

Schloss Drosendorf
Castle hotel, Drosendorf
Tel 02915 23210
schloss-drosendorf.at
Renaissance castle with rambling rooms; needs restoring.

Zum Goldenen Hirschen **Village inn, Göstling an der Ybbs**
Tel 07484 2225
www.hotel-hirsch.at
550-year-old vine-covered inn.

Benediktinerhof **Village hotel, Gumpoldskirchen**
Tel 02252 62185
www.benediktinerhof.at
Well-priced hotel with pretty courtyard in wine village.

Puchbergerhof **Town inn, Puchberg am Schneeberg**
Tel 06766 276982
www.puchbergerhof.at
17thC inn with pretty, quiet garden; vegetarian options.

Hotel Belvedere
Restaurant-with-rooms, Semmering Tel 02664 2270
www.belvedere-semmering.at
Excellent food and welcome; large swimming pool.

Hotel Amadeus **City bed-and-breakfast, Vienna**
Tel 01 533 8738
www.hotel-amadeus.at
Cherry-red, white and gold furnishings; central location.

Hotel Alma
City hotel, Vienna
Tel 01 533 2961
www.hotel-alma.com
Individually designed rooms with gold-stencilled walls.

Hotel Attaché
Town hotel, Vienna
Tel 01 505 1818
www.bestviennahotels.at
Friendly hotel with modern exterior; business and family.

Hotel-Pension Museum **City pension, Vienna** Tel 01 523 4426
www.hotelmuseum.at
Popular with visiting professors and art lovers.

Hotel Rathaus – Wein & Design **City hotel, Vienna**
Tel 01 400 1122
www.hotel-rathaus-wien.at
Wine and design hotel popular with wine lovers.

Hotel Topazz
Boutique city hotel, Vienna
Tel 01 532 2250
www.hoteltopazz.com
Award-winning eco-friendly luxurious hotel – ultra modern.

3601 Dürnstein 64, Wachau

Tel 02711 253
e-mail saengerblondel@aon.at
website www.saengerblondel.at

Nearby Weissenkirchen (5 km);
Krems (7 km); Melk (30 km); Maria
Taferl (45 km); Vienna (85 km);
Maria Zell – narrow-gauge railway
(95 km).
Location in Dürnstein, not
overlooking river; car parking
outside, 7 garage spaces
Food breakfast, lunch, dinner,
snacks
Price €€ (10% discount on week-
long stays)
Rooms 16; 15 double, 1 single, all
with bath or shower; all rooms have
phone, TV, fan, hairdryer, wi-fi
Facilities 3 dining rooms; garden
Credit cards MC, V
Children accepted
Disabled not suitable
Pets accepted
Closed mid-Nov to mid-March
Proprietors Schendl family

Gasthof Sänger Blondel
Town hotel

According to legend, the minstrel Blondel discovered the place where King Richard I of England was im-prisoned by singing the monarch's favour-ite song beneath the castle battlements. Did it real-ly happen here? Who knows, but the old walled town of Dürnstein and its ruined castle are still worth a visit, particularly when you stay in this yellow-painted villa.

The Schendls take care over their food, not only following regional recipes, but using plenty of organic produce. Our reporter happily devoured home-made bread and apricot jam, plum dumplings and praline chocolates. The wine list, with its detailed descriptions, makes interesting reading and even better drinking. The family have been in Dürnstein for 300 years and have been innkeepers since 1900. In this much-visited town it would be all too easy to rest on their laurels; fortunately they do not. They are genuinely enthusias-tic about their hotel and always look for-ward to visits from their regular guests.

Rooms are spotless and well appointed. Colours throughout tone with the caramel-coloured oak panelling, and the quiet terrace garden is full of flowers. Looming above is the heavily decorated blue tower of the Stiftskirche. Once a week there is an evening of zither music and there are bicycles for guests to use.

3485 Grafenegg 12

Tel 02735 26160
e-mail grafenegg@moerwald.at
website www.moerwald.at

Nearby Krems (11 km); Danube
River (6 km); vineyards.
Location in countryside, near village
of Haitzendorf; ample car parking
Food breakfast, lunch, dinner,
snacks
Price €€
Rooms 9 double, all with bath or
shower; all rooms have central
heating, phone, TV, minibar, safe
Facilities 3 dining rooms, bar;
terrace
Credit cards AE, DC, MC, V
Children accepted
Disabled not suitable; restaurant
accessible
Pets accepted
Closed Jan to Mar; restaurant only,
Mon, Tue
Manager Toni Mörwald

Restaurant & Hotel Grafenegg **Castle inn**

Dynamic chef Toni Mörwald is in charge here. He has other catering interests, but the hotel side of the business retains the charm that attracted us here in the first place.

The impressive 19thC Gothic-style Grafenegg Castle belongs to Duke Metternich-Sandor, and this castle inn has a flair and elegance reminiscent of a French château. The castle itself is well known for its classical music concerts, which take place in the enormous indoor riding school.

Despite the grandeur of the complex, the hotel has an aura of intimacy, with comfortable bedrooms decorated in Laura Ashley style. Toni Mörwald has added mini-bars and safes, as well as a variety of expensive dining experiences, particularly in the summer months. The menus feature game, wild fowl and fish specialities, as well as cakes and ice creams in the afternoon. Toni's attention to detail extends to making his own chocolates and he is happy to prepare elegant, but again pricey, picnic hampers for guests who want to explore the surrounding woods.

3511 Klein Wien, Furth-Göttweig

Tel 02736 7218
e-mail office@schickh.at
website www.schickh.at

Nearby Stift Göttweig monastery (1 km).
Location beneath hill-top monastery of Göttweig; ample car parking
Food breakfast, lunch, dinner, snacks
Price €
Rooms 7 double, all with bath or shower; all rooms have central heating, phone, satellite TV
Facilities 3 dining rooms, bar, conservatory; garden, railway-carriage diner, bakery
Credit cards not accepted
Children welcome
Disabled access to restaurant only
Pets accepted
Closed never; restaurant only, Wed, Thurs
Proprietors Schickh family

Landgasthof Schickh
Restaurant-with-rooms

It's right next to the railway station, but it gets our vote because of its food, the surroundings and the professional yet friendly host. The building is low, painted yellow and right next to the single-track Krems St. Pölten line, mercifully silent at night and with very little traffic during the day, although there is the occasional blast from a locomotive. Railway enthusiasts insist on having bedrooms overlooking the line. Everyone, however, likes to have a drink in the 80-year-old railway carriage in the garden, furnished to resemble a Viennese café.

All three dining rooms are attractive, although different in size and decoration. Regulars, including the Viennese acting fraternity, book tables in the one which suits their mood. They also sit in the conservatory, heated in winter, roof open in summer, or out in the large garden, shaded by horse chestnut trees. The house specialities are lobster and crab. Other popular dishes include veal *entrecôte* with truffle puree and chicken cordon bleu and chestnut rice with cream.

Förthofer Donaulände 8, 3504 Stein an der Donau

Tel 02732 83345
e-mail hotel.foerthof@netway.at
website www.gourmethotel-foerthof.at / www.hotel-foerthof.at

Nearby Krems (3 km); Stein old town (1 km); Dürnstein (4 km); wine museum.
Location on road looking south over Danube; car parking outside
Food breakfast, lunch, dinner, snacks
Price €€
Rooms 20 double, all with bath or shower; all rooms have central heating, phone, TV, radio
Facilities 2 dining rooms, TV room; terrace, heated swimming pool
Credit cards DC, MC, V
Children welcome
Disabled not suitable
Pets accepted
Closed never
Proprietor Helga Figl

Gourmethotel am 'Förthof'
Restaurant-with-rooms

Frau Figl's young team of chefs clearly know their business, serving up modern versions of traditional specialities such as *Tafelspitz* and garlic soup, which you can eat on the upper terrace or in the elegant dining rooms. Hearty appetites might find the portions a little scant, but a recent reporter found that the 'detail, presentation, delicacy and freedom from ostentation were peerless'. The inn is a wino's delight, with a wide range of award-winning wines by the glass and a most knowledgeable wine-waiter. Emperor Josef II used to stay here, because it was the best place for hunting in the area. It's the only hotel in Krems on the river Danube.

Frau Figl encourages local artists by displaying their work and there is often a huge painting on an easel near reception. You may, or may not, like what is on show when you visit. The bedrooms are decorated in country style, with paintings from Frau Figl's artists hanging on the white walls. Ask for a room at the back to avoid traffic noise.

Week-long programmes are offered, with lectures and tours on themes of churches, castles, museums and wine. 'A wonderful interlude between the pace of Vienna, and grace of Salzburg.'

Weitental 34, 3295 Lackenhof

Tel 07480 5300
e-mail office@jagdhof.at
website www.jagdhof.at

Nearby Ötscher mountain (2 km); Wienerbruck (12 km); Mariazell (16 km).
Location at foot of Ötscher mountain; ample car parking
Food breakfast, lunch, dinner, snacks
Prices €€-€€€
Rooms 23; 16 double, 3 single, 4 suites for 4-6 people, all with bath or shower; all rooms have central heating, phone, TV, wi-fi
Facilities 3 dining rooms, sitting room, bar, spa; terrace, heated outdoor swimming pool, garden, winter sports nearby
Credit cards AE, DC, MC, V
Children welcome
Disabled not suitable
Pets accepted
Closed 2 weeks after Easter, 2 weeks Nov, Chistmas Eve to Boxing Day
Proprietors Borbath family

Hotel Jagdhof
Resort health hotel

You do not have to take the cure to feel healthy here: just gazing on the scenery is therapeutic. The 20-year-old building was remodelled, using all natural fibres and materials in furnishings. It has been refurbished since then, and some visitors still find the decoration a little dated, but others have called it 'modern rustic'.

The motto in the kitchen is 'natural and light', with an emphasis on whole food menus incorporating plenty of organic fruit and vegetables. Regional specialities are also offered, plus homemade breads and herb schnapps. The *Biostuben* is a no-smoking zone, as are the Tower Suites and one entire floor of bedrooms.

Fitness fans swim in the heated outdoor swimming pool, play tennis on the clay court, practice golf shots on the driving range and hike the 150 km of marked trails. Fly-fishing, paragliding and river-rafting can be arranged. In winter, the ski lift on Ötscher mountain is just 150 m away. We would be happy to stay put and have massages, cosmetic treatments and spa baths.

Just before we went to press we were told of a rumour that the hotel was about to be sold, but we were unable to confirm this with the hotel before publication. Reports welcome.

3622 Mühldorf bei Spitz/Donau

Tel 02713 8221
e-mail reservierung@burg-
oberranna.at
website www.burg-oberranna.at

Nearby Spitz (5 km); Wachau
Museum (10 km); Krems (20 km).
Location on crest of hill above
village; ample car parking
Food breakfast, snacks
Prices €-€€€€
Rooms 6; 4 double, 2 single, all with
bath or shower; all rooms have
central heating, phone, TV, radio; 7
apartments with kitchenette
Facilities breakfast room, sitting
room, bar, TV room; terrace, garden
Credit cards AE, MC, V
Children very welcome
Disabled not suitable
Pets accepted
Closed Nov to Apr
Proprietors Nemetz family

Burg Oberranna
Castle hotel and apartments

Special experiences rarely come cheaply,
but this one is worth every penny. The
Nemetz family rescued this romantic,
Renaissance castle from dilapidation a
decade ago. Standing on a hill above the
Danube valley, a castellated wall protects
the 900-year-old building with its steep
grey roofs, sheer white walls and windows
high above ground level. The crypt beneath
the handsome, Romanesque chapel is 200
years older; the oldest, in fact, in Austria.
Oberranna is secluded, with views to
every point of the compass over wooded
hills, valleys and pasture. The interior has
been sympathetically restored, the
beamed ceilings and white arches balanced
by thick Persian carpets and clusters of
pictures, a traditional *Kachelofen* and a
grandfather clock.

Bedrooms and apartments have well-
chosen antique furniture; one of the best is
the single with a four-poster baroque bed,
curtained in green. Bathrooms are rather
small, perhaps because of the difficulty in
building them into such a massive struc-
ture. We would happily while away the
time watching deer grazing in the inner
moat while sipping one of the manager's
home-made apple or apricot brandies.

Zeughausgasse 239, 3511 Palt

Tel 02732 70446
e-mail office@weinresidenz.at
website www.weinresidenz.at

Nearby Stein an der Donau (3 km);
Krems an der Donau (3 km); Vienna
(55 km); hiking and cycling trails.
Location follow the road from
Donau, then turn right towards Palt
– hotel is on the left-hand side;
airport transfers on request
Food breakfast
Price €€
Rooms 14 double, all with bath or
shower; all rooms have satellite TV,
hairdryer, wi-fi
Facilities breakfast room, wine
cellar with sitting room; terrace,
vineyard
Credit cards MC, V
Children welcome
Disabled some ground floor
bedrooms
Pets by arrangement
Closed never
Proprietors Geraldine and
Christian Sonnleitner

Weinresidenz
Sonnleitner **Village pension**

Sitting at the heart of Austria's burgeon-ing wine territory, the Weinresidenz Sonnleitner is an interesting mixture of old and new. The views are ancient ones – gnarled vines twist and tug their way on all sides, punctuated by only a handful of prem-ises and the stunning abbey of Göttweig.

Inside the hotel, all is new. The large bedrooms are a little plain but light and airy. Reception and the breakfast room, full of wood panelling and mood lighting, are rather more fetching, while the stone-clad wine cellar and sitting room are altogeth-er captivating for those interested in tast-ing one of the drops from the several well-represented local vineyards.

Christian and Geraldine run their prop-erty with flair and kindness, and are always happy to talk about their wines and to rec-ommend activities in the local area.

Well-executed and warm, this is a great stop-over or a destination all of its own.

Kleinau 34, 2651 Reichenau, Rax

Tel 02666 53633
e-mail office@knappenhof.at
website www.knappenhof.at

Nearby cable car to Rax Alps.
Location on southern slopes of Rax;
ample car parking
Food breakfast, lunch, dinner,
snacks
Prices €€€-€€€€
Rooms 24; 20 double and single, 4
suites, all with bath or shower; all
rooms have central heating, phone,
satellite TV
Facilities 3 dining rooms, 2
conference rooms, TV room, spa,
massages, wi-fi; terrace, riding and
hunting nearby
Credit cards AE, MC, V
Children welcome
Disabled limited facilities
Pets accepted
Closed never
Manager Clemens Keller

Knappenhof
Mountain hotel

The drive from Reichenau to the
Knappenhof is a thoroughly enjoyable
one through lush pastures and orchards.
The hotel, built in 1907, stands on the
southern slopes of the Rax mountains,
which offer guided hikes, mountain biking,
climbing and kayaking – all organized by
the hotel.

In 2011 the whole hotel was renovated
to modern standards, but carefully preserving the character of the building.
Bedrooms are in relaxing shades of blue
or green, with white walls hung with metal
deer heads or deer-shaped lamp stands.
Two rooms at the back are rather gloomy;
the rest have splendid views.

Kurhotels sometimes have a rather aus-
tere atmosphere, as if healthy regimes pre-
clude enjoyment, particularly where food
is concerned. Previous chefs have had
other ideas, cooking imaginative food that
is full of both flavour and variety. A new
head chef started just before we went to
press – reports would be welcome on on
how he changes the food.

3610 Weissenkirchen, Wachau

Tel 02715 2201
e-mail office@raffelsbergerhof.at
website www.raffelsbergerhof.at

Nearby Wachau Museum.
Location on edge of village, overlooking square; own car parking
Food breakfast
Price €€
Rooms 13; 11 double, 2 single, all with bath or shower; all rooms have central heating, phone, TV, minibar, radio; some hairdryer
Facilities breakfast room
Credit cards MC
Children welcome
Disabled not suitable
Pets accepted (€7 per night)
Closed Nov to end April
Proprietor Claudia Anton

Raffelsberger Hof
Village inn

A gem, pure and simple. Who would not want to stay in this late-Renaissance house on the edge of the village? Turn off the main street down a little lane towards the Danube and suddenly you are in a flower-filled square. Wisteria and vines climb over this former ship master's house, where the stables once housed the horses that pulled the Danube barges.

Outside, a statue of St. John of Nepomuk stands in a small niche; inside, a stern stone face spouts water into a tiny pool and ancient steps lead up to reception. Claudia Anton is the second generation of her family to run this *pension*. Her antique-dealer father restored the 16thC building, then filled it with eye-catching objects. In the breakfast room, a Biedermeier cabinet displays gold-embroidered Wachauer *Brettlhaube*, the traditional bonnets of the region. Even the locks, handles, hinges and light fittings are finely-crafted and worthy of notice. Views from the vaulted rooms and arcades are either into the garden with its walnut and cherry trees or out towards the late-Gothic church and hills. Bedrooms are attractively furnished, a few with brightly painted feature walls that manage not to overpower the rest of the room, and modern bathrooms; two have views of the Danube.

No. 1, 3924 Schloss Rosenau

Tel 02822 582210
e-mail schloss.rosenau@wvnet.at
website www.schlosshotel.rosenau.at

Nearby Zwettl (10 km).
Location deep in country, near
Zwettl; ample car parking
Food breakfast, lunch, dinner,
snacks
Prices €€-€€€
Rooms 18; 5 double, 13 suites, all
with bath or shower; all rooms have
phone, satellite TV, radio, CD
player, hairdryer, safe, minibar
Facilities 3 dining rooms, TV room,
spa, indoor swimming pool; fishing
and riding nearby
Credit cards AE, MC, V
Children very welcome
Disabled 5 bedrooms accessible
Pets welcome
Closed mid-Jan to mid-March
Manager Margit Zulehner

Schloss Rosenau
Country castle hotel

This small, Baroque mansion, complete
with clock tower, nestles in a small
wooded valley near the Czech border. It is
only 10 km from Zwettl but our reporter
needed a good map to find it. Rose bushes
and statuary line the approach, while
inside every inch of wall space is decorated, every alcove bears a fresco. In contrast,
bedrooms are simply decorated; some
have heavy, dark furniture, others have
honey-coloured pine beds, but all have
plain white walls.

The restaurant has built quite a reputation for its Waldviertel specialities such as
local game, often combined with berries
and mushrooms in the autumn. In the
spring, menus include fresh asparagus and
shrimp soup and deep-fried elderflowers.

What takes visitors aback, however, is
the museum of freemasonry, the only one
in Europe. It is an authentic 18thC lodge,
complete with symbols and regalia. All
quite a contrast to the indoor swimming
pool, mini-golf and tennis courts.

'A classy establishment but not as
expensive as you might expect,' said one
reporter. Some recent guests have been
impressed by the wheelchair access to five
bedrooms.

Dürnstein

Zur Himmelsstiege 122, 3601
Dürnstein

Tel 02711 206
e-mail info@pfeffel.at
website www.pfeffel.at
Food breakfast, lunch, dinner
Prices €-€€
Closed Jan
Proprietors Pfeffel family

Gartenhotel Pfeffel
Town hotel

Situated just outside Dürnstein on the riverside road, the building is modern, but the general look is pleasantly old-fashioned. Oleanders, geraniums and a walnut tree add colour to the entrance. The hotel expanded in 2010, making it too large for a full page, but we keep it in the guide because our first impression: 'Nice, jolly owner; nice, jolly place', still rings true.

Views change with every flight of steps: the sitting area and terrace look out on the hills; most of the bedrooms look over the Danube. Like other hoteliers in this region, the Pfeffels produce their own wine and special dishes range from fish and lamb to nettle-cream soup. There is now a penthouse spa with five saunas, a heated outdoor swimming pool and a sun terrace.

Dürnstein

3601 Dürnstein, Wachau

Tel 02711 212
e-mail hotel@schloss.at
website www.schloss.at
Food breakfast, lunch, dinner
Prices €€€-€€€€
Closed never
Manager J C Thiery

Hotel Schloss
Town hotel

When our seasoned reporter first saw this grand hotel overlooking the Danube, he thought it was a tourist attraction, but despite its 45 rooms, it doesn't feel large, let alone hotelish. It's elegant, comfortable and intimate – 'up-market, but not in a showy way'. He also noted that the antiques here are genuine; 'this place just oozes class.'

The bedrooms are all different, but equally elegant and full of character: luxury rooms have gilt mirrors and heavy curtains on huge windows, and even the least expensive double rooms (€209 per night) have chandeliers and exposed beams. The dining room is just as charming as the rest of the building, and the interesting menu is cheaper than you might expect.

Hinterbrühl

Gaadnerstr 34, 2371 Hinterbrühl

Tel 02236 262740
e-mail office@hoeldrichsmuehle.at
website www.hoeldrichsmuehle.at
Food breakfast, lunch, dinner, snacks
Price €€
Closed never
Proprietors Moser family

Die Höldrichsmühle
Village inn

This is where Schubert was supposedly inspired to write the melody of one of his most famous songs, *Der Lindenbaum*. In sunny weather, meals are served on the garden terrace. The formal dining room, in the vaulted cellars, serves fine Viennese cuisine. Popular sweet treats include homemade pastries and the local speciality *Höldrichsmühle Milchrahmstudel* (sweet, cream cheese strudel with vanilla sauce).

Rooms in the extension are modern, well designed and clean. Corridors and staircases are lined with paintings of varying styles; 'some are explicit nudes,' our reporter notes. Only 17 km from Vienna, it is popular both at weekends and for weekday business lunches and conferences. The owners recently added a spa.

Klosterneuburg

Niedermarkt 17-19 , 3400 Klosterneuburg

Tel 02243 32072
e-mail info@schrannenhof.at
website www.schrannenhof.at
Food breakfast
Price €-€€ (half board)
Closed never
Proprietor Veit family

Hotel Schrannenhof
Medieval house and apartments

In the heart of town, the Veit family owns this small, cosy hotel. Carefully converted in 1990, it retains the old arched ceilings, stone floors and outer timberwork.

The bedrooms are plain, but individually furnished, some with cast-iron four-poster bed frames, some with sofas, and there are apartments with small kitchens.

The owners pay attention to detail, with flower arrangements and potted plants in every nook and pumpkin arrangements in October. There is a small paved garden with potted plants and benches.

Laaben

Hauptplatz 28, 3053 Laaben

Tel 02774 8378
e-mail linde@landgasthof-zur-linde.at
website www.landgasthof-zur-linde.at
Food breakfast, lunch, dinner
Price €
Closed Jan; restaurant only, Wed and Thu
Proprietors Geidel family

Landgasthof Zur Linde
Restaurant-with-rooms

In a charming village in the Vienna Woods, the Landgasthof zur Linde is a regular draw for the Viennese who sit in the garden or old *Stube*. Less well-known are the practical bedrooms in the modern building next door. The Geidel family, who took over a few years ago, recently refurbished all the bedrooms, which all now have king-size beds and balconies.

A recent visitor said the restaurant served 'interestingly Austrian' seasonal food, which includes Viennese escalopes and shredded pancakes as well as home-made bread. Everything is sourced locally and the Geidels favour eco-friendly products. The staff here is friendly and it's good value for money.

Mautern

Südtirolerplatz 3512 Mautern

Tel 02732 82937
e-mail linde@landhaus-bacher.at
website www.landhaus-bacher.at
Food breakfast, lunch, dinner
Prices €€-€€€
Closed mid-Jan to end Feb; restaurant only, Mon, Tues
Proprietor Lisl Wagner-Bacher

Landhaus Bacher
Restaurant-with-rooms

Lisl Wagner-Bacher is among Austria's top dozen chefs, and her restaurant, in the middle of a pretty village, is a high temple of cuisine. The next generation has joined the business with just as much success: her daughters Susanne and Christina, who are chefs here, have been internationally praised; and son-in-law and head chef Thomas Dorfer was Austria's Chef of the Year in 2009.

Visitors have mostly praise for this stylish place and even find the €110 price tag for the seven-course menu good value given the quality of food. The stylish fine dining doesn't have to stop when you go home: Lisl offers cooking lessons and has her own cookery book. You can also buy ingredients used in the recipes here.

Mayerling

2534 Mayerling 1

Tel (02258) 2378
e-mail hanner@hanner.cc
website www.hanner.cc
Food breakfast, lunch, dinner, snacks
Prices €€€
Closed 23-24 Dec, early Jan
Proprietors Hanner family

Hanner
Country hotel

Despite the change of hotel name (it used to be the Kronprinz Mayerling), the food in this famous restaurant is as consistent as ever, according to visitors. The Hanner is one of Austria's top 50 restaurants, and has been called 'creative, surprising and unconventional' by reviewers.

Inside, artworks and natural materials make for a peaceful atmosphere. Spacious modern bedrooms are individually done out, and have whirlpool baths. On the terrace, koi carp swim in a geometric pond.

No detail is overlooked by chef Heinz-Viktor Hanner. Herbs are grown in his own garden, the wine list runs to 200 vintages from France, Spain, Italy and Austria, and there is even a *Käse-Somelier* who selects cheeses for ripening in a special cellar.

Payerbach

Kreuzberg 60, 2650 Payerbach

Tel 02666 52911
e-mail steiner@looshaus.at
website www.looshaus.at
Food breakfast, lunch, dinner, snacks
Price €
Closed never
Proprietors Steiner family

Loos Haus
Converted villa

Anyone with an interest in architecture will appreciate this villa, designed by Adolf Loos 85 years ago. This early example of modern functionalism, with built-in furniture, has been altered little. Walls and fittings are painted bright colours (yellow, red, blue and green), decoration is minimalist.

It's a family business: head chef Hanna uses local ingredients in her modern take on regional classics while her husband Adolf Sehn sources game and brother, Norbert Steiner, manages the wine cellar. The restaurant has a two-storey window looking out to the hills, and cosy corners with books or a fireplace.

A hideaway for Viennese. Surrounded by woods and meadows; steep approach; dramatic views.

Raabs an der Thaya

Hotel Thaya
Riverside inn

On the banks of a river, overlooking an 11thC castle. Raabs itself is a sleepy little village in what many Austrians consider to be a backwater which borders the Czech Republic.

From the main street, guests step straight into the bustling *Lärchenstube*, which has a slightly French brasserie air

and four suites are in the annexe. Picture windows look over the garden, or even better, lead on to balconies overhanging the river itself. Decoration is simple; bathrooms are compact but practical.

This is a sports-oriented hotel, with canoeing on the still, green Thaya River. They also organize excursions into the Czech Republic.

der Thaya

Tel 02846 202
e-mail info@hotelthaya.at
website www.hotelthaya.at
Food breakfast, lunch, dinner, snacks
Price €
Closed 2 weeks Feb; restaurant only, Tues dinner
Proprietors Strohmer family

Yspertal

Ysperstrasse 4, 3683 Yspertal

Tel 07415 7265
e-mail gh-schauer@aon.at
website www.hotel-waldviertel.at
Food breakfast, lunch, dinner, snacks
Price €€
Closed mid-Oct to Easter
Proprietors Schauer family

Zur Blauen Traube
Village inn

In one of Austria's prettiest villages, this typical, pink-painted, Waldviertel inn celebrated its 270th birthday in 2012. Run by the Schauer family for three generations, the inn is decorated traditionally, perhaps a little dated in places. The dining room is decorated with pretty pink fabrics and the bar is furnished all in wood. Bedrooms, some with balconies, are functional, and decorated with flowers.

Food is homely Austrian, accompanied by Wachau wines and Herr Schauer's home-made brandy. Guests dine out in a courtyard full of creepers and geraniums. They also relax in the garden and play ten-pin bowling in the bar.

Hiking, mountain biking and fishing nearby. No credit cards.

Vienna

Kirchengasse 41, 1070 Wien

Tel 01 52633990
e-mail hotel@altstadt.at
website www.altstadt.at

Nearby Ulrichsplatz; St Ulrich's church; museums; Hofburg.
Location in attractive street off Burggasse
Food breakfast, afternoon tea
Price €€
Rooms 45; 31 double, 6 junior suites, 8 suites, all with bath or shower; all rooms have central heating, phone, TV, radio, minibar, safe, hairdryer
Facilities sitting room with fireplace, concierge; opera and theatre ticket reservations
Credit cards AE, DC, MC, V
Children welcome
Disabled not suitable
Pets accepted
Closed never
Proprietor Otto Ernst Wiesenthal

Altstadt Vienna
Town hotel

True to form, owner Herr Wiesenthal continues to make improvements to this luxury hotel. He spent 20 years travelling the world, so he knows what he likes and dislikes about hotels. His collection of contemporary art is spread throughout the building. Here, antiques mix harmoniously with modern furnishings in rooms with high ceilings and parquet floors.

Suites on the second floor are large by city standards, they can sleep up to four with comfort. Nine of the rooms were designed by architect Matteo Thun (all damask wallpaper and crystal chandeliers), and fashion designer Lena Hoscheck decorated one of the suites in retro chic. The rooms are high enough for roof-top views to the tower of nearby St Ulrich's church.

The hotel occupies the upper stories of a wealthy burgher's house in Neubau, a well-preserved Baroque quarter of the city that is quiet and residential and just around the corner from the museum quarter. It's just a ten-minute walk from the Ringstrasse and Mariahilferstrasse, which is Vienna's longest shopping street.

You get the feeling that the family enjoy playing host. Nothing seems to be too much trouble, whether it's booking a limousine to the airport or concert tickets.

Vienna

Herklotzgasse 6, 1150 Wien

Tel 01 8926000
e-mail office@altwienerhof.at
website www.altwienerhof.at

Nearby Haydn Museum.
Location near Westbahnhof; own garage
Food breakfast, lunch, dinner, snacks
Prices
Rooms 23; 10 double, 7 single, 4 suites, 2 family, all with shower; all rooms have central heating, phone, satellite TV, internet
Facilities restaurant, breakfast room, bar, conservatory; terrace
Credit cards AE, DC, MC, V
Children welcome
Disabled not suitable
Pets accepted
Closed never; restaurant only, 3 weeks Jan
Manager Sorin Panus

Altwienerhof
City hotel

Don't be put off by the unfashionable location, south of the Westbahnhof in an unattractive part of town: the Altwienerhof is a gem. Its restaurant, rated one of the best, if not the best, in Vienna, attracts local gourmets as well as foreigners, especially the French. The ever-changing menu focuses on fish, but baby lamb and potato strudel are also specialities; the wine list, with French classics and Austrian vintages, also receives rave reviews.

The hotel has changed hands quite recently, but the atmosphere of intimacy and luxury that the previous owner created – both in the alcoves of the restaurant and in the hotel itself – has not changed.

The best bedrooms echo the *belle époque*, with plush velvet and lace, though gilded taps in the en suite marble bathrooms may be too much for conservative tastes. Breakfast is served in the conservatory or, during warm weather, in the courtyard garden, sheltered by cascades of ivy.

A warning to those on slimming diets: the smell of delicious food permeates the premises and piques the appetite.

Vienna

Stubenring 2, 1010 Vienna

Tel 01 512 52 910/19 110
e-mail reservations@arenberg.at
website www.arenberg.at

Nearby CAT airport train (0.5 km).
Location on Stubenring 2 in central
Vienna; car parking
Food breakfast, lunch, dinner
Prices €€-€€€
Rooms 21; 2 double/twin, 2 single,
10 triple, 7 junior suite, all with bath;
all rooms have phone, satellite TV,
air conditioning, minibar, hairdryer,
safe
Facilities restaurant, wi-fi
Credit cards AE, DC, MC, V
Children accepted
Disabled ground floor room
Pets accepted
Closed never
Proprietor Michael Ecker

Hotel-Pension Arenberg
City bed-and-breakfast

Is it small? Yes. Is it charming? Yes, 'and they do try' says our much-travelled reporter. The Arenberg is conveniently placed on the Stubenring, in central Vienna. Photographs in the foyer perhaps tell of a mightier past – George London (concert and operatic bass-baritone) and Gunther Wand (20thC German orchestra conductor) once stayed here. A more recent photograph is of film producer Allan Starski (of *Schindler's List* fame) who visited in 2013. Although it is a part of the Best Western chain, the hotel has been privately owned and run for 60 years – well run, according to our reporter, from the sweet receptionist to 'Frau Mop' who presided helpfully over his 'above average' breakfast.

Rooms are small but adequate and spotlessly clean. Most of the 'antique' furniture is reproduced, but 'contributes to a sense of the genteel', which our reporter liked. For dinner, the owner suggested the Plachutta restaurant, a five-minute walk from the Arenberg, which he also liked. The great and the good of the 21st century go there, which is not surprising. The atmosphere is 'sensationally Austrian and the food the best I have eaten outside of Krems.'

Neustift am Walde, near Vienna

Rathstr 24, Neustift am Walde, 1190 Wien

Tel 01 440 3033
e-mail landhaus@fuhrgassl-huber.at
website www.fuhrgassl-huber.at

Nearby vineyards; *Heurigen* villages; Vienna woods; central Vienna.
Location on main street of picturesque wine village, outskirts of Vienna; own garage
Food breakfast, dinner (200 m)
Price €€
Rooms 22 double, all with bath or shower; all rooms have central heating, phone, TV, minibar, safe, wi-fi
Facilities breakfast room, sitting room, bar, gym; terrace, garden
Credit cards MC, V
Children welcome
Disabled some ground floor access
Pets accepted
Closed New Year's Eve
Proprietors Huber-Krenberger family

Landhaus Fuhrgassl-Huber **Wine-village pension**

Opened in 1991, this *pension* immediately made a name for itself among local connoisseurs of small hotels. Set in the long, rather straggly wine-village of Neustift am Walde, it backs on to a slope covered by orderly rows of vines. Here is your chance to drink wine straight from the vineyard of one of Vienna's most famous *Heurigen*, which just happens to be owned by the same family.

In contrast to the historic *Heurigen*, this hotel is a refreshing combination of old and new. Outside, the cream and white façade is ablaze with azaleas in spring; inside, antique hand-painted peasant wardrobes from Tyrol catch the eye.

Flowers are everywhere, brightening the natural wood and tiled floors. Bedrooms are generous and comfortable, mainly pristine white, with flowered bed linen or upholstry. Our reporter enthused about the light and airy atmosphere, created by large windows looking out on to the garden or into the courtyard. Breakfast is served in the latter on sunny days and half-board guests can have dinner at the Pfiff or Hauerkuchl restaurants (also run by the owners' family) at either end of the road.

Although central Vienna is only half an hour by bus and tram, the bustle of city life seems further away, though the restaurant can get quite busy with tourists.

Vienna

Hernalser Hauptstr 187, 1170 Wien

Tel 01 486 66200
e-mail hoteljaeger@aon.at
website www.hoteljaeger.at

Nearby *Heurigen* villages,
Kongressbad swimming pool.
Location in quiet suburb of Hernals;
ample car parking, garage
Food breakfast, snacks
Price €€
Rooms 17; 10 double, 2 single, 3
family, 2 suites with kitchen, all with
bath or shower; all rooms have
central heating, phone, TV, minibar,
hairdryer, internet, some have air
conditioning, wi-fi, suites have
kitchen
Facilities 2 breakfast rooms; garden,
terrace
Credit cards AE, DC, MC, V
Children welcome
Disabled not suitable
Pets welcome
Closed never
Proprietors Dr. Andrea Feldbacher
and Helene Hartmann

Hotel Jäger
Suburban pension

A stay in the suburbs of Vienna at this century-old family-run business is always delightful. Frau Hartmann retired in 2000, but she is still involved in the hotel, now run by her daughter Andrea who is also helped by her 16-year-old daughter during the summer. Andrea knows exactly what a charming small hotel should be, both as hotelier and as guest, having used our guide to Italy on her holidays.

The 3-storey art nouveau villa is set back from the road, with a beautiful new garden in front of the house. Bedrooms on that side are double-glazed, so noise is not a problem. The garden was redesigned in 2010 and is now the main draw of this arty hotel. It's unusually large for a place so close to the city centre, and is filled with flowers and dotted with small paved sections with tables and chairs where visitors enjoy eating breakfast or relaxing after a long day in the city. All the bedrooms have been refurbished recently and are decorated with paintings from different periods. What else makes this bed and breakfast special? The owners, whose welcome is genuine and whose friendliness is natural.

The two suites are idea for longer stays, especially with children. Tram 43 stops by the hotel and takes 15 minutes to get to the city – you can buy tickets at reception.

Schulerstr 10, 1010 Wien

Tel 01 515 840
e-mail hotel@kvu.at
website www.kvu.at

Nearby St Stephen's Cathedral;
Opera; Musik-Verein; Fiaker tours.
Location central; public
underground car parking close by
Food breakfast and dinner in
restaurant
Price €€€
Rooms 44; 26 double, 9 single,
9 suites, all with bath or shower; all
rooms have central heating, air-
conditioning, phone, TV, radio,
minibar, hairdryer, wi-fi
Facilities large atrium courtyard
with bar, conference room
Credit cards AE, DC, MC, V
Children welcome
Disabled 1 adapted room,
lift/elevator takes wheelchairs
Pets accepted
Closed never
Manager Günter Reiterlehner

Hotel König von Ungarn City hotel

Book well ahead to stay in what is one of the jewels in the crown of Viennese hotels, right in the heart of the old city and only steps away from St Stephen's Cathedral. It's close to the Opera, Musik-Verein and museums and well-connected by public transport. The present building dates from 1746, when it served as the guesthouse of the Archbishop. Now, it is popular with visitors seeking culture, and opera and theatre lovers. Next door, Mozart House is where Mozart composed *The Marriage of Figaro*.

Sitting in the glass-enclosed courtyard, with wood panelling, etched glass and a tree, you can imagine yourself back in the days of the Austro-Hungarian Empire. Portraits line the corridors above, whose windowed galleries are an architectural curiosity. Upstairs, the older bedrooms are decorated traditionally; newer rooms have a more modern twist (see photo above).

The restaurant, with chandeliers lighting the vaulted baroque ceiling, has a high reputation for traditional Viennese and Austrian cuisine as well as a wide selection of fine wine. A recent visitor said 'breakfast was good', but felt it lacked atmosphere.

The 'friendly and very efficient welcome' and the formal atmosphere does not come cheaply but may be worth it for the Viennese experience.

Vienna

Schlenthergasse 17, 1220 Wien

Tel 0664 431 6830
e-mail book@therooms.at
website www.therooms.at

Nearby Naschmarkt; Baroque museum; Riesenrad; Mozart museum; spa; beach.
Location on a side street near the Danube, 3 minutes' walk from underground (Kagran, U1 line); free on-street car parking
Food breakfast, self-catering
Price €
Rooms 4 double, all with shower; all rooms have satellite TV, wi-fi, most have hairdryer, one double has balcony; 3 apartments, all have sitting room, kitchen, washing machine
Facilities breakfast room, wi-fi; terrace
Credit cards AE, DC, MC, V
Children accepted
Disabled not suitable
Pets accepted
Closed never
Proprietor Eva Elbaranes-Koll

The Rooms
Bed-and-breakfast & apartments

The Rooms are four double bedrooms and three apartments. If you choose a bedroom, you can still come and go as you please, just like in an apartment – owner Eva isn't on site all the time, so she gives guests a key.

The style here is Continental-exotic – choose from Asian, Indian, Moroccan and Mediterranean themes. The four bedrooms are in the main *pension* and the apartments are in separate buildings nearby. In some rooms, plain walls are contrasted with colourful fabrics and artwork; in others, warm beige and peach walls are complemented by deep purples and browns.

It's worth choosing the bedrooms just for the breakfast, with home-made granola and jams – apricot with rum, cinnamon and cardamom; quince with pumpkin and rosemary; or strawberry with lavender. It's served on the Indonesian teak table downstairs, overlooking the terrace and garden, with handmade crockery from Israel, cutlery from India and tea cups from Japan.

The closest underground station is just a three-minute walk away, plus there's a Chinese spa nearby and plenty of riverside restaurants along the Danube, some with floating terraces – ask Eva for advice on local eateries.

Annagasse 16 1010 Wien

Tel 01 512 77 510
e-mail info@rkhotel.bestwestern.at
website www.hotel-roemischer-
kaiser.at

Nearby Staatsoper; Stadtpark;
Burggarten; museums.
Location in pedestrian area in heart
of city, public car park in
Mahlerstrasse, 3 minutes' walk from
hotel
Food breakfast, snacks
Prices €€-€€€€
Rooms 24 double, all with bath or
shower; all rooms have central
heating, air conditioning, phone,
TV, radio, minibar, hairdryer
Facilities sitting room, bar, café
Credit cards AE, DC, MC, V
Children welcome
Disabled not suitable
Pets not accepted
Closed never
Proprietor Vision GmbH & Co KG

Schlosshotel Römischer
Kaiser **City hotel**

Another romantic hotel with a history,
this was built as a Baroque mansion in
1684 for Johann Hüber, an Imperial coun-
sellor. Later it became a school for engi-
neering under Maria Theresa. In 1904, the
Jungreuthmayer family took over. Though it
is no longer in Dr Jungreuthmayer's hands,
it retains the old-world flavour his family
took care to maintain.

Chandeliers, arches, mouldings, and gilt
work are preserved, with newer furniture
carefully chosen to blend in with traditional styles. A parlour, with tapestry-covered
chairs, provides a useful meeting place.

Bedrooms come in a variety of sizes and
shapes; some have modern furnishings in
neutral colours, others are so rich with
gold, cream and brocade that the 1990s
push-button telephones and digital clocks
look strangely out of place.

Outside, mischievous carved faces look
down on locals and visitors taking time off
from shopping and sightseeing at the
hotel's pavement café. Annagasse is a narrow street just off the fashionable
Kärntnerstrasse, between the Opera
House and St Stephen's Cathedral. Arriving
by car, use the hotel entrance on
Krugerstrasse.

Vienna

Mariahilfer Strasse 15, 1060 Wien

Tel 01 587 5415
e-mail reception@das-tyrol.at
website www.das-tyrol.at
Food breakfast
Prices €€-€€€€
Closed never
Proprietor Helena Ramsbacher

Das Tyrol
City hotel

Design and history enthusiasts, and shopaholics, will all enjoy a stay at Das Tyrol. Located in the museum quarter, on the Mariahilferstrasse's mile of shopping, this stylish hotel was completely renovated in 2009. The already well-designed public areas now have colourful curtains and modern light fixtures. Bedrooms are decorated in greens and oranges, which blend with dark wood furniture. Personal touches are not forgotten – tables are decorated with vases of fresh flowers or bowls of fruit.

The breakfast buffet is generous, and even the table settings are works of art. In the spa, which can be reserved for private use, the curved ceiling and walls glitter with gold tiles reflecting coloured mood lighting – not to everyone's taste.

Vienna

Seitenberggasse 19, 1160 Wien

Tel 01 486 5162
e-mail office@fleger.at
website www.fleger.at
Food self-catering
Price €
Closed never
Proprietors Annelie and Ernst Fleger

Fleger Apartments
City apartments

Honest, functional apartments in the Vienna suburb of Ottakring, close to an underground station, 15 minutes to the city centre. Their four-star rating puts them above the average, but expect neutral, even bland decoration. They're reasonably spacious, properly equipped and family run since 1988. Plus they can be rented from just two days or long term.

The building stands on a respectable, nondescript street – Ottakring has some pleasantly leafy streets and squares, but this is not one of them; though there is a pleasant internal courtyard.

Vienna

Köllnerhofgasse 6, 1010 A-Vienna

Tel 01 96 11 960
e-mail hotel@hollmann-beletage.at
website www.hollmann-beletage.at
Food breakfast, lunch, dinner, snacks
Prices €€-€€€
Closed never
Proprietor Philipp Patzel

Hollmann Beletage
City hotel

Cruise the website and you'll see that someone here has a sense of humour. That aside, it's a serious operation. In the middle of the old town, it's modern enough for business guests, but relaxed enough to be a holiday base. Every bedroom is large, with an open-plan bathroom – some have sinks on the back of the headboard, with a clawed bathtub behind a curtain (or not, if you prefer). Storage has been designed with ingenuity reminiscent of Ikea – some rooms have whole bathrooms tucked away in cupboards. iPads are standard.

Besides the bedrooms, you're offered cooking courses, and all food is organic, regional and seasonal. There's also a tiny spa with a futuristic circular fireplace (and a treadmill covered with artificial grass).

Vienna

Kärntnerstr 47, 1010 Wien

Tel 01 5129310
e-mail info@operasuites.at
website www.operasuites.at
Food breakfast (in bedroom)
Price €-€€€
Closed 1 week Feb
Proprietor Markus Terkovics

Opera Suites
City pension

For those on a budget, and particularly for opera lovers, this is recommended by a reader who bought standing tickets for the opera and went every night – it's just around the corner from the Vienna State Opera House.

The 12 bedrooms are decorated in traditional Viennese style, with deep red fabrics and chandeliers. Every room has air conditioning, a minibar, a Nespresso coffee machine and free wi-fi. The modern bathrooms all have rainfall shower heads. Breakfast is served in the bedrooms.

Vienna

Hasenauerstr 12, 1190 Wien

Tel 01 3675700
e-mail hotel@parkvilla.at
website www.parkvilla.at
Food breakfast
Price €€
Closed never
Proprietor Wolfgang Bracke

Hotel Park Villa
Suburban art-nouveau hotel

Formerly the Hotel Cottage, this four-storey 19thC villa features huge windows and wrought-iron railings. In the leafy, up-market residential area of Döbling, with two parks next door, it is favoured by academics visiting the nearby university departments. The wine bars of Grinzing and Kahlenberg are nearby and Vienna city centre is a 15-minute bus ride away.

The 21 bedrooms are all decorated in green: green carpets, green upholstry and green marble in the bathrooms mix with yellow or cream walls and red patterned curtains. Most have balconies. Breakfast is served in the pretty, secluded garden.

Vienna

Schubertring 11, 1010 Wien

Tel 01 717 020
e-mail hotel@schubertring.at
website www.schubertring.at
Food breakfast, bar snacks
Prices €-€€€€
Closed never
Proprietor Josef Mühlfellner

Hotel am Schubertring
City hotel

A recent guest raves about the Schubert bar, whose mahogany, marble and brass fittings imitate the style of Adolf Loos (see page 97 for another hotel inspired by his design). Streamlined and masculine, this look continues throughout the hotel: there is not a swirling line, frilly curtain, or gilt-edged moulding in sight. Bedrooms come in all shapes and sizes (and prices), as often happens when old buildings are converted, and corridors are long and winding.

Even though the hotel is right on a busy junction, rooms are quiet (some with skylights instead of windows – not for claustrophobics). It's a favourite of musicians and artists, who enjoy being on the doorsteps of the Musikverein and the Konzerthaus, with the Staatsoper only a short walk away.

Area introduction

We combine two Austrian states in this section, Burgenland and Styria (in German, Steiermark).

Burgenland, the easternmost state of Austria is also the least Austrian – until 1921 it was part of Hungary – and life is lived at a slower pace in warm, dry weather. Accommodation is simpler and cheaper than elsewhere in Austria, ranging from modern seaside-style boxes to rooms in old castles. Because the weather is milder and holiday-makers come primarily in the summer, furnishings are more basic.

Styria has miles of unspoilt countryside and large variations of landscape, ranging from mountains to rolling hills and vineyards. Small, family-run hotels abound for holiday-makers, many environmentally friendly. Graz, the state capital, is rather underrated, but well worth spending time in to explore its old streets.

Below are some useful back-up places to try if our main selections are fully booked:

Gasthof Bärenwirt
Village inn, Aich bei Schladming Tel 03686 4303
www.baerenwirt.com
16thC tavern with good food; skiing and golf nearby.

Villa Kristina
Town hotel, Bad Aussee
Tel 03622 52017
www.villakristina.at
Dated traditional house with lovely garden; light cooking.

Hotel Kogler Family hotel, Bad Mitterndorf
Tel 03623 23250
www.hotelkogler.at
Good location by park; spa; tennis; themed dinners.

Hotel-Restaurant Ohr
Restaurant-with-rooms, Eisenstadt Tel 02682 62460
www.hotel-ohr.at
Award-winning restaurant with modern bedrooms.

Country Inn Birkenhof
Hotel and restaurant, Gols
Tel 02173 2346
www.birkenhof-gols.at
Modern four-star hotel; useful stop on way to Hungary.

Landgasthof Reisslerhof
Farmhouse hotel, Gröbming
Tel 03685 22364
www.reisslerhof.at
Family hotel next to farm and riding school; organic dishes.

Gasthof Ladner
Lakeside guesthouse, Grundlsee Tel 03622 8211
www.lad.at
200-year-old guesthouse near cable car; inexpensive.

Annerlbauerhof
Farmhouse inn, Krieglach
Tel 03855 2228
www.annerlbauer.at
Ideal for low-cost, unpretentious outdoor holidays.

Mariazellerhof
Village hotel, Mariazell
Tel 03882 21790
www.lebkuchen-pirker.at
Recently refurbished; in popular destination; restaurant.

Hotel Gasthof Lercher
Town hotel, Murau
Tel 03532 2431
www.lercher.at
Traditional inn with gourmet food and wine tastings.

Judenburger Hütte
Mountain hotel, near Obdach
Tel 03578 8202
www.judenburger-huette.at
Remote retreat; ski from door; sauna; swimming pool.

Gasthof Hensle
Old inn, St Gallen
Tel 03632 7171
www.hensle.at
Solid inn with 1509-dated beams; useful overnight stop.

Bernstein

7434 Bernstein

Tel 03354 6382
e-mail holiday@burgbernstein.at
website www.burgbernstein.at

Nearby Goberling (9 km); Bucklige
Welt (25 km).
Location in wooded hills above
village; car parking in courtyard
Food breakfast, dinner, snacks
Prices €€-€€€€
Rooms 9; 4 double, 5 suites, all with
bath
Facilities dining room, 2 sitting
rooms, bar; terrace, outdoor
swimming pool; sauna, golf and
riding nearby
Credit cards AE, MC, V
Children welcome
Disabled access to ground floor
bedroom
Pets accepted
Closed Nov to Apr
Managers Andrea and Alexander
Almásy

Burg Bernstein
Town castle hotel

What do you expect from a castle?
This one not only has towers and
fortifications, it has a dungeon complete
with whipping bench, rack, and cells plus
an armoury and an Alchemist's Kitchen.
The public can see all this, plus the former
Knights' Hall. This is now a restaurant and
boasts a splendid early 17thC stuccoed
ceiling by Bartolomao Bianco, portraying
scenes from Greek mythology. Concerts
are held here from time to time.

The rest of the castle is for hotel guests.
They enjoy the sitting rooms, one with
ancestral portraits and a lovely baroque-
tiled *Kachelofen*, another with a huge open
fireplace. Even the staircase excites art
enthusiasts: it is believed to be designed by
Fischer von Erlach, the greatest of
Viennese baroque architects.

As for bedrooms, each is different but
all are furnished with antiques and are vir
tually suites. The atmosphere is of yester-
year: no phones, no televisions, no mini-
bars. On cool evenings, wood-burning
stoves provide whatever warmth is needed. Some bathrooms are decidedly old-
fashioned but these are in some of the
most popular rooms, so guests obviously
take it all as part of the experience.

Heiligenkreuz

Obere Hauptstr 10, 7561
Heiligenkreuz im Lafnitztal

Tel 03325 42160
e-mail info@g-gibiser.at /
g.gibiser@aon.at
website www.g-gibiser.at

Nearby Güssing mineral water
museum; Schlösslberg (4 km).
Location on Hungarian border;
ample car parking
Food breakfast, lunch, dinner,
snacks
Prices €-€€
Rooms 10 double, all with bath or
shower; all rooms have central
heating, phone, TV, minibar
Facilities 3 dining rooms, bar,
terrace
Credit cards AE, DC, MC, V
Children accepted
Disabled not suitable
Pets accepted
Closed Feb, 2 weeks Christmas
Proprietor Gerlinde Gibiser

Gasthof Gerlinde Gibiser **Wayside inn**

Steeply-roofed, thatched cottages are a feature of the flat countryside down here on the Hungarian border, and Edith Gibiser (she ran the hotel before Gerlinde took over and renamed it after herself) cleverly incorporated the style into her hotel, or rather her 'hotel complex'.

The house itself is a solid, square, stone inn complete with terrace dotted with red parasols. Staff are friendly, and Gerlinde does everything she can to make the inn feel like a second home. The restaurant has a reputation for authentic Pannonian dishes, which have a Hungarian influence. *Zigeuner Fleisch* (a mixture of chicken, beef and pork in a paprika sauce) and herb strudel are specialities.

It is the area behind the inn, however, that captivated our reporter. In the lush meadow that climbs the hillside are thatched bungalows that children love to stay in. Each looks like a fairy-tale cabin where Little Red Riding Hood or Snow White would feel at home.

Inside are solid, bright pine beds, tables and chairs with pretty curtains and an individual *Kachelofen*. Parents appreciate the comfort and the modern bathrooms, as well as the TV and covered porches for sunbathing. A nearby pond, occupies city children for hours, studying the wildlife.

Waldsiedlung 2, 7083 Purbach

Tel 02683 5519
e-mail hotel@klosteramspitz.at
website www.klosteramspitz.at

Nearby Purbach (1.5 km); Neusiedlersee (6 km); Eisenstadt (14 km).
Location on hill above town; ample car parking
Food breakfast, lunch, dinner
Price €€
Rooms 17; 14 double, 2 single, 1 suite, all with shower; all rooms have central heating, phone, TV
Facilities 5 dining rooms, sitting room, bar, TV room; terrace, garden, cycling and golf nearby
Credit cards DC, MC, V
Children welcome
Disabled easy access; 2 specially adapted rooms
Pets accepted
Closed Jan to Feb
Proprietors Schwarz family

Kloster Am Spitz
Restaurant-with-rooms

Readers who have toured Burgenland confirm that the Am Spitz represents value for money whether you are a wine-lover or not. The Schwarz family has made a success of the vineyards that surround the hotel and restaurant, which are run by Wolfgang; their brother Thomas runs the winery. Thomas's wines, which have won awards in competitions all over Europe, include the gold-medal winning Blaufränkisch (1992) and silver-medal winning Cabernet Sauvignon/ Merlot (1992). No wonder the Friday evening dinner, complete with a dozen wines, are a great attraction for gourmet weekenders.

The 70-year-old restaurant is in what was once the gatehouse of the monastery and is unusually eye-catching, with a voluted baroque façade. All around are lawns studded with chestnut trees, oleanders and ancient stone walls, which make a fine backdrop for summer dining.

Because this is all so attractive we found the simple, modern bedrooms a little disappointing on our first visit, but we are happy to say that they are much improved since the hotel was renovated in 2004: bedrooms are now modern, light and airy with oak floors. We would happily sleep off a fine meal here. Several readers have appreciated the bedrooms that have been specially adapted for wheelchair users.

Hauptstraße 33, 7081 Schützen am Gebirge

Tel 02684 22970
e-mail restaurant@taubenkobel.at
website www.taubenkobel.at

Nearby Eisenstadt (7 km); Lake Neusiedl (8 km); Vienna (43 km).
Location between Eisenstadt and Neusiedl am See; car parking
Food breakfast, lunch, dinner
Price €€
Rooms 11 double and suites, all with bath and shower; all rooms have TV, hairdryer, yoga mat, port wine selection
Facilities restaurant, bistro, sitting room; garden, swimming pool
Credit cards AE, DC, MC, V
Children accepted
Disabled not accessible
Pets accepted (extra charge)
Closed Jan
Proprietor Walter Eselböck

Taubenkobel
Village hotel

Heading out into the Burgenland countryside from Vienna, this wonderfully airy and elegant place has only eleven rooms, but a reputation which is far larger. Husband and wife team Walter and Eveline Eselböck have turned this village house into a truly special place to visit. They are a great combination: he cooks for the two-Michelin-starred restaurant and the bistro, she designed the interior of the hotel and looks after the guests. The food is incredible and well worth a visit alone – indeed, you may find the Viennese gourmands out in force. Fish will have been freshly caught in the nearby lake, and don't leave without asking for a look at the cheese (more wardrobe than board) – or better yet a generous tasting.

The whole place is surrounded by trailing ivy, lovingly tended plants and well-worn cobbled pathways – and the bedrooms reflect the feeling of airy comfort with their sparkling white bedspreads and large windows, letting in lashings of natural light. We love the ones at the top of the house which have sloping roofs and skylights. A delight.

Lockenhaus

7442 Lockenhaus

Tel 02616 2394
e-mail rezeption@ritterburg.at
website www.ritterburg.at
Food breakfast, lunch, dinner, snacks
Price €
Closed never
Manager Manuel Komosny

Ritterburg Lockenhaus
Castle hotel and apartments

Make sure you reserve one of the nine rooms in the 800-year-old castle itself, rather than the 32 apartments in the large, modern annexe. Behind the towering walls and red-and-yellow shutters are a medieval courtyard, Renaissance stairway, and echoing bedrooms with antique furniture. The apartments are sparsely furnished, and decorated with white, offset with bright, even garish, colours. Each has a balcony and a kitchenette. There are also 14 cheap rooms in the attic for those on a budget.

Traditional group meals are available in the Castle Tavern, served on long tables under vaulted ceilings, and accompanied by minstrels' music. These are eaten with the hands, as they would have been when the castle was built.

Mörbisch

Raiffeisenstrasse 8, 7072 Mörbisch am Neusiedlersee

Tel 02685 8294
e-mail privathotel@das-schmidt.at
website www.das-schmidt.at
Food breakfast, lunch, dinner, snacks
Prices €€-€€€€
Closed Nov to Easter
Proprietors Schmidt family

Hotel Restaurant Schmidt **Holiday hotel**

Readers have been agreeably surprised by the standards set by the Schmidt family, here in a part of Austria less visited by Western Europeans. They make extra effort to accommodate the less mobile: this is one of the few hotels we have found that takes this provision seriously, with a lift/elevator and specially fitted bathrooms in the six suites. Right at the top, they are nicknamed the Storks' nests and decorated in soft blue and beige, with maple and pear wood furniture crafted by a local carpenter.

Modern stained glass is a feature in the 23 other bedrooms, all of which have views of the lake. There is a play area for children, plus a large garden. Herr Schmidt makes his own wine; try his speciality, Welschriesling.

Neusiedl am See

Seestraße 15, 7100 Neusiedl am See

Tel 02167 2489
e-mail hotelleiner@aon.at
website www.hotelleiner.com
Food breakfast, dinner, snacks
Price €
Closed never
Proprietors Leiner family

Hotel Leiner
Town bed-and-breakfast

Bird watchers flock here from all over Europe to spot rare species on the Neusiedl Lake. The lake, 1.5 km from Hotel Leiner, which straddles the Austria-Hungary border, is the second largest drainage basin in Europe. The cheerful welcome offered by the Leiner family appeals to both bird watchers and cyclists – the B10 cycle route circles the lake.

The hotel no longer offers dinner, but there are plenty of restaurants and *Heurige* (Austrian wine taverns) nearby in the town centre (500 m). Bedrooms are plainly furnished. A useful budget address.

Podersdorf

Strandplatz 1, 7141 Podersdorf am See

Tel 02177 24 15
e-mail contact@seewirtkarner.at
website www.seewirtkarner.at
Food breakfast, lunch, dinner, snacks
Price €€
Closed Dec
Proprietors Karner family

Seewirt Karner
Lakeside hotel and apartments

Burgenland offers simpler accommodation than other parts of Austria. The Karner family's holiday hotel on the eastern edge of the Neusiedl lake has echoes of seaside Greece or Spain. The lake view on a hazy day is 'quite stunning, with sailing boats and windsurfers flickering over the water'.

Families will have an enjoyable holiday in the Attila annexe. Here, the white bedrooms, all with pine furniture, most with balconies, are more spacious than in the main hotel. There are also apartments for up to four people, each with a kitchen, a sitting room and a balcony. The unpretentious food is Panonian, reflecting the quasi-Hungarian cuisine using local carp and perch, accompanied by Herr Karner's own wines. The terrace has views across the lake.

Deutschlandsberg

Burgplatz 1, 8530 Deutschlandsberg

Tel 03462 5656
e-mail info@burg-deutschlandsberg.at
website www.burg-deutschlandsberg.at

Nearby Deutschlandsberg (1 km); Stainz (15 km); Bärnbach (30 km).
Location overlooking village; ample car parking
Food breakfast, lunch, dinner, snacks
Price €€

room, bar, meeting rooms, gym; terrace, golf and riding nearby
Credit cards not accepted
Children welcome
Disabled not suitable
Pets accepted
Closed Jan to Mar; restaurant only, Sun **Managers** Jasmin and Karl Kollmann

Burg Deutschlandsberg
Castle hotel

There is a certain thrill about staying in a castle, which is why we continue to include this large medieval pile in the attractive village of Deutschlandsberg, deep in the country. With its drawbridge and foreboding gateways, there are still echoes of the battles fought centuries ago with the Turks and Hungarians.

Once inside the massive walls, however,

of the comforts demanded by international travellers. In 2005, the hotel was taken over by Jasmin and Karl Kollmann, who have recently refurbished all the rooms. Although there are some antiques, most of the furniture is refreshingly simple. Some rooms boast hand-painted country furniture, others have more contemporary fabrics. The restaurant, once the *Rittersaal*, or Knights Hall, is impressive, with a massive beamed ceiling. The bar has a history of its own, since it once graced the Steirerhof Hotel, a landmark in Graz. Despite the veneer of history, the atmosphere is relaxed and guests enjoy their surroundings.

Gniebing 15, 8330 Feldbach

Tel 03152 2741
e-mail office@landhotelwippel.at
website www.landhotelwippel.at

Nearby Feldbach (2 km);
Riegersburg (6 km); Bad
Gleichenberg (10 km); Graz (35 km);
Loipersdorf (58 km).
Location on main road, just outside
town; car parking outside
Food breakfast, lunch, dinner,
snacks
Price €
Rooms 24; 18 double, 5 single, 1
suite, all with bath or shower; all
rooms have phone, satellite TV, wi-
fi, some have balcony/terrace
Facilities 4 dining rooms, 2 sitting
rooms, bar; 2 terraces, garden, golf
nearby
Credit cards AE, DC, MC, V
Children very welcome
Disabled accessible
Pets accepted
Closed never; restaurant only, Wed
Proprietors Stefan and Viktoria
Wippel

Landhotel Wippel
Town inn

Wayside inn in the east of Styria, in
the heart of what locals call
'Austria's garden'. When the Herbst family
moved on, the inn was renamed after the
new owners, Stefan and Viktoria Wippel.
The interior is decorated mostly in spruce
wood that shows the grain, or elegant
cherry-wood. Some rooms are decorated
in themes such as Tom's Cabin or Aviary.
The big garden is crammed with fruit trees
and children's climbing frames.

All this is merely a backdrop for the
restaurant, which is renowned for its
Styrian specialities, which range from
Kalbsrahmbeuschel (veal lung ragout) and
salads dressed with pumpkin seed oil, to
everything chanterelle (stew, risotto,
roasted on the side). They will even provide a ham and eggs breakfast for visitors
feeling homesick.

The clientele includes businessmen during the week; otherwise, families with small
children enjoy the safety of the garden as
well as the indoor swimming pool at the
town's leisure centre, 200 m away. Recent
visitors have praised the helpfulness of the
staff. All in all, we rate this as a very pro-
fessionally-run place.

Kapfenstein

8353 Kapfenstein

Tel 01357 300 300
e-mail hotel@schloss-kapfenstein.at
website www.schloss-kapfenstein.at

Nearby Schloss Riegersburg; Schloss Kornberg.
Location on peak of Kapfensteiner-kogel; ample car parking
Food breakfast, lunch, dinner, snacks
Prices €€-€€€
Rooms 15 double, all with bath or shower; all rooms have central heating, phone, TV, wi-fi
Facilities 2 dining rooms, sitting room; 3 terraces
Credit cards MC, V
Children very welcome
Disabled not suitable
Pets accepted
Closed mid-Dec to early Mar
Proprietors Winkler-Hermaden family

Schlosswirt Kapfenstein
Country castle hotel

A steep road leads to this small castle dating from the 11thC. It was built on an extinct volcano and this hilltop position provided early warning of invading Turks and insurgent Hungarians centuries ago; nowadays, the view across rolling hills into Hungary and Slovenia is peaceful, with vineyards rather than armies marching in regular rows.

The style is pleasant and comfortable rather than designer-deluxe; nevertheless, guests give a high rating for the personal atmosphere. The Winkler-Hermaden family have run the hotel for over 35 years, establishing a reputation for hospitality that is matched by the quality of their wines.

On the 40 hectares (nearly 100 acres) of vineyards on rich volcanic soil, they grow ten types of grape, including traditional Austrian varieties such as traminer, grauburgunder and sauvignon blanc. From the main variety, Blauen Zweigelt, comes their popular Olivin. This is left in barrels, made from local oak, stored in the 17thC *Löwenkeller*. Food is light, creative and Styrian, featuring game in the autumn, lamb in the spring, plus garden-grown herbs and vegetables.

Kitzeck

Steinriegel 25, 8442 Kitzeck

Tel 03456 2347
e-mail office@weinhof-kappel.at
website www.wein-wellness-hotel.at
/ www.weinhof-kappel.at

Nearby own vineyard with shop.
Location on hilltop among vines;
ample car parking
Food breakfast, lunch, dinner,
snacks
Prices €€-€€€
Rooms 17; 15 double, 1 single, 1
suite, all with bath or shower; all
rooms have central heating, phone,
TV, radio, wi-fi, terrace/balcony
Facilities 2 dining rooms, sitting
room, TV room, spa, indoor and
outdoor swimming pools; terrace
Credit cards MC, V
Children welcome
Disabled not suitable
Pets not accepted
Closed Jan, Feb
Proprietors Kappel family

Weinhof Kappel
Vineyard hotel

The conversion here of five bedrooms to *Biozimmern* reflects the influence of the Green movement in Styria. It comes as no surprise to us, since the dignified demeanour of Herr Kappel bespeaks a man who is serious about his business and serious about his wine. We were mightily impressed by this stylish modern hotel at the top of a steep, winding road.

Kitzeck, near the Slovenian border boasts that it is the highest wine-growing region in Europe (560 m) and it was the vineyard that brought Gunther Kappel here in the first place, some 35 years ago. The ancient wine cellar, complete with splendidly carved and gilded casks, houses his pride and joy, especially the Welsch-riesling, the Muscatel and Morillon (or Chardonnay). The food is enterprising; a speciality is stuffed chicken breast in a Riesling sauce. Blue and white sunshades dot the leafy terrace outside; honey-coloured wood and pink tablecloths lend a comfortable yet formal air to the dining room which has enviable vistas over the vineyards. Just as much care has been taken over the bedrooms, which are bigger than average, often with balconies, pale pine panelling and pots of flowers. The spa has two saunas and two steam baths and there are both indoor and outdoor swimming pools.

8965 Pruggern 65

Tel 03685 22692
e-mail farmreiterhof@gmx.at

Nearby Pruggern (2 km); Gröbming
(5 km).
Location high above village; own
car parking
Food breakfast, snacks
Price €
Rooms 5 double, all with shower; all
rooms have central heating, TV,
kitchenette
Facilities dining room, sitting room
with TV, sauna; terrace, outdoor
swimming pool, barbecue, children's
play area; winter sports and riding
nearby
Credit cards not accepted
Children very welcome
Disabled not suitable
Pets not accepted
Closed Christmas
Proprietors Gerharter family

Farmreiterhof
Country hotel

Forget every tired cliché about Alpine
hotels and Alpine vistas. This is the real
thing. Deep in the countryside, the only
morning sound we heard was the tinkling
of cowbells in the pasture below the
house. From our balcony, we watched
deer scuttling from the garden into the
pine forest.

No wonder we felt envious of the regulars who come here year after year to ski
in winter and hike or climb the mountains
in summer. The house dates from 1872 and
has been in the family for six generations.
The Gerharters are natural innkeepers,
making little separation between their life
and that of the guests.

The cooking is home-style and filling,
with dishes such as *Kasnockerln* (cheese
noodles) and *Ennstaler Krapfen* (doughnuts
filled with brown crumbly cheese) which
are best partnered with schnapps. Peaks
such as Grimming, Kammspitze and
Dachstein provide names for the bedrooms which, like the rest of the hotel,
have rustic, homely comforts.

8972 Ramsau am Dachstein 233

Tel 03687 81223
e-mail info@alpengasthof-peter-
rosegger.at **website** www.alpen-
gasthof-peter-rosegger.at

Nearby Dachstein mountains.
Location on high plateau; approach
via Kulm, follow signs to Vorberg
(no. 389); ample car parking
Food breakfast, lunch, dinner,
snacks
Prices €€-€€€ (half board)
Rooms 12; 6 double, 2 single, 4 fam-
ily, all with shower; all rooms have
central heating, TV, wi-fi, balcony
Facilities dining room, sitting room,
TV room, table-tennis room, sauna;
terrace, garden
Credit cards MC, V
Children very welcome
Disabled easy access
Pets accepted
Closed after Easter to end May,
early Nov to mid-Dec
Proprietors Fritz, Christoph and
Barbara Walcher

Peter Rosegger
Mountain chalet hotel

A display of mountain-climbing equipment by the front door gives a clue to
the favourite summer-time activity at this
chalet-style inn, set on a plateau beneath
the Dachstein ridge. Fritz Walcher is a
well-known mountain guide and, in winter,
he leads cross-country ski and snow-shoe
safaris to secret valleys and huts.

As for the name, 'we did not want
another Dachsteinblick or Alpenrose, so
chose the famous Styrian romantic poet'.
Pictures relating to his life hang on the
walls, while villages with a Rosegger connection provide names of bedrooms. All
have a little entrance hall and large cupboards, while the family rooms at ground
level have doors leading into the garden, so
children (and pets) can go straight outside.

The food is renowned: expect home-
made bread, local trout, goat cheeses and
butter from local farms, and teas made
from mountain herbs grown on the terrace. Organic produce, vegetarian dishes
and even flour-free recipes are all served
up in the cosy dining rooms where guests
congregate for dinner.

In summer, guests get a free Dachstein
Summer Card, which gives access to cable
cars, public transport, museums and swimming pools

8272 Sebersdorf

Tel 03333 25030
e-mail office@obermayerhofen.at
website www.heiraten-im-schloss.info

Nearby Stift Vorau (25 km); castles; wildlife park; thermal spas.
Location on low hill, near Vienna-Graz motorway; own car parking
Food breakfast, dinner
Prices €€-€€€
Rooms 24 double, all with bath or shower; all rooms have central heating, phone, TV, radio, minibar, hairdryer
Facilities 2 dining rooms, sitting room, bar, billiard room, spa; terrace, park, swimming pond; golf nearby
Credit cards AE, DC, MC, V
Children accepted
Disabled not suitable
Pets not accepted
Closed early Jan to end Feb
Proprietor Graf Kottulinsky

Schlosshotel Obermayerhofen **Castle hotel**

'The honeymoon suite would not have been beneath the dignity of Elizabeth Taylor' was our reporter's verdict. It was meant as a compliment, for he reckoned this hilltop hotel was 'the last word in luxury' and ideal for affluent romantics.

Bedrooms are named for the Austrian noble families and all are on a grand scale. Plain colours such as cream, apricot and butter-yellow provide the background for antiques and Persian carpets. Some have four-posters, in others fabric hangs from a coronet above the headboard. Even bathrooms are generous in size, with potted plants, huge towels, and the latest in fittings, including some whirlpool baths. For those without, there is also a whirlpool in the spa, as well as a sauna and steam bath.

A hotel only since 1986, the estate has been in Count Kottulinsky's family since 1777. Like so many castles in Austria, the Renaissance arcades and staircases of the inner courtyard contrast with the plain exterior. Inside, chandeliers glitter, parquet floors shine with polish, and huge windows let in plenty of light. In the ceremonial hall, an 18thC fresco depicts a fanciful jungle scene, complete with palm trees and growling leopard. Above the staircase the family coat of arms depicts an eagle's claw inside a heart-shaped shield. The private chapel may be used for weddings.

8625 Turnau 34

Tel 03863 2234
e-mail anfrage@kirchleitn.at
website www.kirchleitn.at

Nearby Kapfenberg (14 km);
Mariazell (24 km).
Location in heart of village in valley;
own car parking
Food breakfast
Price €€
Rooms 15; 7 double, 5 single, 3
suites, all with bath or shower; all
rooms have central heating, phone,
satellite TV, minibar, kitchenette,
suites have balcony, fireplace; 3
apartments with kitchen
Facilities dining room, sitting room,
bar; terrace, riding and winter sports
nearby
Credit cards not accepted
Children very welcome
Disabled not suitable
Pets accepted
Closed Nov to mid-Dec
Proprietors Knapp family

Pension Kirchleit'n
Country hotel and apartments

Irmgard Knapp's welcome was 'like being mothered and pampered by a favourite aunt in the country', said our reporter when he visited this enchanting village house, with verandas covered in different varieties of geraniums. The men of the family belong to a long line of carpenters, which explains the lovingly carved staircase and the distinctive light-and-dark pine panelling in the dining room. The house dates back to 1750 when it was built as a *Bauernhof* (farmhouse) with the usual 2 cows, some pigs and chickens. Since 1954, the Knapp family have expanded and improved it, all with their own hands.

Our reporter was particularly taken with the rooms in the old house, which have exposed beams and small square windows; many also have balconies. At the very top are small, cosy rooms 'like a dolls' house.' The new suites, on the other hand, have whitewashed walls and furniture of light-coloured pine with peasant floral decoration. There are also three self-catering cottages in the grounds. Beehive is for two people and has a terrace. The two Mountain House apartments have two floors and sleep two to six people. Views are across the valley or over the garden with fruit trees and the village church behind.

Aigen im Ennstal

8943 Aigen im Ennstal 13

Tel 03682 225200
e-mail office@putterseehof.at
website www.putterseehof.at
Food breakfast, lunch, dinner,
snacks
Price €
Closed Nov
Proprietors Dornbusch family

Landhotel-Gut Puttererseehof **Village inn**

This 250-year-old village inn is family-oriented; it's a safe, friendly spot for children with its large garden, where parents can relax and play miniature golf with their children. Windsurfers and boats are available on the small lake, just a five-minute walk from the inn. It's popular also as a base for fishermen, cyclists and walkers.

In winter, a free ski bus to the Planneralm stops outside, or those with cars can drive 15 minutes away to the larger ski resort at Tauplitz. Putterersee freezes over in winter, and the nearby Loch Ness pub rents out ice skates.

The Puttererseehof also owns the Panneralm, an apartment directly on the piste, sleeping up to nine people.

Altaussee

Fischerndorf 60, 8992 Altaussee

Tel 03622 71302
e-mail hotel@seevilla.at
website www.seevilla.at
Food breakfast, lunch, dinner,
snacks
Price €€€
Closed early Dec to mid-Mar
Proprietors Maislinger-Gulewicz
family

Hotel Seevilla
Lakeside hotel

Standing among summer homes where the road reaches a dead end at the lakeside, the Seevilla has been run by the same family since 1978. Modern comforts include a glamourous indoor swimming pool with a recently refurbished spa. Families like the attic bedrooms, with pale wood beams and rooftop views. The restaurant (fish specialities) is light and airy, with picture windows overlooking the lake.

This resort was a favourite of composers and writers in the 19thC. Arthur Schnitzler and Gustav Mahler visited; so did Brahms. Classical music evenings continue the tradition. Outside, little has changed by the Altaussee; lilacs still bloom in spring while the birch and ash, chestnut and maple trees provide shade from summer sun.

Graz

Kaiser-Franz-Josef-Kai 30, 8010
Graz

Tel 0316 80700
e-mail office@schlossberg-hotel.at
website www.schlossberg-hotel.at
Food breakfast
Price €€€
Closed Christmas
Proprietors Marko family

Schlossberg Hotel
Town hotel

We include this hotel despite the fact that it has well over 30 bedrooms. Our reporter was insistent that we have somewhere nice to stay in Graz; this is extraordinarily elegant as well as having character and charm.

This amalgamation of two 15thC bourgeois houses could not be better placed. Step off the embankment and back in time. The hotel's entrance hall retains its stout pillars and vaulted ceiling. Owner Helmut Marko's motto is 'art, individuality and sincerity'; everywhere antique furniture maintains the sense of history. The bedrooms are carefully furnished, often with whitewashed walls and even more antiques. Breakfast is served on the roof garden in summer; swimming pool; spa.

Kitzeck

8442 Kitzeck, Höch am
Demmerkogel/Sausal

Tel 03456 2328
e-mail office@steirerland.co.at
website www.steirerland.co.at
Food breakfast, lunch, dinner, snacks
Price €
Closed Jan, Feb
Proprietors Ruth and Maria Stelzer

Hotel-Restaurant
Steirerland **Country hotel**

Although the building is a standard, traditional chalet, it boasts a striking hilltop position, with views to the Austrian and Slovenian Alps and a huge, covered terrace surrounded by vineyards. Head chef Ruth Stelzer and service chef Maria Stelzer are charming hostesses. They serve delicious Austrian dishes featuring local game, seasonal ingredients, herbs from their garden and wild mushrooms from the woods.

Bedrooms are modern and prettily decorated, with pine furniture, plain walls and red or green upholstry and fabrics. Most have subtle art on the walls. Bathrooms are tidy and modern.

Krakauebene

8854 Krakauebene 55, Klausen

Tel 03535 8334
e-mail info@schallerwirt.at
website www.schallerwirt.at
Food breakfast, lunch, dinner
Price €
Closed Apr, Nov to mid-Dec
Proprietors Joseph Schnedlitz

Schallerwirt
Guesthouse and apartments

The Schnedlitzs' simple hotel is a place for relaxation, high in the Tauern range. It's a small haven for ramblers and mountain climbing enthusiasts, suitable for every season; Joseph is an experienced mountaineer and can be booked for hiking tours. The skiing here is suitable for all abilities, so it's popular with families with children. After a taxing day on the mountains, guests can relax with a massage or spa treatment.

Bedrooms are fitted out with different types of wood and decorated individually. Each of the four apartments have a living room, kitchen/dining area, sauna, terrace and two bedrooms.

Joseph manages the restaurant, which serves fresh local food. He also runs yodeling, folk music and folk culture workshops.

Mühlen

Jakobsberg 2, 8822 Mühlen

Tel 03586 30077
e-mail info@tonnerhuette.at
website www.tonnerhuette.at
Food breakfast, lunch, dinner, snacks
Price €€ (minimum 3-night stay)
Closed 3 weeks after Easter, Nov
Proprietor Reinhard Ferner

Tonnerhütte
Mountain hotel and huts

To discover this place, our fearless reporter drove up 'a vertical, unmetalled road to a mountain hut at the end of the world'. When he reached the top he was met with fabulous views from Jakobsberg across the valley.

Bedrooms are standardized, decorated with pine. The two self-catering huts are rustic and have kitchenettes, though breakfast and a four-course dinner in the restaurant can be included. All ingredients are sourced from local organic farms.

The main activity is hiking, but there's skiing at uncrowded slopes (lift nearby). An inexpensive option for families. Perfect for getting back to nature.

Obdach

Hauptstrasse 23, 8742 Obdach

Tel 03578 2201
e-mail office@groggerhof.at
website www.hotel-groggerhof.at
Food breakfast, lunch, dinner, snacks
Price €
Closed never; restaurant only, Mon and Mar
Proprietors Robert and Eva Ederer-Grogger

Groggerhof
Village inn

On the main street of Obdach, this 380-year-old inn has a growing reputation for its food thanks to Eva Ederer-Grogger, who runs the hotel with her son Robert. Visitors and locals enjoy Eva's authentic Styrian cooking, with as many as a dozen wines available by the glass. The inn is an *Echt Steirisch Botschafter* ('real Steirisch ambassador'), which means that all produce is high quality and organic.

Bedrooms are functional, with cable TV and wi-fi. Most are large (except, of course, those in the attic); all are cosy and have modern bathrooms. The restaurant prices range from €5,90 to €24, but guests can get half-board for an extra €15 per night. Large garden with swimming pool; sauna.

Oberhaag

Unterhaag 88, 8455 Oberhaag

Tel 0699 104 10533
e-mail held.e@gmx.at
website www.pilchhiasl.at
Food self-catering
Price €€
Closed never
Proprietors Held family

Pilch Hiasl & Höllberg
Self-catering farmhouses

Two self-catering chalet-style holiday homes off the beaten track in the south of Steiermark near the Slovenian border. They look new, but are 300 and 150 years old respectively. The former farm buildings have been immaculately restored by hands-on owners with attention to every detail. Hiasl sleeps six and Höllberg four. 'We thought it could have been boring' writes a satisfied guest, 'but in fact the days flew by.' This guide looks for self-catering places with imaginative extras – and you definitely get them here: wine, beer and juices at cost in the cellar; oil, eggs, jam and honey in the fridge on arrival; breakfast food delivered each week day; loads of toys for kids; 'hard to know where to start enthusing' says another guest.

Radstadt

Forstauer Str. 17, 5550 Radstadt

Tel 06452 6789
e-mail info@seitenalm.at
website www.seitenalm.at
Food breakfast, lunch, dinner
Prices €€-€€€
Closed never
Proprietors Hanni and Peter
Arnold

Die Seitenalm
Mountain resort and apartments

Popular with families wanting a base for summer and winter sports. This traditional chalet-style hotel is surrounded by meadows and woodland and has magnificent mountain views. Die Seitenalm is situated in its own grounds and has a petting zoo, pony-riding farm and playground. Parents are also catered for, with a relaxing spa area, which has an indoor swimming pool, a sauna and a gym.

Bedrooms vary from family rooms to three-room apartments. A recent visitor said it was 'warm and cosy, but also fresh and light.' He praised the friendliness of the staff and their special touches, such as free fruit and cakes in the afternoon. Good value for money.

Stadl an der Mur

Steindorf 11, 8862 Stadl an der Mur

Tel 03534 2237
e-mail murtalerhof@murau.at
website www.murtalerhof.at
Food breakfast, lunch, dinner,
snacks
Price €
Closed never
Proprietor Johann Lassacher

Murtalerhof
Modern hotel and apartment

A bright hotel popular with rafters, but rather lacking in character. However, Johann Lassacher's authentic Styrian dishes, served in the cavernous dining room are much appreciated by the rafting enthusiasts who hurtle down the Mur river (€40 per person). There is also a steep bike trail for the very fit, and hiking. In winter, there is skiing at Kreischberg (7.5 km), Turracher Höhe (20 km) and Obertauern (37 km).

When guests are not busy with activities, they have enough to do indoors; there is a bowling alley, a children's play area and a sauna area. The 22 bedrooms are plain but functional and there is an annexe with an apartment.

Area introduction

Carinthia (German, Kärnten) is Austria's Riviera, with the massive Tauern range protecting this southernmost state from weather extremes. A belt of picturesque lakes, running east to west, provides that Mediterranean feeling – the biggest is the Wörthersee, where the water can reach 28° C (82° F) in summer. We also like Carinthia's small lakes, such as the Faakersee and the more remote Weissensee.

In winter, Carinthia is blessed with the sunny, southern slopes of the Tauern and the Karawanken range. It's long been an international playground, so hotel standards are high. Bad Kleinkirchheim's small, family-run hotels, are typical Carinthia's accommodation at its best. The road leading up to the Grossglockner, the highest peak in Austria, is an impressive drive, with fine hotels along the way offering riding and downhill skiing. Klagenfurt, the capital, with its old centre, is a pleasant base.

Below are some useful back-up places to try if our main selections are fully booked:

Hotel Lärchenhof
Mountain hotel, Afritz
Tel 04247 2134
www.laerchenhof.co.at
Run by sports mad family;
tennis, swimming; skiing.

Eschenhof Resort hotel, Bad Kleinkirchheim
Tel 04240 8262
www.eschenhof.at
Family-run mountain resort;
perfect for families.

Bio Hotel Jesch
Village hotel, Diex
Tel 04232 7196
www.gasthof-jesch.at
Organic converted farm:
popular with families.

Inselhotel
Island hotel, Faakersee
Tel 04254 2145
http://inselhotel.at
Luxury island hotel: tennis,
surfing, fishing and walks.

Hotel Post
Wayside inn, Grosskirchheim
Tel 04825 26736
hotelpost.sevenspire.net
Popular with hikers in summer; pleasant garden.

Schlosshotel St. Georgen Converted castle, Klagenfurt
Tel 0463 468490
www.schloss-st-georgen.at
Brightly decorated castle; 5
minutes from Klagenfurt.

Villa Verdin
Lakeside hotel, Millstatt am See
Tel 069912 181093
http://villaverdin.at
19thC house with romantic
tower on the Millstättersee.

Naturgasthof Schlosswirt Guesthouse, Ossiach
Tel 65053 92589
www.schlosswirt-ossiach.at
Unpretentious organic cooking, homemade cakes; dock.

Gasthof Tell
Village inn, Paternion
Tel 04245 2931
www.gasthof-tell.at
Jolly 700-year-old inn;
Carinthian specialities.

Hotel Mosser Town hotel, St Veit an der Glan
Tel 04240 507
www.suppenkasper.at
Budget base to explore
medieval town; local dishes,

Art Lodge
Mountain lodge, Verditz
Tel 04247 29970
www.art-lodge.com
Unique modern art lodge;
organic and vegetarian food.

Villa Rainer
Lakeside villa, Wörthersee
Tel 04272 2300
www.rainer.at
Luxury villa on lake: three
jetties, sauna, whirlpool, golf.

Krokusweg 2, 9546 Bad
Kleinkirchheim

Tel 042 408 262
e-mail mauerwirt@eschenhof.at
website www.mauerwirt.at

Nearby Spittal (30 km); Villach (40
km); Klagenfurt (50 km).
Location in the centre of Bad
Kleinkirchheim; car parking
Food self-catering, half board
available (1.5 km)
Prices €-€€
Rooms 8 apartments for 2-7 people,
all with bath or shower; all
apartments have kitchen
Facilities sauna, wi-fi, bicycle hire
Credit cards MC, V
Children accepted
Disabled 2 apartments accessible by
terrace
Pets accepted
Closed never
Proprietors Hildegard and Gerhard
Ortner

Landhaus Mauerwirt
Apartment hotel

We like these apartments – they don't skimp on space, and the interior decoration (as we went to press) was new, clean, and pretty – in fact quite feminine, with squashy pillows, colourful throws, and pleasing pine furniture and panelling everywhere. Plus, you can light your own fire in a lovely tiled stove (having collected wood from an outhouse).

Outside, it looks nothing special, but it is a bit of a discovery – it's not widely known about. The location is in the village centre, just ten minutes on foot from the ski lift. There's a washing, cleaning and ironing service and, if you don't want to cook, there's a half-board deal on offer at sister hotel Eschenhof (see p. 000), 1.5 km away (from where you collect your key when you arrive). It's family friendly, with a children's play area, table tennis and other facilities. A well-priced self-catering operation that is thoughtful and offers more than just the basics.

Egg am Faakersee

Egger Seepromenade 8, 9580 Egg
am Faaker See

Tel 04254 2375
e-mail genuss@kleineshotel.at
website www.kleineshotel.at

Nearby Faaker See (150 m); Villach
(6.5 km).
Location in meadows above lake;
ample car parking, garage
Food breakfast, lunch, dinner,
snacks
Price €€ (half board)
Rooms 16; 12 double, 4 suites, all
with bath or shower; all rooms have
central heating, phone, TV, radio,
hairdryer, safe, minibar, balcony
Facilities dining room, sitting room;
terrace, garden, lakeside sauna,
childrens play area, own dock, golf
nearby
Credit cards AE, DC, MC, V
Children welcome
Disabled not suitable
Pets not accepted
Closed Nov to March
Proprietors Tschemernjak family

Kleines Hotel Kärnten
Lakeside hotel

We have heard nothing but praise
from readers for this contemporary small hotel. 'To create a hotel to
match the view' was the aim of the
Tschemernjak family. The view is a panorama across Faaker See to the Mittagskogel
rising above other mountains.

The hotel is unashamedly modern, with
rooms decorated in soft grey and suites in
yellow, green, red or blue. The dining
room, sitting room, and corridors all boast
original works of art.

During the day, you can relax in the
lakeside sauna, which sits on stilts among
the reeds. Those with young children will
be thankful for the playhouse, complete
with climbing, library and video areas. It
can even accommodate children overnight
while parents enjoy a peaceful evening.
Dinner is informal and can be enjoyed
under the apple trees, on the terrace, or
the restaurant.

There are hiking and cycling trails, water
sports and a golf course nearby, but many
guests, prefer to relax in the garden under
the old trees, admiring that spectacular
view.

Fellacheralm

Fellacheralm, 9564 Patergassen bei
Bad Kleinkirchheim

Tel 04275 7201
e-mail office@almdorf.com
website www.almdorf.com

Nearby Falkert (5.5 km); Bad
Kleinkirchheim (6 km);
Turracherhöhe Pass (11 km).
Location near Patergassen, follow
signs for Falkert; car parking
Food breakfast, lunch, dinner
Price ⊜⊜⊜⊜
Rooms 21 huts, 4 hunting lodges, 3
chalets, all with baths and shower; all
have TV, iPod dock, wi-fi, 2
bedrooms, kitchen, balcony, terrace,
garden; 1 tree house
Facilities restaurant, private dining
room, wine cellar, spa; terrace, golf
and tennis nearby
Credit cards AE, DC, MC, V
Children welcome
Disabled not suitable
Pets accepted
Closed mid-Mar to mid-Apr
Managers Rupert Simoner and
Werner Müller

Almdorf Seinerzeit
Mountain huts and lodges

This is ultimate luxury self-catering: the owners describe the set up as 'not a simple holiday accommodation, but your home for the time of your stay,' and they are spot on. Traditional mountain huts, hunting lodges, chalets, a restaurant, bathing house, spa and two ponds make up the small mountain village of Fellacheralm. The buildings are all made with natural materials – there are even traditional wooden bathtubs on some of the terraces. Each hut is separate, with its own external door, and comes with books and games for children, plus a private garden; the four hunting lodges have their own mini wine cellars and the chalets have saunas in the bathroom.

The main restaurant, Gasthaus Fellacher, is not for vegetarians – traditional, regional dishes, such as grilled venison medalions, use game hunted in the nearby forest. For dessert, we recommend the *Kaiserschmarrn* (caramelised pancake). For a special occasion, guests can book either what claims to be the 'smallest restaurant in the world', the *Holzknechthütte* (up to four people), or the wine cellar (up to six).

The nearby Nockberge mountains offer hiking and mountain biking in summer, or snow-shoe walking and skiing – slopes at Bad Kleinkirchheim, Falkert or Turracher Height – in winter.

9844 Heiligenblut

Tel 04824 2215
e-mail office@romantic.at
website www.romantic.at

Nearby Grossglockner (12 km).
Location off main road above
village; ample car parking
Food breakfast, dinner, snacks
Prices €-€€€
Rooms 13; 3 double, 2 single, 8
suites, all with bath or shower; all
rooms have central heating, phone,
TV, radio
Facilities dining room, 3 sitting
rooms, bar, TV room, table-tennis
room, gymnasium, sauna, solarium
Credit cards AE, MC, V
Children very welcome
Disabled not suitable
Pets accepted (not in restaurant)
Closed after Easter to mid-June,
Oct to mid-Dec
Proprietors Senger family

Haus Senger
Mountain hotel

Not many sports stars have turned to
hotel-keeping as successfully as Hans
Senger, who represented Austria at the
1952 Olympic Games in Oslo. He ran this
small hotel, a careful mixture of old and
new wedged into a steep hill above
Heiligenblut, until Rosemarie and Andreas
Senger took over several years ago.
Rebuilt in 1966, it looks like an old farmhouse thanks to the 400-year-old beams
and planks rescued from an old barn.
These, along with the hundred-year-old
beams and three crackling open fireplaces,
give the hotel the atmosphere holidaymakers dream about.

Upstairs, bedrooms are decorated in
country style with solid wooden furnishings and balconies that look out to the
Grossglockner (3,800 m) and its surrounding mountains.

Menus range from Italian to local
Austrian dishes, with regular Wednesday
fondue evenings. There is also a health and
fitness area with a sauna and steam bath,
which blends in cleverly, and guests ski out
and ski back from a side door. A hotel that
is better in reality than in its brochure.

Heiligenblut

Hof 45, 9844 Heiligenblut,
Oostenrijk

Tel 04824 411 4700
e-mail info@hotel-kaiservilla.com
website www.hotel-kaiservilla.com

Nearby Heiligenblut; Bergbahen;
Grossglockner.
Location 5-min walk from middle of
village and ski slopes; ample car
parking, garage
Food breakfast, dinner, snacks
Price €€
Rooms 13 suites, all with bath or
shower; all rooms have cable TV,
safe, sitting room, wi-fi, most with
balcony, some with hairdryer
Facilities restaurant, sitting
room/bar, spa, safe, ski storage,
terrace, wi-fi
Credit cards MC, V
Children accepted
Disabled ground floor access
Pets accepted (extra charge)
Closed Nov
Proprietors Family van Dijk – de
Haast

Hotel Kaiservilla
Mountain retreat

'Forget the chalets and geraniums, this is totally different from any Austrian hotel I have ever stayed in', says a trusted reporter, and several readers agree that this 1930s villa is special. The villa was originally named Villa Kaiser Franz Josef after the previous owners were granted the use of the Kaiser's name in 1864, and when the van Dijk – de Haasts took over they renamed it the Kaiservilla. It has been completely renovated, and reopened in the summer of 2013.

Suites are spacious and decorated mainly in Alpine style. Instead of ornate furniture and gilt, a few well chosen pieces of furniture are set against plain or coloured walls and pale wood floors. Some rooms boast views of the church and the Grossglockner, Austria's highest mountain.

In winter, reception can set you up with a ski pass, in summer, the Nationalpark Kärnten Card is free with stays of at least two nights. The ski slopes on Grossglockner are not too far, and skiers will appreciate the seasonal, local and organic food in the restaurant or good wines in the *après-ski* bar after a long day on the slopes. Then relax on the comfy sofas in the sitting room by the open fire, looking out to Heiligenblut and the mountains.

Kötschach-Mauthen

9640 Kötschach-Mauthen 24

Tel 04715 269
e-mail info@sissy-sonnleitner.at
website www.sissy-sonnleitner.at

Nearby Lienz (25 km); Spittal an
der Drau (40 km); Lake Wörthersee
(80 km); Klagenfurt (100 km);
museum; Hercules Temple.
Location in middle of village; ample
car parking
Food breakfast, lunch, dinner,
snacks
Price €€
Rooms 12; 5 double, 5 suites, 2
apartments, all with bath or shower;
all rooms have central heating,
phone, TV, minibar
Facilities dining room, sitting room,
library, bar, terrace, garden; fishing,
golf and skiing nearby
Credit cards AE, DC, MC, V
Children very welcome
Disabled not suitable
Pets accepted
Closed 1 week after Easter, mid-
Nov to mid-Dec
Proprietors Sonnleitner family

Sissy Sonnleitner's Kellerwand Restaurant-with-rooms and apartments

Sissy Sonnleitner is a star, voted Austria's Chef of the Year in 1990. Yet she does not work in Vienna, Salzburg, or even a posh ski resort, but in the village of Mauthen. Find it on the River Gail, a few minutes' drive from the Italian border. Apart from inspiration derived from family holidays in France and Germany, she is self-taught. Her repertoire combines Carinthian and Friuli dishes: she fills pasta Austrian-style, with white cheese, potatoes and herbs but stuffs dumplings Italian-style, with pumpkin.

Kurt Sonnleitner's wine cellar scores for its competitive prices and wide range of vintages from Italy, Bordeaux, Burgundy and Austria. Breakfast is served under the arches in the peaceful courtyard. The 500-year-old Kellerwand, with yellow walls and blue shutters, is the oldest building in Mauthen and has been in the family for more than 300 years. A half-way house for travellers between Venice and Vienna, it merits more than an overnight stay. Those who settle in for a fortnight on half-board are never offered the same dish twice. Bedrooms match the high standards of the cooking: Thonet furniture and Ralph Lauren fabrics with Carrara marble in the bathrooms.

Weissensee

9762 Techendorf am Weissensee

Tel 04713 2221
e-mail office@seehotelenzian.at
website www.seehotelenzian.at

Nearby Weissensee.
Location on hillside above lake;
ample car parking
Food breakfast, lunch, dinner,
snacks
Price €€
Rooms 23; 16 double, 1 single, 6
lake-side suites, all with bath or
shower; all rooms have phone, TV,
central heating, wi-fi,
balcony/terrace
Facilities sitting room; terrace,
garden, tennis court, boats, lakeside
spa, riding and winter sports nearby
Credit cards MC, V
Children welcome
Disabled not suitable
Pets accepted
Closed mid-March to mid-May,
mid-Oct to mid-Dec
Proprietors Cieslar family

Seehotel Enzian
Weissensee **Lakeside hotel**

Several readers have written in to recommend this delightful hotel overlooking Carinthia's highest lake, the
Weissensee. This provides year-round
sport since the water reaches 24° C (75°
F) in summer, and freezes in winter, allow-
ing skaters and cross-country skiers to
whizz across the snow and ice.

On a dead end road is the Enzian, built
by the grandparents of current owner
Christine Cieslar (the fourth generation),
whose family heirlooms such as clocks, a
wedding veil, and photographs add character. The Enzian (gentian) theme appears in
carvings on shutters and in the blue of
tablecloths on the terrace. Inviting armchairs and good reading lamps give the sitting room the look of a private house,
while the well-maintained bedrooms are
medium sized, mainly with white walls and
floral curtains.

Where the rest of the hotel is light and
airy, the *Almhütte*, just outside, is a dark,
cosy cabin that has been turned into a
pub, perfect for *après-ski* or late evening
schnapps. Dinner is a five course affair
with a salad and cheese bar. As well as the
garden and clay tennis court, the sailing
school is a bonus for youngsters. The new
spa has a sauna, a herbal steam bath and a
panoramic view of the lake.

Hallegger Str 131, 9061 Klagenfurt
am Wörthersee

Tel 0720 505561
e-mail reservations@schloss-
hallegg.at
website www.schloss-hallegg.at

Nearby Lake Wörth (3 km);
Krumpendorf (3 km); Klagenfurt (5
km); Pörtschach (10 km); Velden (17
km).
Location in woods, high above
Krumpendorf and Klagenfurt; ample
car parking
Food breakfast
Price €
Rooms 6 double, all with bath or
shower; all rooms have central
heating, minibar
Facilities dining room, sitting room;
tennis, riding, fishing and golf
nearby
Credit cards not accepted
Children very welcome
Disabled not suitable
Pets accepted
Closed Oct to mid-May
Proprietor Frau Yulia Haybäck

Schloss Hallegg
Castle hotel

'The best place in the world to have
breakfast.' That was the reaction of
our reporter who, like all first-time visitors, was open-mouthed at the views.
Where else in the world can you sip coffee and munch rolls outdoors on top of
castle ramparts? Far below, the land drops
away sharply and in the distance, beyond
the trees and fields, are the twin towers of
Maria Saal.

The 800-year-old castle, built on a rocky
outcrop, is large enough to garrison a
small army. Enter the huge portal and you
expect to see knights in armour. Instead,
roses fill the courtyard and old-fashioned
sleds and carriages shelter in the cloisters.
Two more stories of arches climb to the
steep wood-shingled roof. Everything is on
a huge scale, with high ceilings and wood
floors. Bedrooms could sleep whole families, while the medieval hall could be a film
set. Forty metres long, 9 metres high, with
vicious-looking weapons on the wall, it
cannot look much different than it did
when Otto II of Hallegg lived here. Open
only in summer, guests walk in the woods,
fish on the private lake, play tennis and
golf, and peep into the tiny chapel in the
tower, big enough for only two pews.

Bad Bleiberg

Bleiberg Nötsch 131, 9530 Bad Bleiberg

Tel 04244 2249
e-mail pension@lindenbauer.co.at
website www.lindenbauer.co.at
Food breakfast
Price €
Closed early Jan to end Mar
Proprietors Lindenbauer family

Gartenpension Linden-bauer **Village guesthouse**

You will get more than just a warm welcome here. Hildegard and Karl Lindenbauer are those rare type of hosts who can intelligently anticipate needs – and meet them without being obtrusive. Staying here is like staying with friends – and their family ownership goes back nearly 30 years, so their track record is consistent. Plus there's been major reinvestment recently – another good sign.

The grounds here are large and well looked after, with a backdrop of low mountains. In winter, there's cross-country skiing and skating on the lakes. In summer, there's swimming in the lakes, and mountain walks.

Bodensdorf

Gerlitzenstrasse 55, 9551 Bodensdorf

Tel 04248 296 21
e-mail info@hotel12.at
website www.hotel12.at
Food breakfast, lunch, dinner
Price €€€
Closed early Nov to mid-Dec
Manager Christoph Glaser

Hotel 12
Town art hotel

Art hotels are commoner in Germany and Austria than in Western Europe, and we usually have mixed feelings about them. This one is sincere, rather than gimmicky, with different artists' work displayed on plain white walls in each of the 12 rooms, named after creatures from the Chinese zodiac.

It's in a terrific location, high in the Carinthia mountains, with stunning views. Maybe the restaurant is a little over the top in some respects – they serve own-brand wine and cigars – but the food has a reputation. But above all guest after guest reports a genuinely laid-back atmosphere and a personal welcome.

Feld am See

9544 Feld am See

Tel 04246 2274
e-mail urlaub@landhotel-linden-hof.at
website www.landhotel-lindenhof.at
Food breakfast, lunch, dinner
Price €€ (half board)
Closed 3 weeks after Easter, mid-Oct to mid-Dec
Proprietors Hannes and Angelika Nindler

Hotel Lindenhof
Country inn

Cyclists – come here. A member of the Association of Biking Hotels in the Alps, this hotel is the place for those wanting to explore the Alps on two wheels. The owner is a certified biking guide and takes guests out on tours in the Nockberge area.

Set beside a splashing fountain and a church, the Lindenhof is at the heart of the quiet lakeside village of Feld am See. Locals still drink in the *Stube*, with its pale wood, bright turquoise seats and deep window sills. Outsiders flock to the modern-rustic dining rooms for award-winning cooking.

In winter, cross-country enthusiasts ski around the lake, but the nearest downhill is at Bad Kleinkirchheim. Basement fitness room; stylish and modern spa area; massages; tennis courts; beach on the lake.

Friesach

Hauptplatz 11, 9360 Friesach

Tel 04268 25100
e-mail metnitztalerhof@burgen-stadt.at
website www.metnitztalerhof.at
Food breakfast, lunch, dinner
Price €€
Closed never
Proprietors Bucher family

Metnitztalerhof
Restaurant-with-rooms

An atmospheric old inn dating back to the 1300s in a dominating position in an interesting medieval town – but don't come for the rooms. Although clean and properly equipped, they are standardized, and their decorative scheme is unimaginative (which is perhaps putting it politely). However: many visitors feel that that the food and the welcome more than make up for this. The restaurant, which specializes in Carinthian noodle dishes, is rated as one of the top eating places in the region, and you're looked after by the Buchers, a dedicated and experienced husband and wife team who will give you an 'old school' welcome. Don't miss a visit to the medieval wine cellar.

Grosskirchheim

Döllach 100, 9843 Grosskirchheim

Tel 04825 26761
e-mail info@schlosswirt.net
website www.schlosswirt.net
Food breakfast, lunch, dinner, snacks
Price €
Closed mid-Oct to Jun
Proprietors Sauper family

Hotel Schlosswirt
Wayside inn

You need time to get the best out of this inn on the famous Grossglockner road. Ride, hike, take horse-driven carriage rides, or merely admire the wildlife and flowers.

The old *Stuben* have the obligatory horns on the walls. The food is honest, regional cooking with south-Tyrolean influences. Afternoon tea is served in the little parlour off the cosy bar in winter. The cheerful bedrooms have plain, solid furniture (made in the village) brightened by hand-painted details above the bedheads.

Behind the hotel is a small *Schloss* which the Sauper family renovated as a challenge. It doesn't contain bedrooms – they're all in the main house – but it makes a charming feature. Ski-bus from hotel door; outdoor swimming pool.

Liesing

No. 8, 9653 Liesing

Tel 04716 303
e-mail gaestehaus.ortner@aon.at
website www.gaestehaus-ortner.at
Food breakfast, lunch, dinner
Price €
Closed early Jan to early May, mid-Oct to mid-Dec
Proprietor Ortner Adelheid

Gästehaus Ortner
Mountain hotel and apartments

Hotel? Holiday home? Self-catering? In fact it's all three, which is why we include this versatile family-run place in the Carinthian mountains. Rent a room, as in a hotel, and eat breakfast and dinner downstairs. Or take an apartment with a kitchen (going half-board if you wish). Or rent the nearby holiday home, a self-contained small dwelling suitable for two to five, again eating in the restaurant as and when you want.

Further twists to the usual self-catering formula include a wine cellar where they sell bottles at keen prices – and they make their own schnapps. Set at 1,043 m on a slope in the lowish mountain scenery of the Lesachtal.

Pörtschach

Kogelweg 4-6, 9210 Pörtschach am Wörthersee

Tel 04272 25910
e-mail info@landhaus.at
website www.landhaus.at
Food breakfast, lunch, dinner
Prices € –€€
Closed never
Proprietor Waltraud Faeser

Das Landhaus Hauptmann **Lake hotel**

Asafe mid-price choice almost on the Wörthersee (see also our suggestions on pages 130, 138 and 143) – don't expect flair. It's up a track a little way from the road in farmland on a small hill that gives the lake views a bit of extra punch. If it weren't for the location it probably would-n't be in this guide because it's too much of an ordinary hotel. The bedrooms are standard, with monotonous green and purple colour schemes – more like hotel rooms than bedrooms. However, the welcome is friendly, the food is okay and it's peaceful. The basics are right, it's well run and a real bonus is the hotel's own swimming jetty on the lake, a ten-minute walk away.

Schiefling

Kirchenstraße 121, 9535 Schiefling am Wörthersee

Tel 04274 3004
e-mail info@haus-kaiser.com
website www.haus-kaiser.com
Food breakfast
Price €
Closed never
Proprietors Spitzer family

Haus Kaiser
Country hotel and apartments

The charm is almost all in the price. Two people can stay here in a double room for 66 euros or less in high season, including breakfast, so we include it as a budget option in the popular Wörthersee area – see our other recommendations on pages 130, 138 and 143. The rooms and four apartments are clean, pleasant enough, but no more than you would expect for the price. What you might not expect is the location: it's surrounded by wide green slopes running gently down to the lake, and there are mountain views. The swimming pool is big. Family friendly.

Velden am Wörthersee

Am Corso 9-11, 9220 Velden am Wörthersee

Tel 04274 26150
e-mail info@villabulfon.at
website www.villabulfon.at
Food breakfast, lunch, dinner, snacks
Price €€€
Closed never
Proprietor Mr Mahnki

Villa Bulfon
Town hotel

Quite a long way outside our normal territory – it has 35 rooms and is very much a conventional hotel with smart but standardized decoration (white leather banquette-sofas everywhere). Its charm is in the location, in big grounds beside the Wörthersee, which include a lakeside restaurant like a top country club and a smart beach club i.e. a manicured area where you rent (at a price) swanky sun loungers. The building has a long history (back to 1481), so it has a bit of character and tradition. The lake's first bathing hut was put up here in the 19th century, and in the 1900s it had a spell as a casino – relics of which are preserved in the new Rum-Bar (cigars on sale). Prices are reasonable.

Weissensee

Techendorf 39, 9762 Weissensee

Tel 04713 2203
e-mail hotel@harrida.at
website www.harrida.at
Food breakfast, dinner, snacks (in hotel café)
Price €
Closed Nov to May
Proprietor Frau Kolouch and Herr Attila

Hotel Harrida
Suburban hunting lodge

You can't escape the panoramic setting here – every room has a balcony or terrace overlooking either the Weissensee (turquoise and warm in summer, frozen in winter) or the surrounding mountains. Nor can you avoid the family-run character and Austrian authenticity of the place. Much of the ground floor is decorated with wood-panelling, exposed beams and ornaments, such as the carved creatures in the reception area. Hunting lodges tend to be compact, so the bedrooms – with pretty painted furniture – and bathrooms are small, but there is plenty of outdoor space, including a beach, and a sunny terrace. Guests praise the four-course dinners and wine selection, Some report a lack of meatless dishes, but vegetarian meals are available – on request.

Area introduction

This is the French-speaking part of Switzerland, bordering France – which English drivers cross *en route* from the Channel Ports to the Alps. Valais, the large canton to the south-east, also French speaking, has its own section (pages 203-211).

Here you find two of Switzerland's most international cities, Geneva and Lausanne, sitting on the shores of Lake Geneva, with a generally balmy climate, vineyards growing down to the water's edge and a near-distant backdrop of mountains.

Geneva is a disappointing city for small hotels with character and charm. We have some suggestions, but don't expect them to reach our ideal standards. The least lacking are the places on the hillsides overlooking the lake – useful bases for walking or relaxing. To the north-east, in the mountains, and on the smaller lakes further north, are some rural retreats, some quite rustic, others smart country house hotels.

Below are some useful back-up places to try if our main selections are fully booked:

Port Gitana
Lakeside hotel, Bellevue-Geneva Tel 022 774 3148
www.port-gitana.ch
Quiet rooms looking out to
harbour; busy restaurant.

Major Davel
Lakeside hotel, Cully
Tel 021 799 9494
www.hotelaumajordavel.ch
Most rooms have view of
vine-terraced peninsula.

Du Midi Restaurant-with-rooms, Delémont
Tel 032 422 1777
www.hoteldumidi.ch
Award-winning, well-priced
restaurant near station.

St Gervais
City hotel, Geneva
Tel 022 732 4572
www.stgervais-geneva.ch
Budget hotel, one minute
from train station and lake.

Tiffany
City hotel, Geneva
Tel 022 708 1616
www.hotel-tiffany.ch
Art nouveau hotel with
bright furniture; two studios.

La Fleur de Lys
Old inn, Gruyères
Tel 029 621 08
www.hotelfleurdelys.ch
300-year-old mansion with
beams and wood-panelling.

Le Debarcadère **Lakeside apartments, Lausanne at St Sulpice Tel** 079 289 9509
www.ledebarcadere.ch
Louis XVI and colonial-
style; all have lake views.

Auberge de Vers-chez-Perrin **Village inn, Vers-chez-Perrin Tel** 026 660 5840
auberge-verschezperrin.ch
Sophisticated country inn
with comfortable bedrooms.

Masson
Lake-view hotel, Montreux
Tel 021 966 0044
www.hotelmasson.ch
19thC house with walnut
furniture; wooded gardens.

Maisonforte SA, Bursins, 1183 Nyon

Tel 078 778 1141
e-mail info@lerosey.ch
website www.lerosey.ch

Nearby Rolle (4 km); Nyon (8 km);
Geneva (30 km); Lausanne (33 km).
Location halfway between Geneva
and Lausanne (33 km), 5 minutes
from Rolle and Geneva Lake
Food breakfast, dinner (twice week-
ly)
Prices FFFFF
Rooms 4 double, all with en-suite;
all rooms have internet
Facilities dining rooms, drawing
room, garden, vineyard
Credit cards AE, MC, V
Children welcome
Disabled not accessible
Pets welcome
Closed never
Proprietor Pierre Bouvier

Chateau Le Rosey
Converted medieval castle

A notable retreat for wine lovers; this much-rebuilt château with roots in the 1300s, sits comfortably in the middle of a small vineyard and soaks up the surrounding atmosphere. A ground-floor wine cellar sits in the heart of the building and opens on to the castle's enclosed central courtyard where, weather permitting, 15 different wines are available for tasting.

It has been painstakingly renovated over six years by owner Pierre Bouvier, and most of the château is open to guests. Each of the four bedrooms offers spectacular views of the surrounding vineyards. The bathrooms are covered from floor to ceiling with colourful mosaic tiles. The style throughout is contemporary yet respectful of the historic building, with plenty of open space, light and exposed beams. Creams and greens are used to complement the country house feel.

Dinner is served twice a week for private receptions by an outside chef who creates dishes of your choice from produce grown in the orchard and kitchen garden. The château hosts regular gastronomy events, with chefs coming from far and wide to create dishes that complement the château's wine.

This is fairly recently opened, a new find on the north shore of Lake Geneva, about half way between Geneva and Lausanne

Clarens near Montreux

1815 Clarens, Montreux

Tel 021 964 4411
e-mail contact@ermitage-mon-
treux.com /
ermitage.krebs@bluewin.ch
website www.ermitage-
montreux.com

Nearby Château de Chillon (4 km).
Location overlooking lake; ample
car parking
Food breakfast, lunch, dinner,
snacks
Prices FFFF-FFFFF
Rooms 7; 5 double, 1 single, 1 suite,
all with bath or shower; all rooms
have central heating, phone, TV,
radio, minibar, hairdryer
Facilities dining room; terrace, gar-
den; winter sports nearby
Credit cards AE, DC, MC, V
Children welcome
Disabled not suitable
Pets accepted
Closed Christmas and New Year;
restaurant only, Sun, Mon
Proprietors Etienne and Isabelle
Krebs

L'Ermitage
Restaurant with rooms

Most people come here for the food, among the best in the west of Switzerland; some come for the art on die walls; others turn off the busy route 9 for the calm of the lake. 'I'd come for a bath,' writes a guest. That bath is in the suite, standing in splendour upon a plinth; 'look straight ahead, as you slide into the bub-bles, out on to the lake with the snow-capped Mont Blanc framed in the window'.

Each bedroom is different, some with plain walls, some with patterned wallpaper, many with large prints that manage to blend with colour schemes such as butter-cream and moss-green or tones of pink. All have welcoming fruit and flowers; five have balconies. Not everyone will like them all – if possible, choose one to suit your taste.

The point of the place is the stylishly modern restaurant. The Krebs have been here since 1990 and each year the food seems to get better. Local ingredients fea-ture in dishes such as veal chop with morels and sea bass with broccoli polenta. The wine list is long, with an impressive number of fine wines. Desserts are deca-dent, for example, chocolate cake with red berries and pistachios, or strawberry and grenadine molasses tacos.

Place de l'Eglise 6, 1232 Confignon

Tel 022 757 1944
e-mail info@auberge-confignon.ch
website www.auberge-confignon.ch

Nearby Geneva (5 km); Mont Salève
(6 km); lake; airport.
Location in small village; ample car
parking
Food breakfast, lunch, dinner,
snacks
Price FF
Rooms 14 double, all with bath or
shower; all rooms have central heat-
ing, phone, TV, radio
Facilities restaurant, bar; terrace,
garden
Credit cards MC, V
Children welcome
Disabled not suitable
Pets accepted
Closed never; restaurant only, Sun
eve, Mon
Manager Sergio Schoener

Auberge de Confignon
Village inn

The setting is almost perfect: on the
corner of a traffic-free village green
with a fountain, flowers and views over
Geneva and the mountains of the Salève. It
even has the village church nearby. Yet this
idyll is so close to the city that the number two trolley bus stops just at the end of
the road, so guests can become temporary
commuters, returning each evening to
rural peace broken only by the church
clock chiming.

Our reporter felt at home as soon as he
walked inside. The bar and restaurant are
the focal points of the hotel and of the village, where business is done and the con-
versation is animated. Bedrooms aren't
fussy and have a Scandinavian look: white
with touches of colour, the occasional print,
plenty of potted plants and large cupboards
for clothes. Bathrooms are functional.

The inn is closed for refurbishment until
mid-December 2013 and, as we went to
press, no information was available on
prices, opening dates, or the number of
rooms available, so we haven't changed
this information – contact the hotel when
it reopens for up to date details. Even so,
it's a useful base for sightseeing and is
worth visiting just for the restaurant.

Coppet near Nyon

1296 Coppet

Tel 022 960 8000
e-mail info@hoteldulac.ch
website www.hoteldulac.ch

Nearby Château de Coppet (150 m); lake.
Location between main road and lake in Coppet; car parking on street; private boat mooring
Food breakfast, lunch, dinner, snacks
Price FFF
Rooms 19; 12 double, 7 suites, all with bath or shower; all rooms have central heating, phone, TV, radio, minibar
Facilities dining room, 2 sitting rooms, bar, lift/elevator; terrace, garden; riding, sailing nearby
Credit cards AE, DC, MC, V
Children welcome
Disabled not suitable
Pets accepted
Closed never
Proprietor O. Schnyder

Hôtel du Lac
Lakeside hotel

When the local 18thC Château de Coppet was new, this hotel was already old. For 350 years it has offered hospitality to travellers. Arcades and façades present a decorative face to the Grande-Rue but the focus is the lake on the other side. Here you can swim, lie back on a sun lounger, or dine on the semi-circular curve of terrace, underneath an orange and white-striped awning. Bedrooms are large (you pay a premium for a view of the lake) but the suites are enormous. Our reporter was ready to move into one which even had a kitchen. The exposed joists of the attic ceiling are a dramatic feature, while the largest even has a private patio set into the slanting roof. He was less enthusiastic about the deep turquoise bathrooms.

With doors the thickness of an arm and heavy wooden furniture, the atmosphere is like a gentlemen's club, particularly in the plush smoking room and large bar with its grand piano. 'Inviting armchairs, pity about the piped music,' was the reaction. In the restaurant, roasting is the order of the day, with the meat, poultry and fish turning on spits over the wood fire creating an almost medieval impression.

Cully

1 place de l'Hôtel-de-Ville, 1096
Cully

Tel 021 799 2131
e-mail info@aubergeduraisin.ch
website www.aubergeduraisin.ch

Nearby Lake Geneva (100 m);
Lausanne (8 km); Lavaux and
Dézaley vineyards.
Location on main square; car park-
ing on street
Food breakfast, lunch, dinner,
snacks
Prices FFF-FFFF
Rooms 10; 9 double, 1 single, all
with bath or shower; all rooms have
central heating, phone, TV, radio,
minibar, hairdryer
Facilities 3 dining rooms, bar; ter-
race
Credit cards AE, DC, MC, V
Children welcome
Disabled limited access
Pets accepted
Closed never; restaurant only, Sun
Manager Peter Hasler

Auberge du Raisin
Renovated inn

A model of what hotels should be but
rarely are. Gilded grapes hang outside,
while the interior looks like a well-kept
church, with stone floors, large, simple furniture and wooden ceilings. Our reporter
had nothing but praise for this inn dating
from the 13thC.

Flowers are everywhere, not in formal
arrangements, but looking as if they have
just been brought in from the garden. A
vase of asters or poppies brightens the
bedrooms, named for people with a Swiss
connection, such as Chaplin, Rousseau,
Dali, or Stravinsky. All are beautifully furnished with eye-catching artwork and
antique furniture. 'If you can't stay long
enough to try them all, try one at the top
under the ceiling joists, one with a four-
poster bed or, in chilly weather, one with a
wood burning stove.'

There is no garden but the terrace
above the dining room is peaceful enough
for birds to nest in the bay tree. Chef
Peter Hasler's cooking features fish from
the lake. Typical dishes on his menu
include: spicy *foie gras*; lobster casserole
with mint coulis; veal with mushrooms and
chive cream; and lemongrass steak with a
red wine sauce.

1204 Geneva, rue Puits-St-Pierre 1
GE

Tel 022 310 9172
e-mail reception@hotel-les-armures.ch
website www.hotel-les-armures.ch

Nearby Cathedral, Town Hall,
Arsenal, Tavel House.
Location in old town pedestrian
area; car parking by hotel porter
Food breakfast, lunch, dinner,
snacks
Price FFFFF
Rooms 32; 23 double, 4 single, 5
suites, all with bath or shower; all
rooms have central heating, air con-
ditioning, phone, TV, radio, minibar,
hairdryer, wi-fi
Facilities dining room, sitting room,
bar, lift/elevator, terrace
Credit cards AE, DC, MC, V
Children welcome
Disabled some access
Pets accepted
Closed never
Proprietors Nicole Borgeat-
Granges

Hôtel les Armures
City hotel

Although this hotel is only 25 years old,
it's in a much older building, parts dating to the 15th century. During conversion, upstairs rooms revealed 17thC painted wooden ceilings and very old walls.

The restaurant, on two levels, is rather
grand. On the ground floor level, a dull suit
of armour stands guard over businessmen,
and singers from the nearby opera, who
order up Swiss specialties. Below it, in the
celler, is the second eating area, Carnozet.

The hotel has been recently renovated
and redesigned to encompass a mix of his-
torical and contemporary features.
Tapestries, 17thC paintings and 20thC
pieces decorate exposed walls; marble
bathrooms have modern lighted mirrors.
Our reporter noticed minibars hidden in
antique bureaux.

Open the windows looking on to the
traffic-free old town, smell the fresh flowers in every room and breathe in Geneva.
A word of warning: it is easy to get lost in
the labyrinth of narrow streets in this part
of the city, so take a taxi or follow the map
which is faxed out with all reservations.

Rue du Midi 12, 1248 Hermance

Tel 022 751 1368
e-mail info@hotel-hermance.ch
website www.hotel-hermance.ch

Nearby Geneva; French border;
medieval village on lake.
Location on quiet side-street in old
village north-east of Geneva on the
lake; car parking in street
Food breakfast, lunch, dinner
Prices FFF-FFFFF
Rooms 9; 2 double, 6 suites, 1 sin-
gle, all with bath or shower; all
rooms have central heating, phone,
TV, radio
Facilities dining room; terrace, gar-
den
Credit cards AE, DC, MC, V
Children welcome
Disabled not suitable
Pets accepted
Closed Christmas to New Year;
restaurant only, Tue, Wed lunch
Proprietor Franz Wehren

Auberge d'Hermance
Country inn

This is one of those special little places
you don't tell your friends about.
Although Hermance has more art galleries
than most cities and one or two touristy
shops, it retains the character of a village
and has successfully fought off too many
trappings of the 21st century. The *auberge*
describes itself as 'rustic' and rustic it certainly is: there is not a straight line in the
place. In the restaurant, wreaths of wheat
and loaves of bread are mixed with wood-
en ceilings and country prints in a style
that would have made Laura Ashley feel at
home. Even in spring, it looks autumnal,
thanks to the wood fire that burns all year.

A suite up in the eaves boasts its own
fireplace and some rooms have small windows through which you can look out over
chimney pots. Paintings are everywhere.

Here you eat well (perch fillets *meunière*
style and *Kobier* beef *entrcôte* steak are
specialities) and since there is space
upstairs for only three bedrooms and five
small suites, you feel as though you are
staying with a friend. Book early, particularly on summer weekends.

Route des Monts 31, 1824 Caux-sur-Montreux

Tel 021 961 2591
e-mail contact@hostellerie-caux.com
website www.hostellerie-caux.com

Nearby Lake Geneva (2 km); Montreux (9 km).
Location above Montreux; cogwheel train stop Hauts-de-Caux; by car, 20-min drive; ample car parking
Food breakfast, lunch, dinner, snacks
Price FF
Rooms 6 double, all with bath, 2 with shared facilities; all rooms have central heating, wi-fi
Facilities restaurant, sitting room; garden, terrace, winter sports nearby
Credit cards AE, MC, V
Children very welcome.
Disabled not suitable
Pets not accepted
Closed mid-Dec to mid-Jan; restaurant only, Wed, Thu
Proprietors Rita and Jean-Philippe Wüthrich

Hostellerie de Caux
Chalet hotel

If Heidi's grandfather had run a hotel, it would have looked like this. Perched on the mountain, the Hostellerie de Caux is 1,165 m, or more than 20 hair-pin bends, up the steep road from Montreux. Those in the know, however, take the small, blue cogwheel train to the Rochers de Naye. The stop at Caux is just a three-minute walk from the inn. Although popular for weekend lunches in the 1930s, the standards had fallen, until Jean-Pierre Fath and his Austrian wife decided to escape from the large hotels of Montreux and reignite the hotel's popularity. Rita and Jean-Philippe Wüthrich, their successors, have continued to improve the reputation of Hostellerie de Caux, serving game, *Rösti* and fondues to satisfy the hearty appetites of guests who ski in winter and march along the mountain tracks in summer. In October, Rita and Jean-Philippe offer a hunting menu with boar, venison and wild mushrooms and berries,

Every bedroom has spectacular mountain or lake views, which make up for the rather basic furnishings, although there are comfortable double beds. Bathrooms are small but perfectly adequate. After all, who wants to spend time upstairs when downstairs there is a roaring fire and a bar with a panorama of Lac Léman, the sunset and birds swooping below.

Au Gor du Vauseyon, 2006
Neuchâtel

Tel 032 730 5454
e-mail info@hotel-prussien.ch
website www.hotel-prussien.ch

Nearby gorges, climbing wall;
Neuchâtel; lake.
Location on edge of town; ample
car parking
Food breakfast, lunch, dinner,
snacks
Prices FF-FFFF
Rooms 10 double, all with bath or
shower; all rooms have central heat-
ing, telephone, TV, radio, hairdryer,
minibar, 2 have fireplace
Facilities 2 dining rooms, sitting
room, 2 conference rooms; terrace
Credit cards AE, DC, MC, V
Children very welcome
Disabled not suitable
Pets accepted
Closed 3 weeks during summer, 2
weeks during Christmas and the new
year
Manager Jean-Yves Drevet

La Maison du Prussien
Converted brewery

At the heart of the Swiss watch-making region, Neuchâtel is an attractive city on the shore of Switzerland's largest lake. Home to language schools and education-al institutions, the area is known for the clarity of its spoken French. For 150 years, however, the region was part of Prussia, which explains the name of the hotel, which readers have pressed us to include.

Only a five-minute drive from the rail-way station at Neuchâtel, this tastefully converted former brewery is surrounded by large trees and the ruins of three 16th-19thC mills. The plain stone walls and exposed beams throughout retain the atmosphere of the 18thC building, while bedrooms are named for former owners, such as Suzanne Merveilleux and the brewer, Brasseur Andres. One of the most romantic is the Jean Chambrier room under the eaves, with its vast wooden ceil-ing, grand beams and working log fireplace. All the bathrooms are modern and luxuri-ous; six have double bathtubs.

The conference rooms are used every week for workshops and private functions. The gourmet restaurant, in an adjoining modern conservatory, has an excellent public reputation thanks to the cooking of French chef and manager Jean-Yves Drevet.

Chemin de Châteauvieux 16, 1242
Satigny-Genève

Tel 022 753 1511
e-mail guillaume.lefebvre@chateau-vieux.ch
website www.chateauvieux.ch

Nearby Geneva (10 km); Geneva
airport; vineyards.
Location deep in vineyards, on hill-side overlooking Rhône; ample car
parking
Food breakfast, lunch, dinner
Price FFFF
Rooms 18; 17 double, 1 single, all
with bath or shower; all rooms have
central heating, phone, TV, radio,
minibar
Facilities dining room; terrace
Credit cards AE, MC, V
Children welcome
Disabled not suitable
Pets accepted
Closed 2 weeks in Aug, Christmas
and New Year; restaurant only, Sun,
Mon
Proprietors Philippe Chevrier

Domaine de Châteauvieux **Country hotel**

The mass of French cars and international business executives who regularly find their way to this old stone farm-house, perched on a hill top, are explained by the fine cooking of Philippe Chevrier. He is passionate about his business and sets himself extremely high standards. Our reporter was relieved to discover that he has neither been overwhelmed by expense-account gourmet dining nor fallen prey to the pursuit of yet more Michelin stars.

The place has a rustic feel with wooden beams, stone floors, and a courtyard. A guest tells us how he enjoyed gem after gem from the kitchen, each course matched by wine produced by vineyards visible from the window. 'This is not the paid-to-smile brigade,' he wrote in tribute to the staff, 'they really hope you enjoy every mouthful.' There are rooms as well, furnished in rather plain, traditional style; some have large windows overlooking the Rhône River and surrounding forests. The bountiful breakfast tempted our reporter to indulge once more. 'All this and only a short drive from Geneva and its airport,' he concluded. 'The only thing that will get thinner if you stay here is your wallet.'

1134 Vufflens-le-Château, Morges

Tel 021 804 6868
e-mail ermitage@ravet.ch
website www.ravet.ch

Nearby Morges; Château; vineyards.
Location in village, near church
Food breakfast, lunch, dinner,
snacks
Prices FFF-FFFFF
Rooms 9; 6 double, 3 suites, all with
bath; all rooms have central heating,
phone, TV, minibar, Nespresso
machine, hairdryer, trouser press,
wi-fi, balcony, suites have sitting
room
Facilities dining room, sitting room,
bar, lift/elevator; terrace, garden
Credit cards AE, DC, MC, V
Children welcome
Disabled reasonable access
Pets accepted
Closed 2 weeks in Aug; 3 weeks at
Christmas; restaurant only, Sun,
Mon
Proprietors Ravet family

L'Ermitage
Restaurant-with-rooms

Bernard Ravet has been Switzerland's
chef of the year twice, yet he remains
a modest man. In 1989, the Ravet family,
settled in this little village dominated by a
huge château set in the midst of vineyards.
Much of the 17thC farmhouse remains:
brick floors lead to a bar and sitting room
with a huge 18thC fireplace and blue
painted-wood ceiling. Of the 30,000 bottles in the wine cellar, much is local or
from the New World for, despite his roots
in Burgundy, M. Ravet delights in suggesting
that his guests try something new. He also
distills his own wine, which can be bought
in the little shop, as well as home-made
jams, vinegar, *foie gras* and Isabelle Ravet's
chocolate fondant.

A perfectionist, he insists on baking his
bread in a wood-fired oven and smoking
his own salmon and rabbit. Though the
restaurant is closed on Sundays, guests are
still served breakfast on Sunday morning.

A small room designed for summer dining joins the main building to the extension, whose six rooms and three suites
look over the garden and are decorated
with split cane furniture and large, old
armoires. Our reporter gave an accolade
to the bathrooms for the baths, generous
showers, twin wash-basins, separate lavatory and towels as big as football fields.

Gruyères

Ruelle des Chevaliers 1, 1663
Gruyères

Tel 026 921 8030
e-mail info@chevaliers-gruyeres.ch
website www.chevaliers-gruyeres.ch
Food breakfast, lunch, dinner,
snacks
Prices FF-FFF
Closed Jan to Feb
Manager Pierre Bovay

Hôtel de Gruyères
Mountain inn

Gruyères is a fixture on the tourist trail and car access is restricted; mention that you are staying at the Hôtel de Gruyères (formerly the Hostellerie des Chevaliers), however, and the barricade is lifted. The owners run several businesses in the town, including an inn, a shop and two restaurants, the Chalet Gruyères, which serves traditional fondues and *Raclettes*, and the Poya Pizzeria.

Wood floors, painted beams and old furniture create a traditional look. An underground passageway hung with pictures links the main villa and another, which houses the 34 bedrooms: all have stunning views of meadows and mountains. Ideal for families and those wanting to enjoy the medieval town once the tourists have left.

Morges

Rue de Lausanne 70, 1110 Morges

Tel 021 811 5811
e-mail hotel@fleur-du-lac.ch
website www.fleur-du-lac.ch
Food breakfast, lunch, dinner,
snacks
Prices FFF-FFFF
Closed never
Manager Céline Baudard

Hôtel Fleur du Lac
Lakeside hotel

New owners took over from Rodolphe Schelhert a few years ago, but the hotel is still run with the same enthusiasm.

Although the building isn't pretty, thousands of flowers at the entrance and in the garden soften its lines. Inside, furnishings are old-fashioned but nicely so. All 30 bedrooms face south, with balconies looking over the lake to the distant Mont Blanc. Bedspreads match curtains or chairs; bathrooms can be small but towels are big and fluffy. Those on half-board choose from the *menu du jour* or get a credit for à la carte dishes in the restaurant. There's also a bistro with lighter dishes and a cocktail bar, Le Galion. Private pier – boat rides.

Area introduction

As Switzerland's second largest canton, Bern gets a section of its own. Bern, the capital, has a history older than Switzerland itself and a diverse landscape. We have some useful small hotels on the fringe of Bern, but sadly lack a place to stay that meets our standards in the charming medieval streets of the old city.

From the capital we drove the mountain roads that lead to the famous ski resorts of the Bernese Oberland – the northern Swiss Alps that can claim largely to have inspired the popular image of Switzerland thanks to serious peaks such as the Jungfraujoch (3,470 m) and the Eiger (3,970 m), its nine deep valleys, its thundering waterfalls and its calm lakes, such as Thun and Brienz. Although, as usual, the ski resorts are full of formulaic hotels, we have searched out a selection of small, competitively priced places for both walkers and skiers.

Below are some useful back-up places to try if our main selections are fully booked:

Airport Hotel
Restaurant-with-rooms, Bern
at Belp Tel 031 961 6181
www.airhotel.ch
Near airport control tower;
plain bedrooms; fair value.

Sternen
Suburban hotel, Bern at Belp
Tel 031 819 0011
www.sternen-belp.ch
Budget hotel serving traditional food in big helpings.

Löwen Wayside inn, Bern
at Münsingen
Tel 031 724 3111
www.loewen.ch
Grand hotel with spiral staircase; elegant cooking.

Alpenblick
Ski hostel, Grindelwald
Tel 033 853 1105
www.alpenblick.info
Basic hotel for budget group skiing; restaurant.

Le Grand Bellevue
Village hotel, Gstaad
Tel 033 748 0000
www.bellevue-gstaad.com
Luxury hotel: reopens Dec '13
after complete renovation.

Hirschen Wayside inn,
Langnau im Emmental
Tel 034 402 1517
www.hirschen-langnau.ch
Well-priced 500-year-old tavern with comfortable rooms.

Schönbühl Village hotel,
Schönbühl near Bern
Tel 031 859 6969
www.gasthof-schoenbuehl.ch
Classic hostelry with antique and modern furniture.

Emmental
City hotel, Thun
Tel 033 222 0120
www.thunisst.ch
Contemporary café-hotel serving healthy snacks.

Krone
Old inn, Thun
Tel 033 227 8888
www.krone-thun.ch
Converted bakers' guild house with three restaurants.

Chalet Adler
Self-catering, Wengen
Tel 033 855 4400
adler@wengen.com
Chalet 300 m from
Männlichen cable car.

Sonnegg
Resort hotel, Zweisimmen
Tel 033 722 2333
www.hotel-sonnegg.ch
Modern hotel decorated with wood; 'e-bike' rides; skiing.

Adelboden

Dorfstrasse 22, 3715 Adelboden

Tel 033 673 2151
e-mail hotel@baeren-adelboden.ch
website www.baeren-adelboden.ch

Nearby Reichenbach (18 km);
Interlaken (32 km).
Location in middle of resort next to
public park; underground car parking
Food breakfast, lunch, dinner,
snacks
Price FFF
Rooms 14; 11 double, 3 single, all
with bath or shower; all rooms have
central heating, phone, TV, radio,
minibar, hairdryer, wi-fi
Facilities 3 dining rooms, bar,
sauna, lift /elevator, internet corner;
terrace; hiking pass, use of tennis
courts and swimming pool nearby in
summer, winter sports nearby
Credit cards AE, DC, MC, V
Children welcome
Disabled limited access
Pets accepted
Closed mid-May to mid-Jun, end
Nov to mid-Dec
Proprietors Willen family

Bären
Chalet hotel

Wherever our reporter went in the
Berner Oberland, hoteliers men-
tioned the Bären in Adelboden. Innkeeper
Peter Willen is a lifelong native of the village and in 1989 he bought this building,
which dates back to 1500. The inn exudes
a solid comfort and charm which fights shy
of luxury and goes one up on *gemütlich*.
Bedrooms are named after the peaks in
view and each has a different ambience.
The Fitzer, a corner room, overlooks the
park and the main street. Sniff the scent of
new pine and admire the romantic, white-
curtained, four-poster bed; stretch out –
and it is a special airbed! The Grosslohner,
on the other hand, is for families, with a
spacious mezzanine area for the children
under the extra-high ceiling.

The inevitable *Rösti*, served up in a cast
iron skillet, is the pride of Peter Willen's
Speisesaal, where *Raclette* and fondues are
also on offer. In the à la carte restaurant,
the menu encompasses a full range of
French and German dishes. Busy in winter
and summer, Adelboden attracts many
Dutch and Belgians, especially families. Do
not look for the jet set here.

Kandersteg

3718 Kandersteg BE

Tel (033) 675 81 81
e-mail info@doldenhorn.ch
website www.doldenhorn-ruedihus.ch

Nearby Adelboden (9 km);
Grindelwald (30 km); Bern (55 km).
Location in meadows below
mountains; ample car parking
Food breakfast, lunch, dinner,
snacks
Prices FFF
Rooms 9; 7 double, 1 single, 1 suite,
all with bath or shower; all rooms
have central heating, phone, radio,
hairdryer, some have 4-poster bed; 1
apartment with terrace
Facilities 4 dining rooms, sitting
room; terrace, garden, winter sports
and heated swimming pool nearby
Credit cards AE, DC, MC, V
Children very welcome
Disabled not suitable
Pets accepted
Closed restaurant only, Wed, Sep to
Jun
Proprietors Maeder family

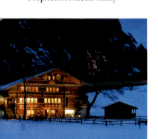

Ruedihus
Mountain chalet and apartment

'Never have I seen a better-preserved example of authentic Oberland style and atmosphere,' our reporter wrote wistfully, wishing he could stay longer. The setting is 'cinematic': open pastures ringed on three sides by mountains. Sitting in the flower garden, under maple trees, 'I hear only the occasional moo of a grazing cow'. Waxing poetic, he described the hand-carved patterns on the sun-seared exterior, enlivened by various types of wood and leaded window panes. Although renovated in 1990 to put in modern heating and plumbing, this 18thC house still looks like a museum of traditional life. There are *Kachelofen* and hand-painted chests plus a rocking horse, a miniature farm wagon for children and an embroidery frame with fabric ready to stitch. The generous four-poster bed makes the *Hoch-zeitsstube* popular with newly-weds, and the *Liebesluube* ('Love room'), an external apartment chalet next door, has excellent mountain views from its terrace. Grandma's jam, home-made from mountain berries, appears on the breakfast table and may be bought by the jar. The Maeder family use only Swiss-made products: there is, therefore, no Coca-Cola.

Trubschachen

Dorfstrasse 26, 3555 Trubschachen

Tel 034 495 5115
e-mail info@hirschen-trubschachen.ch
website www.hirschen-trubschachen.ch

Nearby Langnau (4 km); Bern (30 km).
Location at roadside in village; own car parking
Food breakfast, lunch, dinner, snacks
Price F
Rooms 5; 3 double, 2 single, all with bath or shower; all rooms have central heating
Facilities 3 dining rooms, sitting room; terrace, winter sports nearby
Credit cards AE, MC, V
Children very welcome
Disabled not suitable
Pets accepted
Closed Jan, end July; restaurant only, Mon, Tues until 5 p.m.
Proprietors Soltermann-Brunner family

Landgasthof Hirschen
Wayside inn

Here in the Emmental, hospitality and cuisine come naturally, so after a day walking in the valley, visiting farms and watching the famous cheese mature, there can be nothing better than retiring, hungry, to a nearby inn and asking for the local speciality. This is the *Bärnerplatte*, a challenge to the heartiest appetites. 'I did my best, but couldn't finish the mountain of meat and sausages surrounded by sauerkraut and boiled potatoes,' admitted our reporter, who had never felt so full in his life but was ready to breakfast on delicious Emmental cheese next morning. 'The food is as typically Bernese as the rest of this hostelry,' he said; 'I could even hear jolly singing in the bar.'

The family has been running the Hirschen since 1932. Third-generation Jürg Soltermann cooks while his wife Ursual looks after guests. The Rôtisserie, with its rough ceiling-beams and stone wall has more character than other rooms. The overall look is modern-rustic, with lots of wood but no fancy frills; bedrooms, for example, are straightforward, with small, basic bathrooms. Prices are inexpensive for this country, so this is just the place for families, sporty types and anyone travelling on a budget.

Grosshöchstetten

3506 Grosshöchstetten

Tel 031 710 2424
e-mail stegro@bluewin.ch
website www.stegro.ch
Food breakfast, lunch, dinner, snacks
Price FF
Closed never; restaurant only, Mon, Tue
Proprietors Jürg and Therese Stettler-Gfeller

Sternen
Village inn

From the outside, this *Landgasthof* looks like many others we have seen. A former farmhouse, dating from the 18thC. Only 15 km away from Bern, it's a favourite destination of diplomats who want to show their guests a typical rural pub. No wonder the visitors' book boasts signatures such as HRH Prince Philip.

The Stettler family (hotel keepers for 140 years) have been hosts at the Sternen for two generations. Specialities include breaded pork chop and steak or hare flambéed at your table. Hearty appetites are appreciated. Afterwards, calories may be worked off in the *Kegelbahnen* (bowling alleys). Overall, the look is traditional and simple. Upstairs, bedrooms have peasant-style wardrobes and small bathrooms.

Gstaad at Saanenmöser

3777 Gstaad at Saanenmöser

Tel 033 748 6868
e-mail mail@golfhotel.ch
website www.golfhotel.ch
Food breakfast, lunch, dinner, snacks
Prices FFF-FFFFF
Closed Easter to end Apr, mid-Oct to mid-Dec
Managers Siebenthal family

Les Hauts de Gstaad & Spa **Golf hotel**

The hotel has a reputation for entertaining the *beau monde* during Gstaad's social season. Despite the elegant fabrics and designer colours in the entrance, the atmosphere is relaxed. The fairly modernized building is full of antiques, such as the museum-quality Bernese Oberland baby carriages. The bedrooms have hand-carved pine doors, painted wooden beds and large, white-tiled bathrooms. As for food, guests choose from Belle Epoque (classic French), Winter-Garten (half-board), Bärengraben (Swiss – *Raclette* and fondue) and Dolce Vita (strictly Italian).

Although next to a working farm, there is nothing rustic here; this is a retreat for city folk who enjoy sports, particularly skiing and the new 18-hole golf course.

Interlaken

Hauptstrasse 11, 3800 Matten-Interlaken

Tel 033 822 1545
e-mail info@hirschen-interlaken.ch
website www.hirschen-interlaken.ch
Food breakfast, lunch, dinner
Price FF
Closed Nov; restaurant only, Tues
Proprietors Nicole Sponsors and Jacqueline Feuz

Hirschen
Traditional town inn

Originally a farmhouse, dating from the 1500s, this hostelry is popular with families and the restaurant here is known for its variety of meat dishes.

New wood blends with ancient timbers as antiques do with modern, but traditionally styled furniture. Bedrooms vary in size but all are comfortable and pleasantly decorated, even if they would not win any design awards. Who cares, when breakfast can be had on the balcony with the Jungfrau standing out against deep blue sky? We would be happy to settle in and forget the crowds of tourists in nearby Interlaken.

Owners Nicole Sponsors and Jacqueline Feuz have only recently taken over this inn, and are keeping up standards.

Kandersteg

3718 Kandersteg BE

Tel 033 675 8181
e-mail info@doldenhorn.ch
website www.doldenhorn-ruedihus.ch
Food breakfast, lunch, dinner, snacks
Prices FFF-FFFFF
Closed restaurant only, Tue, Sep to Jun
Proprietors Maeder family

Doldenhorn
Forest hotel

This is a hotel where regulars settle in and stay, often for three or four weeks in the summer. The Maeder family, who also own the nearby Ruedihus (page 159), have been here for 50 years, and their inn is an intriguing blend of old and new. The first thing you see in the lobby is a huge antique working telephone. An even bigger cowbell summons the receptionist. Bedroom keys, however, are electronic.

In the gourmet restaurant, starched while linen and striped silk chair upholstery create a formal look while the opposite effect is achieved in the *Burestube* by oval pine tables, hanging lamps and unfinished plank floors. Each bedroom is different; many have paintings of local mountain scenes. Bathrooms are functional.

Lauenen bei Gstaad

Dorfstrasse 41, 3782 Lauenen

Tel 033 765 3022
e-mail info@geltenhorn.ch
website geltenhorn.ch
Food breakfast, lunch, dinner, snacks
Prices F-FF
Closed Nov; restaurant only, Tue, Wed, lunch Mon to Sat
Manager Elsbeth Mösching

Geltenhorn
Mountain inn

Exploring the valley that leads SW from Gstaad, via Ober-Gstaad, you'll find the village of Lauenen – a pleasant relief after the fur-wrapped plutocracy of its famous neighbour and relatively undeveloped for tourism. The Geltenhorn has a good reputation with locals who eat there; there's a pleasant atmosphere in the dining room; fairly priced home-style food (the chefs are amusing characters); and simple, cheap bedrooms. A useful budget stopover, and a great base for the five-star walking and climbing country beneath the Wildhorn and Geltenhorn mountains above the village. The Lauenensee, a local beauty spot, is a short drive beyond the village. The post bus stops opposite the hotel in a big expanded road car park – not great, but OK.

Mürren

3825 Murren

Tel 033 855 1826
e-mail blumental@muerren.ch
website www.muerren.ch/blumental
Food breakfast, dinner
Price FF
Closed mid-Apr to early Jun, mid-Oct to mid-Dec
Proprietors Ralph & Heidi von Allmen

Hotel Blumental
Mountain chalet

There are almost endless accommodation choices even in a small ski resort such as Mürren, so we try to single out places with something extra. Here, it's the sincere friendliness of the owners, Ralph and Heidi, along with their can't-do-enough-to-help attitude.

Blumental is recommended by a trusted reporter who describes the interior as predictable-traditional but pleasing Swiss chalet-style. Some of the rooms in the main part are maybe a little dark, not so in the newish annexe at the back. Try for a room with a view of the three famous peaks of the northern Alps – Jungfrau, Eiger and Mönch.

near Schangnau im Emmental

6197 Schangnau im Emmental

Tel 034 493 7777
e-mail hotel@kemmeriboden.ch
website www.kemmeriboden.ch
Food breakfast, lunch, dinner, snacks
Prices FFF-FFFFF
Closed Dec; restaurant only, Mon, Tue, Jan to May
Proprietors Invernizzi family

Kemmeriboden Bad
Mountain inn

When it was built over 160 years ago, the sulphur springs provided the attraction here. They still do, but now visitors also come for the canoeing, fishing, walking, and mountain climbing in summer, and the skiing in winter. Summer weekends can be busy, but it never feels overcrowded.

The original house contains large, traditional bedrooms, many with antique furniture but modern beds. In the extension, some bedrooms can sleep up to six, with a double bed and two sets of bunks. The balconies are useful for drying boots and jackets. There are also separate, simpler rooms without private bathrooms for groups.

In winter, igloos are built around the grounds and furnished with either beds or tables and chairs for fondue evenings.

Spiez

Schachenstrasse 39, 3700 Spiez

Tel 033 655 6666
e-mail hotel@belvedere-spiez.ch
website www.belvedere-spiez.ch
Food breakfast, lunch, dinner, snacks
Price FFFF
Closed 2 weeks Feb
Proprietor Markus Schneider

Strandhotel Belvédère
Lakeside hotel

Many consider the Bay of Spiez to be one of the most beautiful in Europe, with its landmark 11thC tower, its 12thC church and sailing boats on the water. The Belvédère is just above the water, with a beautiful garden filled with flowers and herbs – rosemary, thyme, lavender and sage are the signature herbs of the restaurant's dishes, which feature fish from the lake.

The Blue Room, used for breakfast, is grand with high ceilings, twin grandfather clocks and velvet floor-to-ceiling curtains. Bedroom decoration follows subtle flower themes and all have been updated with orthopaedic beds – as well as wi-fi for the more modern guests. The spa has recently expanded, adding a wider range of treatments and an outdoor pool.

Area introduction

Canton is the Swiss term for province and here we include those on the northern border with Germany; in central Switzerland with Lake Lucerne at their centre; and in the country's north-east corner, bordering Lake Constance (Bodensee) and extending south into the mountains.

Basel and Zurich are the main centres of the German-speaking northern cantons, good for shopping, museums, architecture and culture, and their edible specialities. The central cantons, with Lucerne at their hub, were the birthplace of Switzerland seven centuries ago. They are rich in history and the name of legendary marksman William Tell crops up frequently. Highlights of the north-east cantons are the old villages on Lake Constance; the brightly painted towns such as Appenzell; the rich meadows rising to snowy peaks; and Schaffhausen, on the Rhine, with its medieval guildhalls.

Below are some useful back-up places to try if our main selections are fully booked:

Hirschen
Country inn, Amriswil
Tel 071 411 7971
www.hirschen-amriswil.ch
Award-winning cooking with
Italian influence; quaint inn.

Bären
Town hotel, Lachen
Tel 055 451 9999
hotelbaeren-lachen.ch
Useful stop just off N3; road-
side terrace; simple comforts.

Marina Lachen
Harbourside hotel, Lachen
Tel 055 451 7373
www.marinalachen.ch
Modern hotel with popular
Italian-style pizzeria.

Bad Schauenburg
Country hotel, Liestal
Tel 061 906 2727
www.badschauenburg.ch
Top-class, expensive restau-
rant attracts Basel gourmets.

Ambassador
Bed-and-breakfast, Lucerne
Tel 041 418 8100
www.ambassador.ch
Efficiently run new hotel in
heart of city; garden terrace.

Baslertor
City hotel, Lucerne
Tel 041 249 2222
www.baslertor.ch
Only hotel in Lucerne with
outside pool and Jacuzzi.

Sonnegg Restaurant with
rooms, Lucerne at Meggen
Tel 41 377 4400
www.sonnegg-meggen.ch
Useful base for exploring the
area; specializes in fish dishes.

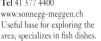

Zum Bären Restaurant-
with-rooms, Nürensdorf
Tel 01 838 3636
www.baeren-nuerensdorf.ch
Refreshing alternative to airport hotels; fine cooking.

Roter Turm
Town hotel, Solothurn
Tel 032 622 9621
www.roterturm.ch
Useful base in medieval city;
pretty views from roof terrace.

Linde
Village inn, Stans
Tel 041 619 0930
www.hotel-linde.ch
Restaurant attracts gourmets;
Persian rugs in bedrooms.

Chäseren Village guest-
house, Wald-Schönengrund
Tel 071 361 1751
www.chaeseren.ch
Appenzell-style house popular with skiers; rustic rooms.

Helmhaus
City hotel, Zurich
Tel 044 266 9595
www.helmhaus.ch
Family-run design hotel with
Gisèle Mengis paintings.

Dorfstrasse 35, 4303 Kaiseraugst

Tel 061 811 1111
e-mail mail@landgasthof-adler.com
website www.landgasthof-adler.com

Nearby ferry stop for Basel (800 m)
Rheinfelden (4 km); Basel (10 km).
Location in middle of village; own
car parking
Food breakfast, lunch, dinner,
snacks
Prices F-FF
Rooms 8; 5 double, 3 single, all with
shower; all rooms have central
heating, TV, radio, wi-fi
Facilities 2 dining rooms, sitting
room; terrace
Credit cards AE, DC, MC, V
Children welcome
Disabled not suitable
Pets accepted
Closed never
Proprietor René Nicaise

Landgasthof Adler
Restaurant-with-rooms

'A typical *Landgasthof*, the heart of village social life' was the description
of this inn, full of old world charm and hospitality. After 17 years in charge of this
17thC inn, Martine Sarbach and Walter
Höhener decided to retire and, in January
2013, René Nicaise took over. His motto is
'the customer is king' and, under his management, the inn has continued to offer
charm and hospitality.

Bedrooms are straight-forward and
simple, with wood furniture; those up in
the eaves have more room. Bathrooms are
tiny, with only a shower, but bright and
clean. There are two dining rooms: one
with flower-patterned tablecloths and
smart chairs; the other all wood. Both have
small plants as centrepieces on tables.
Though the terrace opens on to the main
road, there is little traffic. The wine cellar
has bottles from Switzerland, France, Italy
and Spain. There are no stairs down, just a
lift/elevator which our reporter reckoned
was adapted from a fork lift truck.

Close to the Rhine, this is a handy base
for visiting Basel – there is a ferry stop 800
m away, or it's a ten-minute drive along the
motorway. This section of the Rhine marks
the German border – the closest access
point is at Rheinfelden, just 4 km away.

Steinwiesstr 8-10, 8032 Zurich

Tel 044 267 8787
e-mail info@claridge.ch
website www.claridge.ch

Nearby University; Museum of Fine Art; theatre.
Location near middle of city, on east bank; own paid car parking
Food breakfast, lunch, dinner, snacks
Prices FFF-FFFF (reductions for children)
Rooms 31; 13 double/single, 7 twin, 3 single, 3 suites, 5 family, all with bath or shower; all rooms have central heating, phone, TV, minibar, hairdryer, safe, wi-fi
Facilities 2 dining rooms, sitting room, bar, lift/elevator; terrace
Credit cards AE, DC, MC, V
Children welcome
Disabled not suitable
Pets accepted (CHF 25 per night)
Closed Christmas and New Year
Proprietor Beat Blumer

Claridge Hotel Zurich
City hotel

The name has changed, but we still think that visiting this hotel is like visiting a maiden aunt. The 178-year-old house is on a tree-lined street just five minutes' walk from the university. Inside, chandeliers and inviting chairs and sofas add up to a look that is comfortable, rather than grand, and the modern furniture in public rooms prevent it from looking too dated.

Rooms are not designed, but are full of antiques that look as if they have been collected over the years. Every bedroom is different, though, as in many conversions of old houses, bathrooms end up rather small. To compensate they have every modern luxury, with marble basins, cosmetic bars and weighing scales.

The hotel gets its share of business visitore, but also culture-seeking tourists staying here for the Museum of Art, and actors and musicians who relax over drinks in the bar or in the romantic garden.

The Orson's Gourmet restaurant serves international seasonal dishes, and the Orson's Küche.de specializes in German cuisine. In summer, guests can dine in the garden. A recent reporter says that the quiet location is a plus.

Basel

Der Teufelhof Basel
Art hotel

Leonhardsgraben 49, 4051 Basel

Tel 061 261 1010
e-mail info@teufelhof.com
website www.teufelhof.com
Food breakfast, lunch, dinner, snacks
Prices FF-FFFF
Closed never
Proprietors Raphael and Nathalie Wyniger

This unique Basel institution, open since 1989, brings together culture and hospitality. Now run by Raphael and Nathalie Wyniger, it is part gallery, with exhibitions in some of the rooms and corridors, and part hotel.

In fact, there are two hotels here: the Art Hotel with eight bedrooms and a suite; and the gallery hotel with 20 bedrooms and four suites. There are other hotels in Switzerland that look like art galleries, with superb collections of paintings, but here the rooms can claim to be works of art, each designed by a different artist. Their only condition was to maintain a high standard of comfort. You may like some and loathe some.

Basel at Arlesheim

Zum Ochsen
Town hotel

Eremitagestr 16, 4144 Arlesheim

Tel 061 706 5200
e-mail gasthof@ochsen.ch
website www.ochsen.ch
Food breakfast, lunch, dinner, snacks
Prices FFF-FFFFF
Closed Ascension, Christmas Eve
Proprietors Jenzer family

One must never discount suburbia when looking for well-run hotels. Just 15 minutes from Basel is Arlesheim, where many people stay at the Ochsen when attending the nearby homeopathic hospital or going to the huge theatre at Dornach for productions of Shakespeare and Goethe.

'I'd be happy to stay here' commented our reporter, who liked this inn, founded in 1692 by a family of butchers whose descendants help to run the restaurant. When we first visited, the focus was on meat. Now, the restaurant also has several vegetarian options and a range of gluten-free dishes.

Bedrooms are simple: pale colours and furniture in wild pear wood are offset by antiques and paintings. Those on upper floors have cathedral or country views.

Böttstein

Schlossweg 20, 5315 Böttstein

Tel 056 269 1616
e-mail info@schlossboettstein.ch
website www.schlossboettstein.ch
Food breakfast, lunch, dinner
Prices FF-FFF
Closed never
Proprietor Thomas Bischofberger

Schloss Böttstein
Castle hotel

This castle dates from 1520, but a rebuilding programme in 1974 produced 20 standardized bedrooms with all of the standard contemporary comforts. Some may think the price a little high for what you get, but the food and beautiful grounds are a genuine draw.

The chef concentrates on an international menu with a French emphasis: fish, beef and veal, served in one of the three elegant dining rooms, or on the terrace. As well as game and fish, the menu features quail and sausage dishes.

It's a popular place for conferences and weddings, so check in advance.

Kriegstetten

Hauptstrasse 61, 4566
Kriegstettenstrasse

Tel 032 674 4161
e-mail info@sternen.ch
website www.sternen.ch
Food breakfast, lunch, dinner
Prices FFF-FFFF
Closed restaurant only, Sun dinner
Proprietors Manuela & Christoph
Bohren-Pichler

Sternen
Wayside inn

Near the motorway exit for Kreigstetten, the Sternen is a good example of a Romantik hotel group member. The restaurants and *Sternenstube* are elegantly panelled in 19thC style, with some 150-year-old wood tables and Biedermeier antiques. Owners Manuela and Christoph Bohren-Pichler source food both locally and further afield – beef, veal, pork and freshwater fish from Switzerland, poultry and rabbits from France. Vegetarians can discuss a special menu in advance. Manuela also cooks Austrian specialities, such as boiled beef, schnitzel and *Eispalatschinken* (pancakes with ice cream).

Bedrooms are tastefully furnished, with dark wood, plain walls and flowers. All are different and some have balconies.

Amsteg

Gotthardstrasse 88, 6474 Amsteg

Tel 041 884 0101
e-mail info@stern-post.ch
website www.stern-post.ch

Nearby St Gotthard Pass (13 km).
Location in middle of village; ample car parking, some covered
Food breakfast, lunch, dinner
Price FF
Rooms 11; 10 double, 1 single, all with bath or shower; all have central heating, phone, radio, TV, internet
Facilities dining room, sitting room, bar; terrace, garden
Credit cards MC, V
Children very welcome
Disabled not suitable
Pets accepted
Closed Jan to Easter
Proprietors Remo Vetter and Rolf Welti

Stern und Post
Old coaching inn

The last major event in Amsteg was more than 200 years ago, when the entire village burned down, so 1789 in these parts refers not to revolution but to the building of a new Stern und Post. Goethe was a guest here – he argued over the prices with the hotelier, but today's guests are usually satisfied. Changes have been made since Remo Vetter and Rolf Welti took over in 2011 from the Tresch family – who had run this historic inn since 1474. Stern und Post is their first business as hoteliers and they are all the more enthusiastic about it – and ready to please.

After swimming in the Golzernsee or walking in the Maderaner Valley, where better to write your postcards than in the small salon or *Stubli*. Antiques abound, the bar is full of jolly locals and the restaurant looks over the garden and river. Bedrooms are all different but if your stay is short, opt for an older room, such as the single with the bed rescued from the fire. You can still feel 200 years of history here.

Gersau

Dorfstr 12, 6442 Gersau

Tel 041 828 1234
e-mail info@gasthaus-tuebli-ger-sau.ch
website www.gasthaus-tuebli-ger-sau.ch

Nearby Lake Lucerne (100 m).
Location in heart of village, on north side of lake; ample car parking
Food breakfast, lunch, dinner, snacks
Price FF
Rooms 7 double, all with bath or shower; all rooms have phone, TV, wi-fi
Facilities restaurant; garden
Credit cards AE, MC
Children very welcome
Disabled not suitable
Pets not accepted
Closed hotel never; restaurant only, Mon, Tues, Oct to Apr
Proprietors Ralph Zuberbühler and Angelina Kurath

Gasthaus Tübli
Country chalet

'This is the place for me, this is the real Switzerland' was the reaction to this chalet. Dating from 1767, the house has a traditional atmosphere. Ralph Züberbühler took over from Andreas Schmid in 2007, and runs the hotel (well known for its restaurant and collection of Swiss wines) with his partner Angelina Kurath. Both are Swiss, and the cooking here is typically Swiss, with particular emphasis on fresh lake fish. Specialities include perch from the lake, or beautiful beef *entrecôte*, served in the pan. You'll also see cheese fondue, veal in mushroom sauce, *Rösti*, cordon bleu veal and other typical Swiss dishes on the menu. Most guests are families, or retired folk, who want to escape the pressures of modern life and come here for the food and quiet rooms.

This small guesthouse on a quiet back street is not for everyone, however; those who want designer furnishings, Jacuzzis and the latest exercise equipment should look elsewhere. The small bedrooms and bathrooms are decidedly cosy and traditional, just like the warmth of the welcome.

Stadthofstr 14, 6006 Lucerne

Tel 041 410 8888
e-mail hotel@hofgarten.ch
website www.hofgarten.ch

Nearby Lake Lucerne (200 m); central Lucerne (1 km).
Location behind the Hotel Zum Rebstock; car parking on street
Food breakfast, lunch, dinner, snacks
Prices FF-FFFF
Rooms 19; 11 double, 8 single, all with bath or shower; all rooms have central heating, phone, TV, radio, minibar, hairdryer, safe
Facilities dining room, sitting room, bar, lift/elevator; terrace
Credit cards AE, DC, MC, V
Children welcome
Disabled not suitable
Pets accepted
Closed never
Manager Ferdi Sieber

Hofgarten
Converted old house

The best Swiss designers can combine ancient and modern without annoying fans of either period. This is a fine example of that skill. Although part of the city's oldest building, the hotel is hung with contemporary paintings from the collection in the Rebstock, its sister-establishment (page 174). Embedded in the walls are pieces of tile from the days when traditional ceramic ovens were produced here and five bedrooms still use these for back-up heating. All bedrooms, however, have modern furniture and decorations which together look like a work of art. Bathrooms make you want to get up early to make maximum use of everything they offer. There are proper shaving mirrors, baths to stretch out in, big towels to curl up in, and plenty of natural light, thanks to glass walls and doors.

The restaurant also marries old and new: one area has linen table cloths and crystal candelabra; another boasts a multi-hued ceramic ceiling and coloured crystal lights. Both offer Mediterranean food that is delicious and original, served on dinner plates or sizzling in frying pans or steaming in pots, and prepared with fresh ingredients from local farmers and cheesemakers at Lucerne's markets. Our reporter was full of praise. 'What flair, what comfort, what peace, all in the heart of a city.'

6045 Meggen

Tel 041 377 1135
e-mail info@balm.ch
website www.balm.ch

Nearby Lake Lucerne (500 m); Lucerne (4 km); Rigi mountain (9 km); Pilatus mountain (11 km).
Location off main road in centre of Meggen, outside Lucerne; ample car parking
Food breakfast, lunch, dinner, snacks
Prices FF-FFF
Rooms 14 double, all with bath or shower; all rooms have central heating, phone, TV, radio, wi-fi, most have sofa bed
Facilities 2 restaurants, bar; terrace, garden
Credit cards AE, DC, MC, V
Children welcome
Disabled not suitable
Pets accepted
Closed 2 weeks Feb to Mar, 2 weeks Dec to Jan
Proprietors Stofer-Näpflin family

Balm
Country house hotel

This place has been in the Stofer family since 1969, when is was bought by Herr Stofer, an experienced hotelier who knew his business. Sandra and Beat Stofer took over from him ten years ago, but don't rely on his success – they also know what they're doing. They have refurbished the hotel in a fairly modern style, with bedrooms decorated with fresh greens and blues. The rustic, red-painted shuttered windows remain.

There are two restaurants, La Pistache and the Bistro. The former is decorated with modern art on the walls and stone vases. Here, guests can choose from the regular house menu, à la carte, or a 'surprise' seven-course menu, with wines chosen to complement each dish. The smaller, slightly less formal Bistro serves traditional Swiss dishes from 11.30 a.m. until 10 p.m.

We get approving feedback on the Balm. Guests agree that it's relaxing – you're enveloped in leafy grounds, with a terrace overlooking the colourful garden and lawns sweeping down to the lake in the distance.

Buochs

Dorfplatz 2a, 6374 Buochs

Tel 041 624 6677
e-mail info@krone-buochs.ch
website www.krone-buochs.ch
Food breakfast, lunch, dinner, snacks
Prices FF-FFF
Closed never
Managers Peter Furrer and Daniel Michel

Krone
Lakeside hotel

A modernist hotel only five minutes on foot from Lake Lucerne. Managers Peter Furrer and Daniel Michel run the hotel with friendly, helpful staff. In 2011, the place was completely renovated, but it still charges the reasonable prices that have attracted guests for years. The exterior is unremarkable, but inside it's fresh and modern, with pale colours and plain walls.

The two restaurants are popular with locals, serving modern Swiss dishes relying on regional produce. One is full of light, with floor-to-ceiling windows looking on to the terrace; the other is atmospheric, decorated with dark wood. The 16 bedrooms are spacious, all with bathroom, TV, minibar and wi-fi. Free parking nearby.

Lucerne

St Leodegarstr 3, 6006 Lucerne

Tel 041 417 1819
e-mail hotel@rebstock-luzern.ch
website www.rebstock-luzern.ch
Food breakfast, lunch, dinner, snacks
Prices FFF-FFFF
Closed never
Proprietor Ferdi Sieber

Hotel Zum Rebstock
City hotel

The owner of this 600-year-old hotel, Ferdi Sieber, is an art lover, with 30 years' worth of collecting displayed on the walls. Just as the paintings are original, so every room is different: here an art deco influence, there a striking colour scheme; nothing is uniform. 'It's not so unusual,' says Herr Sieber 'after all, is every room the same in your home?'

That sense of individuality continues with the food in the three restaurants. Eating here is like going to a dinner party at the house of a first-rate cook; nothing here is mass-produced. Local specialities include Lucerne's own *Chügelipastete* (veal vol-au-vent). The breakfast buffet shows the same care. 'It could go on for ever,' enthused our reporter. 'Go and see for yourself.'

Schwyz

Am Hauptplatz, 6430 Schwyz

Tel 041 811 1922
e-mail info@wrsz.ch
website www.wrsz.ch
Food breakfast, lunch, dinner, snacks
Prices FF-FFF
Closed Christmas, New Year
Proprietor Sepp and Ida Trütsch-Reichmuth

Wysses Rössli
Town hotel

The old town of Schwyz saw the origins of the Swiss Federation in 1291. The hotel, which dates from the 17th century, but was rebuilt 35 years ago after a fire, has a prime position on the stunning main square. In 2008, retired TV presenter Sepp Trütsch took over, boosting the hotel's profile with his cookbook of Schwyz specialities based on dishes at the Wysses Rössli.

Although bedrooms are plain, mattresses are excellent. Some guests have complained that the bells of the church opposite are noisy, but to our reporter they sounded 'like a grandfather clock in the hall'. Corner bedrooms have views of the mountains as well as the old town, which is even more atmospheric when the sightseers have gone home.

Weggis

Gotthardstr 4, 6353 Weggis

Tel 041 390 1151
e-mail info@hotel-du-lac.ch
website www.hotel-du-lac.ch
Food breakfast, lunch, dinner, snacks
Price FFF
Closed never
Proprietor Ani Jonuzi

Seehof Du Lac
Lakeside hotel

Weggis offers almost as much to fans of water sports as it does to walkers and climbers, and this 170-year-old inn is right on the lake. Inside, the bedrooms have all been recently refurbished and are decorated in warm greens and yellows. The more expensive bedrooms have balconies overlooking the water, but the cheaper ones at the back have a fine view of the Rigi mountain and are quiet enough since most road traffic uses the bypass.

British regulars are fond of this staid old lady, a friendly soul who welcomes you and, in the restaurant or on the terrace with a lovely view of the lake, offers her specialities: fish and fondue.

Grimm 27, 9030 Abtwil

Tel 071 313 2525
e-mail info@saentis-blick.ch
website www.saentis-blick.ch

Nearby St Gallen (4 km); Lake
Constance (14 km).
Location on hillside among farms;
ample car parking
Food breakfast, lunch, dinner,
snacks
Prices FF-FFF
Rooms 13; 12 double/single, 1 suite,
all with bath or shower; all rooms
have phone, TV, radio, minibar, safe,
hairdryer, wi-fi, some have balcony
Facilities restaurant; terrace, garden
Credit cards AE, DC, MC, V
Children welcome
Disabled not suitable
Pets accepted
Closed never; restaurant only, Mon
Manager Sami Debbabi

Säntisblick
Mountain hotel

Asense of adventure is needed to find
this hotel, perched high on a hill above
St Gallen and looking down on Abtwil.
From this village, drive uphill, first through
seemingly endless suburbia and then fields.
Persevere, despite the absence of signs; the
reward is a country inn set among farms.
These provide horses for riding and the
surrounding coutryside has walking, hiking
and cycling trails.

Walk through the small bar into the
restaurant or on to the terrace where
there are weekly barbecues in fine weather. Meals feature veal and venison as well
as seafood dishes such as fried perch with
saffron and spinach and Mediterranean-
style salmon and tiger prawns. From both
the restaurant and the terrace the panorama is breath-taking: the entire Säntis
region spread out below. This century-old
house has been modernized but still has
plenty of wood. Bedrooms are not luxurious but have modern comforts.

Although the hotel is simple, with wonderful views, our reporter thought that
the prices were a bit expensive for what is
on offer. Perhaps you are paying for the
view. There have been mixed reports since
the new management took over in 2012.
Reports welcome.

Appenzell

Landsgemeindeplatz, 9050
Appenzell

Tel 071 788 1515
e-mail info@hotel-appenzell.ch
website www.hotel-appenzell.ch

Nearby Lienz (10 km); St Gallen (10 km); Säntis mountain (10 km); Vaduz (23 km).
Location on main square; own car parking nearby
Food breakfast, lunch, dinner, snacks
Price FFF
Rooms 16; 13 double, 2 single, 1 suite, all with bath or shower; all rooms have central heating, phone, TV, radio, minibar, internet
Facilities dining room, sitting room, lift/elevator, terrace; winter sports, swimming nearby
Credit cards AE, DC, MC, V
Children welcome
Disabled 2 accessible rooms
Pets accepted
Closed Nov
Proprietors Sutter family

Appenzell
Historic hotel

Usually, we are suspicious of hotels that drape themselves in flags but the Appenzell's decorations are all part of the extraordinary main square of a town famous for its multi-coloured houses. The checkerboard facade of butter-yellow and purple, the silhouettes of medieval towns-folk and those long banners are part and parcel of the Appenzell effect.

It would be easy to cash in on the regular show of camera-carrying tourists by running a hotel that is merely adequate, but Margrit and Leo Sutter have worked hard to make this a special place. On the ground floor is Leo's popular *Konditorei*, full of home-made temptations such as *Biberli* and *Züngli* (local cookies), cakes, ice-cream and jellied fruit confections. In summer, visitors sit outside beneath striped sunshades, lunching on salads, trout, pork chops and vegetarian risottos, perhaps with a glass of freshly-pressed strawberry and pear juice. In the evening, the restaurant inside has more sophisticated fare and, of course, Leo's desserts. Bedrooms are imaginatively decorated using soft blues, pinks and greens, and the small bathrooms were updated some twenty years ago.

Appenzell

am Landsgemeindeplatz, 9050
Appenzell

Tel 071 788 1111
e-mail info@saentis-appenzell.ch
website www.saentis-appenzell.ch

Nearby St. Gallen (20 km); Zürich
(90 km).
Location on main square; own car
parking
Food breakfast, lunch, dinner,
snacks
Prices FFF-FFFF
Rooms 36 double, all with bath or
shower; all rooms have phone, TV,
radio, central heating, minibar
Facilities 2 dining rooms, sitting
room, bar, lift/elevator; terrace,
garden, winter sports and hiking
nearby
Credit cards AE, DC, MC, V
Children welcome
Disabled reasonable access
Pets accepted
Closed mid-Jan to end Feb
Proprietors Heeb family

Säntis
Ancient inn

Appenzell is a star on the tourist route
in this part of Switzerland – it's full of
houses with brightly painted exteriors
showing folk scenes and folk motifs. There
are plenty of places to stay, but if it's within your budget, it's worth seriously consid-
ering Säntis. It's on the town square, and
brightly painted along with the rest, but
not just a pretty face. It happens to be the
only four star in town, which indicates its
quality, but, of course, we rate hotels on
other factors as well.

The Heeb family are hands-on owner-
managers (we met the friendly Stefan) and
there is an intimate, relaxed buzz in the
public spaces downstairs, including the
attractive dining room with its green
ceramic stove. In the right conditions you
can eat outside, on the square, under an
awning and here we enjoyed the three-
course set menu, which non-residents
clearly think is fair value.

Upstairs the rooms are as neat and as
comfortable as you would expect, but with
some standardized colour schemes and
fittings. There is a useful choice of interconnecting family rooms.

'We never stop making changes' says
Stefan Heeb, who can claim to run the
area's best-known inn.

Arbon am Bodensee

Romanshornerstr 15, 9320 Arbon

Tel 071 447 8484
e-mail info@frohsinn-arbon.ch
website www.frohsinn-arbon.ch

Nearby St Gallen (12 km);
Appenzell (20 km); Zurich (70 km).
Location in village; ample car
parking
Food breakfast, lunch, dinner,
snacks
Prices FF-FFF
Rooms 13; 10 double, 1 single, 2
attic family, all with bath or shower;
all rooms have central heating,
phone, TV
Facilities restaurant, dining
room/bar; terrace, garden
Credit cards AE, DC, MC, V
Children welcome
Disabled not suitable
Pets accepted
Closed never
Proprietors Erwin and Monika
Schönau

Gasthof Frohsinn
Town brewery hotel

This is a must for beer enthusiasts, and
anyone else wanting something out of
the ordinary. It's no longer owned by the
Surbeck family who started brewing here,
but current owners Erwin and Monika
Schönau have kept the Frohsinn brewery
going. Down in the basement, the beer cellar has a vaulted roof dating from medieval
times, wooden benches and a sprinkling of
locals, even early in the morning. Sacks full
of barley stand ready for the two copper
mash tuns, or vats, presided over by the
brew master. Twice a week, 500 litres of
lager are produced, with a stronger brown
beer made in winter as well.

The modern Allegro restaurant has
large windows with views over vineyards
towards the lake. Sample the Italian cooking (antipasti and home-made pasta) here
and then head down to the *Braukeller*; or,
settle in downstairs at the start of your
night for veal sausage with *Händl* mustard,
fresh pretzels or cheese salad – accompanied by seasonal beer. If you prefer an
evening out, the cellar serves set menus
(vegetarian, fish or meat) at lunch.

As for the rest of the hotel, bedrooms
are small, neat and plain, 'strictly for sleeping', bathrooms (most with shower only)
are 'just for a quick wash'.

Gottlieben near Kreuzlingen

8274 Gottlieben

Tel 071 666 8060
e-mail info@hoteldiekrone.ch
website www.hoteldiekrone.ch

Nearby Lake Constance (600 m);
Kreuzlingen (4 km); Meersburg (11
km); Stein am Rhein (20 km).
Location in village; limited car
parking on quayside
Food breakfast, lunch, dinner,
snacks
Prices FF-FFFFF
Rooms 25; 19 double, 4 single, 2
suites, all with bath or shower; all
rooms have central heating, phone,
TV, radio, minibar
Facilities breakfast room,
restaurant, cinema, smokers' room,
lift/elevator; terrace
Credit cards AE, DC, MC, V
Children welcome
Disabled not suitable
Pets accepted
Closed Nov to Feb
Proprietors Raphael Lüthy,
Raymond Kronig and Markus
Greter

Krone
Riverside hotel

Many people would be happy to pay to walk round this village whose history dates back to the 12thC. The narrow lanes and half-timbered houses, dominated by the monastery, stand right on the bank of the River Rhine, between the Bodensee and the smaller Untersee. However, it's not been over-visited and still feels like a living town, not a tourist attraction.

This 300-year-old inn, on the tranquil shore of Lake Rhein between Upper and Lower Lake Constance, is only a short distance from the tourist spots in the area. Bedrooms are a mix of old and new, sophisticated and plain. Some have white-washed walls and monochrome furniture, so have extravagant light fittings, heavy classical furniture and fabric-covered walls. The best is luxurious and worth the extra expense for a romantic weekend.

Our reporter enjoyed the restaurant, 'like a gentle-men's club, all polished dark wood' and the exquisite breakfast room. After dinner, guests can retire to the smoker's room for a cigar and glass of whiskey.

The cinema (free for guests) is a small, elegantly decorated room where you can watch classics, blockbusters and family movies. Movies can be requested if you book in advance.

Mannenbach

Seestrasse 4, 8268 Mannenbach am
Untersee

Tel 071 663 4141
e-mail info@seehotel-schiff.ch
website www.seehotel.ch

Nearby Napoleon Museum (4 km);
vineyards; lake.
Location on lake; ample car parking
Food breakfast, lunch, dinner,
snacks
Prices FF-FFF
Rooms 18 double, all with bath or
shower; all rooms have central
heating, TV, hairdryer, wi-fi, some
have balcony
Facilities 2 dining rooms, sitting
room, bar, lift/elevator; terrace,
garden, golf nearby
Credit cards AE, DC, MC, V
Children very welcome
Disabled good access
Pets accepted
Closed mid-Feb
Manager Bettina Buff

Seehotel Schiff
Lakeside hotel

Most members of the Landgasthof association are old wayside inns, so the totally modern Seehotel Schiff comes as a shock, particularly in this area known for its ancient half-timbered buildings. Set on the shore of the Untersee, 'this is more like a Mediterranean hotel', according to our reporter, who picked out the quarry-tiled floor and plain white plaster walls as examples of a 'seaside feel'.

Only 30 years old, the terracotta stucco building with its pale pine balconies is shaded by mature chestnut trees, while the restaurant and terrace look on to the water. Swans paddling past moored motor and sailing boats complete the idyllic scene. With the ferry stop nearby and the cycle path at the door, the Schiff makes a popular stop on a day out but the cooking has a fine reputation, offering fish from the lake such as pike, carp and perch, though some visitors have commented that the food can be overpriced (CHF 40-50 per person). Mannenbach's own vineyards provide the ideal accompaniment, a chilled bottle of Riesling/Sylvaner. Bedrooms are light, bright and neat: white walls and yellow pine complete the holiday atmosphere. There have been mixed reports about the cleanliness of the hotel.

Schaffhausen

Parkstr 18, 8200 Schaffhausen

Tel 052 625 2737
e-mail hotel@parkvilla.ch
website www.parkvilla.ch

Nearby Munot Castle (800 m);
Rhine Falls (2 km); German border
(4 km).
Location in parkland above railway
line; own car parking
Food breakfast, lunch, dinner,
snacks
Prices FF-FFF
Rooms 22; 15 double, 7 single, most
with bath or shower; all rooms have
central heating, phone, TV, radio,
minibar, hairdryer
Facilities 2 dining rooms, sitting
room, bar; terrace, garden, tennis
court
Credit cards AE, DC, MC, V
Children welcome
Disabled not suitable
Pets accepted
Closed never
Proprietor Max Schlumpf

Park Villa
Suburban hotel

'This could be a set for one of Alfred
Hitchcock's films.' That was the first
impression of this house, whose steep
roof, gables and stone facade look rather
forbidding. Don't let that put you off,
though. Built in 1900 by a banker, it had
become a *pension* when Max Schlumpf
bought it and restored the look and ambience of a private home, albeit one of a
rather eccentric grandfather. Forget the
standardization of hotel chains; from the
minute you step into the dark, high-
ceilinged entrance, with its sweeping
wooden staircase and stuffed tiger, you
know this hotel is one of a kind.

The bar is in the former library while
the white-walled breakfast room has large,
arched windows looking into the garden.
There are parquet floors, patterned carpets and most of the furniture is old, if not
antique. The size of bedrooms varies enormously; those in the attic are small, cosy
and more simply decorated than larger
ones below. You may get a bed dating from
1829 or a carved four-poster, but train
spotters should ask for one of the corner
rooms where they can focus their binoculars on the nearby railway line.

Schaffhausen

Rheinquai 8, 8200 Schaffhausen

Tel 052 632 0505
e-mail info@fischerzunft.ch
website www.fischerzunft.ch

Nearby Munot Castle (200 m);
Rhine Falls (3 km).
Location on river bank; car parking
nearby
Food breakfast, lunch, dinner
Prices FFF-FFFFF
Rooms 10 double, all with bath or
shower; all rooms have central
heating, phone, TV, minibar,
hairdryer, safe
Facilities restaurant, dining room,
sitting room, terrace
Credit cards AE, DC, MC, V
Children welcome but not suitable
Disabled not suitable
Pets accepted (extra charge)
Closed never; restaurant only, Mon,
Tue, end Jan to mid-Feb
Proprietors André Jaeger and Jana
Zwesper

Rheinhotel Fischerzunft
Riverside hotel

Once the Fishermen's Guildhall of
Schaffhausen, this is now one of the
most famous restaurants in Switzerland. In
1975, André Jaeger returned from the
Peninsula Hotel in Hong Kong to take over
the family business. Since then he has
developed a cuisine that is a 'perfect blend
of East and West'. Marinated salmon with
Teriyaki sauce, perch-pike fillet with curry
sauce and home-made mango chutney, and
spring chicken 'yin and yang' with sweet
ginger and orange sauce were just a few
dishes on a menu of 'such stunning origi-
nality that I want to eat it all'. The presentation is a photographic dream.

Our reporter was also impressed by
the restaurant itself, with enough space
between tables for private conversations,
beautiful flowers and distinctive floral print
table-cloths. 'No pale blues and pinks here;
this is a design statement.' Bedrooms
show the same flair. The more expensive
have a river view but all are deeply comfortable, with individual colour themes for
paintwork, fabrics and carpets. Chinese
prints abound, looking surprisingly natural,
even on candy-stripe wallpaper. 'Total per-
fection' was the verdict; but book your
table when reserving a room.

8260 Stein am Rhein

Tel 052 741 2144
e-mail rheinfels@bluewin.ch
website www.rheinfels.ch

Nearby German border (1.2 km);
Schaffhausen (17 km); Contance (24
km); lake.
Location overlooking river; car
parking nearby
Food breakfast, lunch, dinner,
snacks
Price FF
Rooms 17 double, all with bath or
shower; all rooms have central
heating, phone, TV, radio, minibar
Facilities 4 dining rooms, sitting
room, bar; terrace
Credit cards AE, DC, MC, V
Children welcome
Disabled not suitable
Pets accepted
Closed Jan, Feb; restaurant only,
Thurs
Proprietors Schwegler-Wick family

Rheinfels
Ancient hostelry

Stein am Rhein is such a touristy town that many travellers avoid its narrow streets and ancient buildings altogether. The secret is to stay overnight; then you can enjoy the medieval atmosphere when the day-trippers have gone home.

The Rheinfels sits on the river-bank next to the bridge; its terrace restaurant overhangs the water where ducks and swans amuse the diners who flock to enjoy Edi Schwegler's cooking. Whether it is fillets of zander, served with a delicate sorrel sauce, or char from the Rhine itself, Edi has a sure touch with fish. An avid hunter, he also serves game in season. The hotel itself is like a huge wooden galleon turned upside down, with stately timbers supporting the curved roof. Climb the stairs, which creak with every step, and full-size suits of armour and stuffed birds stare silently across the landing. At the top of the building, room 35 has rosebud-patterned wallpaper, pink duvets and dark, old beams. A map of the village as it was in 1662 shows each house clearly numbered. The tiny windows look down to the river and bridge. All in all, the hold maintains its medieval feel.

Ermatingen

Fruthwilerstrasse 2, 8272
Ermatingen

Tel 071 664 1133
e-mail adlerermatingen@bluewin.ch
website www.adler-ermatingen.ch
Food breakfast, lunch, dinner
Price FF
Closed mid-Feb to mid-Mar
Proprietor Thomas Albert

Adler
Wayside inn

This towering, half-timbered, blue-shuttered inn is the oldest in Thurgau, dating from 1270. Rebuilt in 1500, famous guests include Goethe, Hermann Hesse and Napoleon III, after whom the restaurant is named. Dine on imaginative fish dishes, including three types of scampi, surrounded by antique wood panelling.

Bedrooms are modern, with fresh blue-painted furniture and yellow and lavender bed linen. Choose a room with a view over the garden or a terrace. The bathrooms are all clean, but some have pastel-pink W.C.s, wash-basins and baths – not for everyone.

Cycling trails along the lake, hiking trails, beach and museum nearby.

Rapperswil

Seequai 1, 8640 Rapperswil

Tel 055 220 8500
e-mail reservation@schwanen.ch
website www.schwanen.ch
Food breakfast, lunch, dinner, snacks
Price FFFF
Closed never
Manager Margrit Riva-Toller

Schwanen
Lakeside hotel

Margrit Riva-Toller believes this hotel should be part of the community. Large and imposing, the hotel dominates the middle of town, in front of the castle and overlooking the lake. Her interest in design ensured that the conversion from old to new retained the character of the building, but in a striking format. Corridors and bedrooms are furnished in dramatic black and white. 'I loved it, but some people won't' commented our reporter.

Much space is devoted to banqueting and meeting rooms for companies from Zurich and although our reporter found the restaurants rather impersonal, he liked the less formal bistro-bar with its high ceilings, terrace and innovative menu.

Schaffhausen

Kirchhofplatz 7, 8200 Schaffhausen

Tel 052 635 7575
e-mail info@kronenhof.ch
website www.kronenhof.ch
Food breakfast, lunch, dinner
Prices FF-FFF
Closed never
Proprietors Peter & Claudia
Pirnstill-Marchesi

Kronenhof
City hotel

This period townhouse built in the 15th century was recently refurbished by new managers Peter and Claudia. They redecorated the bedrooms in typically Swiss style, and added a spa with sauna, steam rooms and gym – free entrance for hotel guests. The restaurant, which is popular with the locals and often fills up in the evening (good sign), serves buffet breakfasts and delicious – albeit rather expensive – food with effusive friendliness.

A recent visitor highlights the hotel's excellent location – just two minutes' walk from the town centre and a gentle stroll to boat rides on Lake Constance. The comfortable beds and intimate setting of Kronenhof will ensure a good night's sleep.

Steckborn

Im Feldbach 10, 8266 Steckborn

Tel 052 762 2121
e-mail info@hotel-feldbach.ch
website www.hotel-feldbach.ch
Food breakfast, lunch, dinner, snacks
Price FFF
Closed never
Manager Yvonne Simml

Feldbach
Modern lakeside hotel

Our reporter was bowled over by this converted 13thC convent, off the main road and through a boat yard, which 'deserves a feature in a design and architecture magazine'. The refectory has an onion-domed tower; a glass-walled walkway gives this two-storey building the look of a medieval cloister; and the colonnaded entrance 'looks like a church'.

The 36 bedrooms, in the modern extension, are all the same, with simple furniture and a touch of colour in the duvets. This is one hotel where disabled travellers will have no difficulty; a wide lift/elevator gives access to the floor above.

This is an extraordinary and harmonious mix of ancient and modern. Free bicycles.

Area introduction

This is Switzerland's largest canton, the country's mountainous eastern chunk, with the Engadine, the deep valley of the River Inn, cutting through it from east to west. With Austria to the north and Italy to the south, the area is strongly influenced by both, and it's here that Romance is spoken by 50,000 people – a linguistic legacy of Roman occupation that sounds familiar but is incomprehensible. Despite the importance of tourism, and especially of the famous ski resorts – for example Davos, Klosters, St Moritz and Arosa – traditional Alpine ways survive. Cowbells are still part of the landscape as cattle make their way from wintering in the valleys to spring mountain pastures. We have recommendations in the ski resorts, but more charming places are in the villages of the Engadine valley. Some of the country's finest chefs work here, and this is the home of *Bündnerfleisch*, air-dried beef sliced paper-thin.

Below are some useful back-up places to try if our main selections are fully booked:

Saluver
Resort hotel, Celerina
Tel 081 833 1314
www.saluver.ch
Popular hotel for sport
lovers; cheerful staff.

Hotel Post
Wayside inn, Churwalden
Tel 081 382 1109
www.posthotel-churwalden.ch
400-year-old family-run inn
serving imaginative food.

Hotel Larix
Chalet hotel, Davos
Tel 081 413 1188
www.hotel-larix.ch
Chalet-style hotel with feel of
private house; ski to door.

Alte Post
Town hotel, Davos Platz
Tel 081 417 6550
www.mountainhotels.ch
17thC restored hotel with
pretty *Stube*; small rooms.

Hotel Surpunt
Town hotel, Flims
Tel 081 928 4444
www.hotel-surpunt.com
Expanded villa, ten minutes'
walk from ski lifts.

Fidazer Hof
Mountain hotel, Flims at
Fidaz Tel 081 920 9010
www.fidazerhof.ch
Health hotel; organic ingre-
dients; sophisticated spa.

Piz Buin
Village inn, Guarda
Tel 081 861 3000
www.pizbuin.ch
Good address for families;
not too close to busy ski areas.

Hotel Spescha
Village hotel, Lenzerheide
Tel 081 385 1424
www.hotel-spescha.ch
Family-run modern hotel
with hillside views.

Kochendörfer's Hotel
Albris Mountain hotel,
Pontresina Tel 081 838 8040
www.albris.ch
Bakery with rooms; special-
izes in fish, cakes and pastries.

Hotel Languard
Bed-and-breakfast, St Moritz
Tel 081 833 3137
www.languard-stmoritz.ch
Run by champion skiers;
some rooms have lake view.

Villa Maria
Villa hotel, Vulpera
Tel 081 864 1138
www.villamaria.ch
Surrounded by hillside golf
course; delightful gardens.

Crusch Alva
Village inn, Zuoz
Tel 081 851 2345
www.cruschalva.ch
Old-world atmosphere; serves
Grison and Swiss specialities.

7050 Innerarosa, Arosa

Tel 081 378 7280
e-mail belri@bluewin.ch
website www.belri.ch

Nearby Arosa (2 km); Davos (13 km); Chur (14 km).
Location at top of Arosa in Innerarosa; ample car parking, 8 garages
Food breakfast only, summer; breakfast, lunch, dinner, snacks in winter
Price FFF
Rooms 18; 12 double, 5 single, 1 suite, all with bath or shower; all rooms have central heating, phone, satellite TV, radio, safe, wi-fi
Facilities dining room, 3 sitting rooms; skiing nearby
Credit cards MC, V
Children very welcome
Disabled not suitable
Pets dogs welcome (extra charge)
Closed after Easter to mid-May, mid-Sep to early Dec
Managers Beerli family

Belri
Mountain hotel

'**A**former girls' finishing school, but don't let that put you off' was the intriguing beginning of the report on this converted chalet, opposite the local museum right at the top of Arosa. The interior is 'like a great-aunt's house', particularly the dark wood-panelled hall and wide staircase that creaks with every step. Upstairs, the students in number 38 probably lay awake in their twin four-poster beds, staring at the carved partridge on the ceiling, while those in number 43, no doubt preferred sitting on the roof-top terrace to studying at the jolly red-painted desk and chairs. In contrast to this remembrance of things past is the spacious, contemporary comfort of the suite with its pretty white organdie curtains and pale wood. There are also five functional bedrooms in the new wing.

This is one hotel where the claim of 'ski out, ski back' really is justified and lifts to the Weisshorn and the Hörnli are only minutes away. At the end of the day, there are three *Stübli* for relaxation and socialising. A recent American visitor said that it had 'the old-fashioned ambience of a New England inn'.

Bever

7502 Bever

Tel 081 851 1616
e-mail reception@chesa-salis.ch
website www.chesa-salis.ch

Nearby St Moritz (8 km); Zuoz (8 km); Italian border (13 km).
Location on the edge of the village; ample car parking, some covered
Food breakfast, lunch, dinner, snacks
Prices FF-FFFF
Rooms 18 double, all with bath or shower; all rooms have phone, TV, wi-fi
Facilities 3 dining rooms, sitting room, lift/elevator, terrace, garden, winter sports and mountain biking nearby
Credit cards AE, MC, V
Children welcome
Disabled not suitable
Pets accepted; stables for horses
Closed mid-Apr to mid-June, mid-Oct to mid-Dec
Managers Jürg & Sibylla Degiacomi

Chesa Salis
Historic house

'**W**orth a whole roll of film' says our reporter of this house that dates back to the 16th century but was embellished by the patrician Salis family who bought it in 1870. 'It's old, it's not practical but we love it,' says owner Jürg Degiacomi, who has run the house with his wife, Sibylla, since 1982.

The restaurant has a fine reputation and serves local and traditional French and Italian dishes. 'We are away from the village, we don't have a swimming pool, so we spoil our guests with good food.' The dining room has a carved front door, matched by an elaborate wrought-iron gate. Off to one side is a small room for private parties that is 'like a doll's house', completely wood-panelled, with bookshelves, an *escritoire* and tiny windows.

Metre-thick walls, paintings, beamed and frescoed ceilings and colourful ceramic fireplaces hint at the building's history. In the reception room, antiques mix with black leather sofas, and the glass counter is highlighted by a modern painting. In the rest of the house, furnishings are traditional.

The bedrooms are all pretty. The best is number 35, tucked under the eaves, with a low ceiling and white-washed pannelled walls painted like a music box. 'If only grandma's house had looked like this' was our reporter's final comment.

Berglistutz 2, 7270 Davos Platz

Tel 081 417 6777
e-mail hotels@mountainhotels.ch
website www.mountainhotels.ch

Nearby Davos Platz railway station
(200 m); Jakobshorn ski lift (150 m);
lake.
Location in middle of Davos;
limited car parking (extra charge in
winter)
Food breakfast, lunch, dinner,
snacks
Prices FF-FFF
Rooms 21; 15 double, 5 single, 1
suite, all with shower; all rooms have
central heating, phone, TV, radio,
safe
Facilities 2 dining rooms, sitting
room, bar, wi-fi; terrace, winter
sports nearby
Credit cards AE, MC, V
Children welcome
Disabled not suitable
Pets not accepted
Closed 3 weeks Easter
Proprietors Davos Klosters
Bergbahnen AG

Davoserhof
Town hotel

Chic and central sums up this hotel,
which is ideal for those who want to
be close to all the facilities of this big, busy
ski resort. Bedrooms are large and furnished with pale-wood built-in cupboards
and desks. Bathrooms are first-rate: white
marble with huge mirrors.

Downstairs, the Buffalo Grill restaurant
serves food in the two dining rooms. With
its old, caramel-coloured wood and traditional carved chairs, the *Davoserstübli* has a
pleasingly masculine look. More feminine is
the honey-toned wood panelling in the
breakfast room. As well as beef steak, the
menu includes buffalo, venison and fish
dishes. There is a lengthy wine list to complement the cooking.

Although the atmosphere seems luxurious and sedate, this is popular with families and the younger generation, who
come for skiing and mountain biking. In
season, the Rotliechtli bar has live music
and stays open until 3 a.m. Happily, this is
well insulated from guests. Some guests
have been disturbed by the chimes of the
clock tower nearby, but earplugs are provided for light sleepers.

Fanas

Alte Kirchgasse 1, 7215 Fanas

Tel 081 325 14 19
e-mail info@hitschhuus.ch
website www.hitschhuus.ch

Nearby Bad Ragaz (12 km); Chur (17 km); Vaduz (20 km): Klosters (21 km); Davos (24 km).
Location near the edge of Fanas; car parking
Food breakfast, dinner
Prices F-FF
Rooms 6 double, all with bath or shower; all rooms have central heating, radio, hairdryer, wi-fi
Facilities dining room, sitting room, library/TV room, lift/elevator; terrace, garden, winter sports nearby
Credit cards not accepted
Children accepted
Disabled arrangements can be made
Pets by arrangement
Closed 2 weeks May, 4 weeks Nov to Dec; restaurant only, Sun
Proprietors Christine Bläuer and Jürg Bühler

Hitsch-Huus
Village hotel

Special, in the best sense… idiosyncratic, maybe homespun, maybe in places a little home-made, but full of the individuality we like to see. It sits in a peaceful road near the edge of the orderly little village of Fanas – a low-key place, unpolluted by mass tourism and somewhat off the beaten track – though accessible (it's near Landquart) from the main north-south and east-west motorways through the Alps. You might want to stay for a charming stopover, or you might want to linger a few days, especially in summer for the Alpine walking and hang gliding (accessed by cable car) and in winter for snow-shoe walks. In terms of skiing it's unsophisticated (1,800m at Grüsch-Danusa) and overshadowed by nearby Klosters and Davos.

The six bedrooms are all different, decorated often in strong colours, and named after exotic places such as Istanbul or Laos – and with (roughly) appropriate furnishings and styling. Very good breakfasts and dinner are offered – the friendly Christine and Jürg do the cooking with ingredients from local organic farmers – and there's Fairtrade honey for your breakfast roll.

Above all, visitors find it cosy, clean, comfortable and affordable, so its sales slogan of *klein aber fein* – small but excellent – is a fair claim.

7551 Ftan

Tel 081 861 0808
e-mail info@paradieshotel.ch
website www.paradieshotel.ch

Nearby Scuol (4 km); Swiss National Park (12 km); Susch (13 km); Müstair (24 km).
Location off small country road, outside village; ample car parking, garages
Food breakfast, lunch, dinner, snacks
Price FFFFF
Rooms 23; 4 double; 4 single, 7 junior suites, 8 suites, all with bath or shower; all rooms have central heating, phone, TV, radio, minibar
Facilities 3 dining rooms, 3 sitting rooms, health spa; terrace, garden; winter sports and hiking nearby
Credit cards AE, DC, MC, V
Children very welcome
Disabled not suitable
Pets accepted
Closed after Easter to end May, mid-Oct to mid-Dec
Manager Meike Bambach

Haus Paradies
Mountain hotel

Serious food-lovers already know the name of this Relais & Châteaux member, thanks to the cooking of Michelin-starred chef Martin Göschel. He uses local ingredients (including Swiss caviar) at his restaurant here, the L'Autezza, which has just seven tables. He serves breakfast all day, with local cheese, dried milk and water-buffalo milk. When L'Autezza is full, guests eat at Stüva Paradies, which serves regional dishes.

'Don't let the cubic-look of the exterior put you off,' warned our reporter, who was ready to unpack and stay for a month; The walls of this 1911 house – originally owned by artist Hans Walter Bayer – are hung with more than 100 works of art. Old meets new where velvet sofas sit on old-fashioned rugs next to modern furnishings. Some period details remain in the public rooms, such as the cembra pine panelling on the walls of the Stüva Paradies, but bedrooms and suites are unashamedly modern, with the accent on comfort. All are different – some have a Scandinavian look, others Provencal-type patterns. All come with binoculars for guests to enjoy the view across the valley to Tarasp Castle and the Swiss Dolomites.

There is also a small spa where guests can enjoy a variety of treatments, and book a Dutch tub on the rooftop.

Guarda

7545 Guarda

Tel 081 862 2132
e-mail info@hotel-meisser.ch
website www.hotel-meisser.ch

Nearby Susch (5 km); Ftan (7 km); Vulpera (10 km).
Location in heart of old mountain village; ample car parking
Food breakfast, lunch, dinner, snacks
Prices FF-FFF
Rooms 22; 14 double, 3 single, 5 suites, all with bath or shower; all rooms have central heating, phone, minibar
Facilities 2 dining-rooms, 3 sitting-rooms; terrace, garden; winter sports, river-rafting nearby
Credit cards AE, DC, MC, V
Children welcome
Disabled not suitable
Pets accepted
Closed Nov to Whitsun
Proprietors Meisser family

Meisser
Mountain village inn

Although Guarda has a population of only 140, it is a well-known tourist destination, thanks to its highly-decorated houses and resident craftsmen. Our reporter was relieved to have climbed the switchbacks from the valley by car, rather than the horse-drawn carriages that brought earlier visitors to this centuries-old inn. Built as a farmhouse in 1645, it was converted to an inn by Benno Meisser's great-great-grandparents. Modern improvements have not always been sympathetic. The box-like restaurant extension has fabulous views over the Engadin Valley to the Swiss Dolomites but lacks the elegance of the old wood-panelled, high-ceilinged dining room.

Bedrooms vary: in one, a handsome carved ceiling, in another, wallpaper that looks like a summer meadow, full of grasses and butterflies. Bathrooms are often problematical in conversions of old houses but there is no excuse for the linoleum floor and cheap, badly-hanging curtains which our reporter saw in one. He hoped that that was due for change in the continuing refurbishment programme. Despite these criticisms, he was impressed by the hospitality and carefully-prepared local dishes. The Meissers are planning a renovation in 2014. We would welcome reports on the changes they make.

Bahnhofstrasse 12, 7250 Klosters Platz

Tel 081 422 2222
e-mail hotel@chesagrischuna.ch
website www.chesagrischuna.ch

Nearby winter sports; swimming, tennis.
Location in the middle of town; car parking
Food breakfast, lunch, dinner, snacks
Prices FFF-FFFFF
Rooms 14; 12 double, 2 single, all with bath; all rooms have central heating, phone, TV, radio
Facilities dining room, sitting room, bar, bowling alley; terrace; winter sports, swimming nearby
Credit cards AE, DC, MC, V
Children welcome
Disabled not suitable
Pets accepted
Closed 6 weeks after Easter, 6 weeks from mid-Oct
Proprietors Guler family

Chesa Grischuna
Chalet hotel

This has been a landmark in Klosters ever since it was built as the original railway hotel 75 years ago. Now it's just a few steps from the Gotschnagrat-Parsenn cable car and it's connected to the Engadine by the Vereina tunnel. Outsiders are attracted all day long to the sunny terrace and the busy restaurant, which serves up caviar and *Châteaubriand* as well as local specialities; in the afternoon, however, pastries are the main draw.

'Old-fashioned in the best sense' was the reaction to furnishings which aim for comfort rather than a designer look. Up the stairs that creak with age, bedrooms have double-thickness doors to ensure a quiet night's rest. The Chesa Grischuna happily manages to satisfy all types: the bar, is famous as an *après-ski* rendezvous with a 'cheery, buzzy atmosphere', while upstairs the sitting room has games and cards, an open fireplace plus a mural detailing the history of Klosters and the Guler family. A recent visitor said 'this continues to be where it's at in Klosters.'

The Guler family has a tradition of gracious hospitality. Their guest book reads like a *Who's Who* of statesmen and princes, actors and artists, but everyone receives the same genuinely warm welcome. Book well in advance.

7250 Klosters Platz

Tel 081 410 2929
e-mail info@walserhof.ch
website www.walserhof.ch

Nearby Davos (8 km); Arosa (18 km); Chur (27 km).
Location on edge of village; ample car parking
Food breakfast, lunch, dinner
Price FFFFF
Rooms 6; 2 double, 4 suites, all with bath or shower; all rooms have central heating, phone, TV, minibar
Facilities dining room, sauna, lift/elevator; winter sports, golf nearby
Credit cards AE, DC, MC, V
Children very welcome
Disabled reasonable access
Pets accepted
Closed mid-Apr to mid-Jun; restaurant only, Sun and Mon in summer, late Oct to early Dec
Managers Silvia and Heribert Dietrich

Walserhof
Chalet hotel

This is one of our priciest places to stay in the Swiss Alps, but you get what you pay for in this Klosters classic. Silvia and Heribert Dietrich worked at Walserhof 21 years ago, back when it was owned by Gabi and Beat Bolliger. They now return as managers, with an eye for quality and an understanding of what makes this place so special. Rooms and public spaces have been refreshed and feel modern. There are now just two double rooms and four suites, but the use of well-chosen colours and pine preserves the welcoming, home-ly atmosphere. The standard of food remains excellent.

Although the hotel is on the road, bed-rooms overlook hillside meadows and mountains on all sides. Whichever room you choose, you're guaranteed a fantastic view. The attention to detail downstairs is repeated upstairs, with comfortable beds and careful mixing and toning of fabrics for curtains, wall coverings and bedspreads.

Each of the suites is named after a let-ter of the Runic alphabet. Colours are gen-erally subdued: pine-green, cool slate-grey and beige. The bathrooms – with *café au lait* marble, large mirrors and double wash-basins – are a delight. Large cupboards are good for families on winter holidays and the ski school is only a minute away.

Via Principala 541, 7031 Laax

Tel 081 921 4466
e-mail info@postaveglia.ch
website www.postaveglia.ch

Nearby museum (50 m); Flims (4 km); Chur (24 km).
Location in heart of village; ample car parking
Food breakfast, lunch, dinner, snacks
Prices FF-FFFF
Rooms 7; 4 double, 3 suites, all with bath or shower; all rooms have central heating, phone, TV, radio
Facilities 3 dining rooms, 2 bars; terrace, garden; winter sports, river-rafting nearby
Credit cards MC, V
Children welcome but not suitable
Disabled not suitable
Pets accepted
Closed mid-Apr to mid-Jun; restaurant only, Mon
Proprietor René H. Meyer

Posta Veglia
Village inn

Laax is one of the prettiest villages in the upper Rhine Valley and the Posta Veglia is arguably the region's prettiest inn. It was originally turned into a hotel in 1978 by Peter Panier, who wanted to create 'the kind of hotel that I always wanted to stay in'. New head chef, René Meyer, bought the hotel in 2002 and has since left the interior mostly untouched.

The stone building with green shutters was once the hub of the community, encorporating schoolhouse, shop and *Stübli*. It is decorated with honey-coloured wood panelling and old furniture and pictures, and there is an old wind-up gramophone in the informal *Beizli* bar-restaurant.

There are several bars and restaurants here: the Remise restaurant, in the converted stables, serves steaks and fondues; upstairs, the old schoolroom is now the *Arvenstübli* (wooden parlour), complete with heart-backed chairs and stern grandmas staring down from sepia photos. Food here is 'market-fresh and seasonal, with Grison's touch'. Each bedroom looks different: swathes of gold fabric above the bed in one, painted *Bauern* furniture in another, a sleigh bed in a single and views of the mountains in the renovated attic *Panoramazimmer*. Nearby there are opportunities for winter sports, river rafting, walks and mountain biking.

Malans

7208 Malans

Tel 081 322 8161
e-mail info@weisskreuzmalans.ch
website www.weisskreuzmalans.ch

Nearby wine villages of Bündner Herrschaft (2 km); vineyards.
Location in middle of village; ample car parking
Food breakfast, lunch, dinner, snacks
Prices FFF
Rooms 4 double, all with shower; all rooms have central heating, phone, TV, radio, minibar
Facilities 5 dining rooms, lift/elevator; terrace
Credit cards AE, MC, V
Children welcome
Disabled 4 special rooms
Pets accepted
Closed two weeks Feb and Jul
Proprietors Family Theus

Weisskreuz
Village inn

We were charmed as soon as we got inside this old inn. The *Bündnerstübli*, two formal dining rooms, are lovely examples of old wood panelling, chandeliers, antique furniture, fresh flowers and baroque clocks. Far below, a giant wine-press in the *Zum Torkel* is 'the wine-making equivalent of the dinosaur, enormous, a magnificent relic of a bygone era'. In the surrounding Bündner Herrschaft vineyards, a new generation of wine makers is impressing wine lovers with chardonnays as well as traditional *Blauburgunder* (pinot noir) and Riesling-Sylvaner grapes.

With its rustic wooden furniture, the *Malanserstube* is the meeting point for locals. The chef cooks traditional *Bündner* dishes such as *Capuns* (sausage wrapped in chard) or *Pizokels* (buck-wheat pasta) using fresh seasonal or regional produce.

Bedrooms have been recently renovated in traditional wood. Bathrooms are first-rate. Disabled guests are well catered for.

7500 St Moritz

Tel 081 838 7000
e-mail info@hotel-meierei.ch
website www.hotel-meierei.ch

Nearby St Moritz (1 km); Silvaplana
(5 km); Madulain (16 km); Italian
border (34 km)
Location on lakeside, 10-minute
walk from station, 10 minutes from
town centre; car parking for hotel
guests only
Food breakfast, lunch, dinner
Prices FFF-FFFF
Rooms 12; 8 double, 3 suites, all
with bath and shower, 1 single with
shower; all rooms have central
heating, phone, TV, minibar, safe
Facilities dining room, breakfast
room, bar, sauna; terrace, children's
play area, private dock, fishing
Credit cards AE, DC, MC, V
Children welcome
Disabled not suitable
Pets accepted
Closed Apr to mid-Jul, mid-Oct to
mid-Dec
Proprietors Degiacomi family

Landhotel Meierei
Lakeside hotel

In what must be the most romantic spot
in St Moritz, the Meierei sits on the far of
the lake, frozen in winter, and commands a
superb view across it to the town and the
mountains beyond. Unless you are a dedicated people watcher, its charm is only
enhanced by its aloofness from the surre-
al, mink-wrapped goings-on in the town
centre. From here, it's a ten-minute walk
along the lakeside path, or, if you prefer, a
sleigh ride, or a taxi ride. Only hotel guests
may arrive in their own cars.

It's not exactly peaceful when you get
there though, especially at meal times, as
the hotel's restaurant is a popular gather-
ing place for lunch and dinner. The traditional Swiss food, with modern twists, is
well regarded; however, the dining room,
with its arched windows overlooking the
lake, is an L-shaped corridor. Though the
bedrooms lack nothing in terms of comfort (the suites have fireplaces), they don't
have much character. But the views are
excellent, especially at night when the lights
of St Moritz twinkle in the distance, and all
is quiet.

7553 Tarasp, Sparsels

Tel 081 861 3060
e-mail chaste@schlosshoteltarasp.ch
website www.schlosshoteltarasp.ch

Nearby Tarasp Castle (500 m); Swiss
National Park (2 km).
Location in heart of old village; car
parking nearby
Food breakfast, lunch, dinner,
snacks
Prices FFF-FFFFF
Rooms 18; 8 double, 2 single, 8
suite, all with bath or shower; all
rooms have central heating, phone,
TV, radio, minibar, hairdryer, safe,
some have iPod dock, Nespresso
machine, non-smoking
Facilities 2 dining rooms, sitting
room, bar, sauna/gym; terrace,
garden; winter sports nearby
Credit cards AE, DC, MC, V
Children very welcome
Disabled not suitable
Pets accepted **Closed** mid-Oct to
mid-Dec, end Mar to end May
Proprietors Rudolf, Daniela and
Gian-Andrea Pazeller

Schlosshotel Chastè
Country inn

Yet another pretty village, yet another
hotel with a fascinating history. The
building dates back more than 500 years
and the *Stüva* still has its tiny trapdoor,
through which the farmer's family would
squeeze to get to the sleeping quarters
above. Rudolf Pazeller's grandfather started the *Stüvetta* in 1912 to cater for work-
ers restoring the castle and, despite subse-
quent expansion, the overall look is traditional. Decorative carving is everywhere,
floors are of glazed terracotta cobbles, and
the old kitchen could be a museum. In
total contrast are the modern exercise
equipment and sauna down below that
were cut out of the granite mountain.

The hotel is full of suprises: gardens and
terraces on different levels, fragrant with
herbs and ablaze with flowers, even a pavil-
ion where the famous local mineral water
is on tap, like beer. As for bedrooms, sit
back in the bath of number 124 and stare
straight at the castle; lean on the balcony
of number 119 and imagine it full of hay
when it was the barn. Our reporter
admired the four-poster beds and carved
ceilings but could do without the bur-
gundy-coloured wallpaper in number 120.

Celerina

Via San Gian 7, 7505 Celerina

Tel 081 837 0101
e-mail hotel@rosatsch.ch
website www.hotelrosatsch.ch
Food breakfast, lunch, dinner,
snacks
Prices FF-FFF

Closed Easter to mid-Jun,
Christmas to mid-Jan
Manager Michael Stutz

Chesa Rosatsch
Riverside inn and apartment

Down a quiet side street, an ornate sign marks the 300-year-old Chesa Rosatsch, right by the Inn River. The cheerful, primrose-yellow annexe has the same deep windows and sloping roof as the main house where, by using natural materials such as untreated wood, stone and linen in the bedrooms and apartment, the effect is traditional with a modern twist.

The Stüvas restaurant, with its mellow wood panelling and ornate door lock, is dedicated to lighter, gourmet dishes, while the trendy Uondas restaurant cooks crispy meat dishes in a wood-fired oven. The bar, with its array of malt whiskies and cigars, has become a fashionable spot.

An ideal base for the St Moritz ski runs, or summer walks along the Engadine Valley.

Klosters

7250 Klosters

Tel 081 422 4545
e-mail info@steinbock-klosters.ch
website www.steinbock-klosters.ch
Food breakfast, lunch, dinner
Price FF
Closed end Oct to early Dec
Manager Marc Demisch

Steinbock
Town hotel

Opposite the well-known Walserhof (page 195), a shortish walk from Klosters' centre, the main cable car and the railway station, is this less opulent and less expensive option.

Inside, it feels smaller than its 34 rooms. Overall, the style is impeccable 'Swiss chalet' – the pleasant bedrooms are all a little different, but couldn't be anything but hotel rooms. Traditional Swiss style continues, nothing if not consistent, into the restaurant and bar, which are cosy, even intimate. Comfort at a fair price.

Lenzerheide at Sporz

7078 Lenzerheide at Sporz

Tel 081 385 8585
e-mail hotel@guardaval.ch
website www.guardaval.ch
Food breakfast, lunch, dinner, snacks
Price FFFFF
Closed never
Managers Christine Abel & Matthias Wettstein

Guarda Val
Country inn

'Luxury in the farmyard, cows and *haute cuisine* – you have to see it to believe it' read the report on this four-star hotel in the middle of the Maiensäss (1,600 m), just above Lenzerheide. Regulars come three or four times a year, treat it like their country home and expect to have 'their' room. That could be one of the gable suites, high under the roof with tiny windows; or Stailetta, the split-level studio suite straight out of a design magazine.

The main building dates from 1810 but looks medieval, with a gallery in the gourmet restaurant. In a former cowshed the informal Crap Naros restaurant serves traditional *Spätzle*, fondue and *Raclette*.

In winter, guests store their equipment in a ski room which, in summer, is the dairy.

Lenzerheide at Valbella

7077 Valbella-Lenzerheide

Tel 081 384 3535
e-mail hotel@seehof-valbella.ch
website www.seehof-valbella.ch
Food breakfast, lunch, dinner, snacks
Price FF
Closed never
Managers Roberto Pisilli

Seehof
Lakeside hotel

The yellow, blue and pine restaurant is the focal point of a visit here. Chefs Roberto and Marco cook delicious and well-presented dishes with fresh, seasonal produce. The influence is Italian, with tagliatelle with black truffles and risotto on the menu. Some recent visitors have found the prices expensive, others feel the price is fair compared to other restaurants nearby.

Bedrooms are large and plain with pine furniture against white walls; all have lake views. Bathrooms are modern with white tiles and black marble. Family-friendly and cheerful, the Seehof is popular with active types who like the great outdoors.

Savognin

7460 Savognin

Tel 081 684 1161
e-mail pizmitgel@bluewin.ch
website www.hotel-pizmitgel-savognin.ch
Food breakfast, lunch, dinner, snacks
Prices FF-FFFF
Closed Nov to mid-Dec
Proprietors Waldegg family

Piz Mitgel
Wayside inn

Eccentric, yet appealing, this old hotel was carefully renovated by the Waldegg family. Where else can you eat breakfast in a former ballroom or collect mountain herbs and flowers with a botanist? Most of the bedrooms have sitting areas and the family rooms, all with a mezzanine level, can sleep up to five.

As well as the botanist activities, there are early morning wildlife photography sessions in summer; in winter there is skiing and a weekly tobogganing party. After exploring outdoors, guests can come back to the heated outdoor swimming pool or relax in the small sauna area with a Jacuzzi and infrared cabin. No credit cards.

Silvaplana

7513 Silvaplana

Tel 081 838 7878
e-mail hotel@hotelalbana.ch
website www.hotelalbana.ch
Food breakfast, lunch, dinner, snacks
Prices FF-FFFF
Closed after Easter to July, Nov
Proprietors Malvika & Daniel Bosshard-Jürisaar

Hotel Albana
Resort hotel

When Malvika and Daniel Bosshard-Jürisaar took over a few years ago, they followed a hotelier couple who had kept up a fine reputation for this hotel, just a short drive from St Moritz. Recent visitors report that the hotel is as stylish (and expensive) as ever.

The 33 bedrooms and suites are bright and practical, with local *Arvenholz* (larch), crisp white duvets and equally spotless bathrooms. The informal *Spunta-Engadina* serves modern dishes and there is a buffet at the Thai restaurant on Sundays (takeaway available). Nearby, there is kite flying on Lake Silvaplana or e-bike riding in summer; free use of cable cars all year. When the hotel is closed, its sister, Julier Palace, next door (open all year) is worth a visit.

Area introduction

The two southernmost cantons of Switzerland mainly border Italy (the west end of Valais also borders France). Valais is large, mountainous and French speaking, with the artery of the Rhône Valley running west to east. Ski resorts are reached up twisting roads both sides of the valley, among them Zermatt and its iconic mountain, the Matterhorn, standing in a chain of other superb 4,000-m-plus peaks. Places to stay in the ski resorts are, as usual, pleasant but formulaic, but we have found a useful number of outstanding, small, owner-managed enterprises.

Italian-speaking Ticino extends quite deep into northern Italy. This is the warm, south side of the Alps – sunshine, lakes, mountains and flowers. Most of our recommendations overlook the spectacular lakes, Lugano and Maggiore. Bellinzona is the canton capital, but Lugano is the hub.

Below are some useful back-up places to try if our main selections are fully booked:

Hotel Riposo
Town hotel, Ascona
Tel 091 791 3164
www.hotelriposo.ch
In old quarter; garden; swimming pool on roof terrace.

La Comanella Suburban
villa, Comano near Lugano
Tel 091 941 6571
www.hotel-la-comanella.ch
Modern hotel in chestnut
forests above Lugano.

Hotel de Moiry
Village hotel, Grimentz
Tel 027 475 1144
www.hotel-grimentz.ch
Large meals and comfortable
bedrooms for hikers/skiers.

Zurigo
Resort hotel, Locarno
Tel 091 923 4343
www.hotelzurigo.ch
Handy lakeside base; modern
style with some period pieces.

Colibri Resort hotel,
Lugano at Aldesago
Tel 091 971 4242
www.hotelcolibri.ch
Views over Lake Lugano and
mountains; good restaurant.

Le Forum
Modern hotel, Martigny
Tel 026 722 1841
www.hotel-forum.ch
Some of the finest cooking in
Valais; typical 1960s design.

Albergo Olivone e
Posta Village hotel, Olivone
Tel 091 872 1366
www.hotel-olivone.ch
Strictly for sporty types; restaurant serves rabbit terrine.

Fletschhorn
Forest hotel, Saas Fee
Tel 027 957 2131
www.fletchhorn.ch
Rustic hotel with restaurant;
excellent views (1,800 m).

Au Manoir d'Anniviers
Village hotel, Vissoie
Tel 027 475 1220
www.aumanoir.ch
Traditional inn; 'fighting
cow' scenes in dining room.

Auberge de Vouvry
Wayside inn, Vouvry
Tel 024 481 1221
www.aubergedevouvry.ch
Simple rooms in 18thC inn;
traditional Valais dishes.

Riffelalp Resort
Mountain hotel and apartments, Zermatt
Tel 027 966 0555
www.riffelalp.com
Luxury hotel; ski to door.

Le Besso
Village hotel, Zinal
Tel 027 475 3165
www.le-besso.ch
Keen walker owner leads
hikes; mountain views.

Belalp

Belalp Retreat, 3914 Blatten bei
Natters

Tel 027 923 2043
e-mail info@hamiltonlodge.ch
website www.hamiltonlodge.ch

Nearby Blatten bei Natters (1.5
km); Brig (7 km); Zermatt (42 km).
Location North of Rhone Valley;
20-minute walk from Belalp
Food breakfast, lunch, dinner
Prices FFF-FFFFF
Rooms 19 double, family and single,
all with shower; all rooms have TV,
hairdryer, safe, wi-fi
Facilities restaurant, sitting room,
TV room, massage, sauna,
whirlpool, luggage transportation,
wi-fi; terrace
Credit cards AE, MC, V
Children welcome, cots available
Disabled 1 room with specially
adapted bathroom
Pets welcome in apartments only
Closed end Oct to mid-Dec
Proprietors Jacqueline and John
Wegink, Birgit and Jaap van
Wagensveld

Hamilton Lodge & Spa
Mountain Lodge

Some ten years ago, Dutch couple
Jacqueline and John Wegink left their life
in Holland to become hoteliers. They found
a disappointing hotel in Belalp (2,100 m),
perched on the Aletsch glacier – the largest
in the Alps – and surrounded by snowy
peaks. Seeing its potential, they persuaded
the owners to sell, and transformed it into
an elegant, cosy hotel that lives up to the
owners' motto: 'Feels like home'.

The 19 bedrooms are individually decorated, with hand-made quilts and views of
the surrounding mountains. The public
spaces have just as much charm: an open
fireplace, comfortable armchairs, wooden
furniture. Lunch and dinner are served in
the restaurant. The menu has local and
international dishes. The tableware was
produced exclusively for the hotel's 'Hip
Heidi' theme, featuring Heidi riding a blue
elephant across a white background.
Recent guests have commented on the
friendly staff, who help create a warm and
homely atmosphere.

The location is wonderful for summer
mountain walks or in the winter for unde-
manding ski slopes. Guests can ski straight
to the hotel and the slopes reach 3,200 m,
so snow is guaranteed until April.

Champéry

Rue du village 114, 1874 Champéry

Tel 024 479 5858
e-mail info@beausejour.ch
website www.beausejour-hotel-switzerland.co.uk

Nearby Avoriaz (7 km); Morzine (12 km); Les Gets (15 km); Geneva (60 km); restaurants; shops.
Location in own small garden; off-road parking
Food breakfast
Prices FF-FFF
Rooms 18; 13 double and twin, 3 single, 2 family, all with bath or shower; all rooms have phone, TV, iPhone docking station, safe, mini-bar
Facilities breakfast room, sitting room, ski equipment storage
Credit cards MC, V
Children accepted
Disabled not suitable
Pets accepted
Closed May, Oct to Nov
Proprietors Sophie and Philippe Zurkirchen

Art Boutique Hotel Beau-Séjour B & B hotel

Something a little different: not a hotel, not a traditional B & B, but a bed-and-breakfast 'hotel' in an authentic Swiss chalet with above-average facilities, run by Sophie and Philippe Zurkirchen. Guests keep coming back for the combination of individuality and thoughtful touches, such as free afternoon tea in winter, with a generous selection of cakes.

On the main street of Champéry, an unspoiled mountain village in the Portes du Soleil skiing area (linking 12 resorts), the views from all the balconies are terrific: the big feature is the Dents du Midi range.

Inside, Sophie's interior design talent is obvious. Each of the bedrooms is different, but, as you would expect from the area, full of pine furniture. Rooms are decorated with mostly white walls, cosy, rural fabrics and imaginatively-placed graphics and murals, again the work of Sophie. The overall feel is a nice blend of contemporary and traditional charm. It's a successful renovation of an old building, but perhaps some of the bathrooms are smallish, though the bedrooms themselves are roomy enough.

The cable car is 400 m from the front door. In 2013 Beau-Séjour won first place (joint with three others) in a list of the 100 most welcoming hotels in Switzerland.

Champex-Lac

1938 Champex-Lac

Tel 027 783 1114
e-mail info@le-belvedere.ch
website www.le-belvedere.ch

Nearby Orsieres (3 km); Martigny
(8 km); Gt St Bernard Pass (15 km);
Vevey (52 km); Lausanne (65 km);
Fribourg (85 km).
Location in woods at edge of lake-
side village; ample car parking
Food breakfast, lunch, dinner,
snacks
Price FF
Rooms 9; 5 double, 1 single, 3 fami-
ly, all with bath and shower; all
rooms have central heating, TV,
hairdryer, balcony
Facilities dining room, sitting
room, bar; terrace, garden
Credit cards MC, V
Children welcome
Disabled not suitable
Pets accepted
Closed mid-Nov to mid-Dec
Proprietors Favre family

Belvédère
Mountain inn

This inn is unashamedly informal and decidedly quirky. The sitting room has a lived-in look no decorator could hope to achieve, with books, binoculars and authentically-ageing peasant-style furnishings. Duck into the low-ceilinged bar, and smells of country cooking assault the nostrils at almost any time of day.

Local specialities and old Favre family recipes are served in the dining room and on the terrace, which both look out to the Grand-Combin massif. Fresh organic ingredients are used whenever possible – often picked straight from the garden next door.

The narrow upstairs corridors and ceilings are lined with a local red pine, much of which was replaced several years ago with disconcertingly fresh wood, albeit in the the traditional style. Many of the small-ish bedrooms have views from the Grand Combin down the valley to Orsieres. This inn has acquired a cult status among cultivated folk from Geneva, who ignore the small bathrooms, and enjoy what is a successful blend of kitsch and basic comforts.

It's just five minutes from the village centre and a quiet base for hikers wanting to avoid hotels filled with large walking groups on the Haute Route.

Crans-Montana

Chemin du Mont-blanc 1, Plans
Mayens, 3963 Crans-Montana

Tel 027 486 6060
e-mail info@lecrans.com
website www.lecrans.ch

Nearby Crans (1 km); Wildhorn
mountain (9 km); Martigny (38 km).
Location above the village of Crans,
5-min drive from center; car parking
Food breakfast, lunch, dinner,
snacks, room service
Price FFFFF
Rooms 13; 10 double; 3 suites, all
with shower and Jacuzzi; all rooms
have central heating, phone, TV,
CD/DVD player, minibar, safe, wi-fi
Facilities dining room, sitting
room, bar, TV room, Cigar Lounge;
terrace, garden; winter sports, hiking
and golf nearby
Credit cards AE, DC, MC, V
Children welcome
Disabled one suitable room
Pets accepted
Closed end April to early June, end
Oct to mid-Dec
Manager Paola Masciulli

LeCrans Hôtel & Spa
Mountain-resort hotel

Luxury is an understatement here. This ski-in, ski-out hotel has the biggest terrace and the best view in Crans-Montana, offering a retreat well away from the bustle of busy downtown Crans itself, crammed with Rolls Royces and Gucci shoppers. All rooms face south, enjoying a view of the Rhône Valley, described as one of the best anywhere in the Alps.

Downstairs, top French chef Pierre Crépaud prepares traditional French and Valais dishes in the hotel's restaurant, LeMontBlanc, where the circular fireplace is large enough to roast a VW 'Beatle' in, while flowers in huge copper pots hang from rafters. The food is classic yet light, the kind you can eat three times a day with relish and still not get fat. The wine-list features local Valais names such as Dôle and Fendaut, rounded out with superb Bordeaux and Burgundy vintages. For a special occasion, guests can sit at *Le table d'hôtes* and be served by the chefs.

After dining, relax in the cinema room or in the spa (free for guests), which has both indoor and outdoor swimming pools, a Jacuzzi, sauna, hammam and four infrared cabins. Outside, a basketball hoop awaits the energetic.

Zen Steckenstrasse 60, 3920
Zermatt

Tel 079 916 1372
e-mail info@chalet-zen.com
website www.chalet-zen.com

Nearby ski lift to Schwarzsee and
Klein Matterhorn (100 m); Zermatt
centre (800 m).
Location 2-minute walk from main
lift to mountains; 10-minute walk
from Zermatt centre
Food breakfast, afternoon tea, dinner
Prices FFF-FFFF
Rooms 4 double, all with bath or
shower; all rooms have satellite TV,
hairdryer, toys, books, games, 1 has
fireplace; 1 apartment in annexe
Facilities 2 sitting rooms with fire-
places, dining room, computer, bar,
massages, wi-fi; outdoor hot tub
Credit cards not accepted
Children welcome
Disabled lift/elevator
Pets small ones by arrangement
(extra charge)
Closed never
Manager Cassie Westbrooke

Chalet Zen
Chalet hotel and apartment

Discreet, even anonymous, set back
from the road up a flight of steps, this
British-owned chalet is a useful Zermatt
address for those who want something
private, perhaps exclusive, for a party of
family or friends. It has four smartly conventional, if not luxurious double bedrooms, all in excellent taste; bunk beds
sleeping two; three south facing with
Matterhorn views; a relaxing downstairs
sitting room with breakfast bar and fireplace; and, upstairs, another living/eating
area with a full view of the Matterhorn.

Run by a dedicated chalet manager,
housekeeper and cook (good food), it
offers all the comforts and convenience of
a small hotel, including a massage room,
while being essentially a private house. It's
at the southern end of town, a ten-minute
walk from the centre, and a highly conven-
ient two-minute walk from the bottom
station of the ski lift that serves the
Matterhorn Paradis and Schwarzee
Paradis ski areas.

Zen? It's not oriental, except for a statue of Buddha in the hall. The name arises
from the street address, and, coincidental-
ly, the owner's connections with Japan and
their interest in Asian art.

There is also an apartment in an annexe
for those who want the option to dine out
(self catering and B & B available).

Champex-Lac

1938 Champex-Lac

Tel 027 782 6151
e-mail info@hotelglacier.ch
website www.hotelglacier.ch
Food breakfast, lunch, dinner,
snacks
Price FF
Closed after Easter to mid-May,
Nov to mid-Dec
Proprietors Yves & Isabelle Biselx

Glacier
Lakeside hotel and apartments

This more than 100-years-old lakeside hotel is ideal for families. There are plenty of activities on offer, from tennis to fishing, and in winter, Alpine and cross-country skiing. Mountaineers have always been regulars, welcomed by four generations of the Biselx family. Bedrooms are comfortable, with a bath or shower, phone, TV and radio. Some have a lake view.

Less than 100 m from the hotel, at the foot of the ski slopes, are the Chalets du Lac: number 1 is an attic apartment; number 2 is a two-bedroom apartment on two floors. Both have sitting room, balcony, kitchen and ski locker. There are also five apartments sleeping up to five in the Sporting Residence. Half-board is available and guests can use all the hotel facilities.

Les Marécottes

Place de la Télécabine 9, 1923 Les
Marécottes

Tel 027 761 1666
e-mail info@mille-etoiles.ch
website www.mille-etoiles.ch
Food breakfast, dinner
Prices F-FF
Closed end Mar to mid-May, last
Sun in Oct to mid-Dec
Proprietors Berner-Mol family

Aux Mille Etoiles
Chalet hotel

Ingrid and Hansruedi Berner-Mol are the second generation to run this genuinely family-oriented hotel. Les Marécottes is a skiing and hiking resort in the Vallée du Trient, between Martigny and Chamonix. It's conventionally decorated, spacious and full of chalet atmosphere.

The main sitting room looks on to the indoor swimming pool, which opens out into the garden. The rustic-style restaurant has a mountain-view terrace. The bedrooms are decorated with natural woods, and junior suites have a balcony looking over the Trient valley. Family suites have a separate room for children, with bunk beds.

The ski slopes above the hotel are the only spot in Valais where the Matterhorn and Mont Blanc are visible at the same time.

Saas Fee

3906 Saas Fee

Tel 027 958 1000
e-mail hotel.allalin@saas-fee.ch
website www.allalin.ch
Food breakfast, lunch, dinner,
snacks
Prices FFF-FFFF
Closed May
Proprietors Eva & Sabrina
Zurbriggen

Allalin
Village resort hotel

This hotel has been owned and managed by the Zurbriggen family for four generations. It was first built in 1928, then demolished and rebuilt in a similar style in 1984. All 30 bedrooms have been recently refurbished into modern, bright and spacious rooms, with panoramic views from the private balconies. The four split-level suites are popular with families.

The candlelit Walliserkanne restaurant, with 350-year-old larch beams, is the domain of chef Yohan Brunon-Zurbriggen. His menus feature light meat and fish dishes, as well as vegetarian choices. Half-board guests are treated to a six-course dinner.

Local paintings, carvings and wood panelling blend with modern comforts, giving the public rooms character.

Saas Fee

Dorfstrasse 61, 3906 Saas-Fee

Tel 027 957 2676
e-mail info@zurmuehle-saas-fee.ch
website www.zurmuehle-saas-fee.ch
Food breakfast, lunch, dinner
Price FF
Closed mid-Apr to mid-Jun, end
Oct
Proprietors Ariette and Peter Welti

Zur Mühle
Restaurant with rooms

Ariette Welti's grandfather was one of Saas Fee's first mountain guides and her father won a gold medal in the 1948 Olympics. Now the Mühle is one of the most popular restaurants in town, known for its cheese and meat fondues. Guests eat in the wood-panelled dining room, then have a drink at the *après-ski* bar on the terrace, watching the sun set behind the pistes.

The three bedrooms look out over the slopes and glacier. Inside, decoration is traditional; outside, the large wooden face above the entrance and the stag skull hung with mistletoe on the terrace give a quirky edge to this popular hotel.

Zermatt

Riedstrasse 2, 3920 Zermatt

Tel 027 966 7600
e-mail hotel@julen.ch
website http://julen.ch
Food breakfast, lunch, dinner,
snacks
Prices FF-FFFFF (last-minute
offers available)
Closed never
Proprietors Julen family

Romantikhotel Julen
Mountain resort hotel

Since 1937 the Julen has been a fixture in this car-free village, famous for its winter sports, but equally attractive in summer for hiking, climbing and summer skiing. Paul-Marc Julen and his wife are the third generation to run the hotel, together with their parents, Paul and Daniela.

Rooms are spacious and comfortable, with a touch of luxury. Although many of the guests are international, it still has the feel of a family hotel. In winter, everyone still heads for the *Schäferstübli* (sheep room) restaurant, decorated in traditional Alpine style, with red and white, and wood panelling. It has always had a good reputation: the locally-reared lamb dishes, enjoyed with Valais wines, are a highlight.

Zermatt

3920 Zermatt

Tel 027 966 4400
e-mail info@schlosshotelzermatt.ch
website www.schlosshotelzermatt.ch
Food breakfast, lunch, dinner,
snacks
Prices FFF-FFFF
Closed mid-Oct to end Nov
Proprietors Alex and Pamela Perren

Schlosshotel
Mountain hotel and apartments

Not really a castle, the Schlosshotel is half 150-year-old wooden chalet, half new stonework; inside, 'eclectic' was the description of furnishings. The oldest part of the building is the barn-like restaurant, which looks like hundreds of other fondue and *Raclette* places all over Valais.

South-facing bedrooms have balconies with Matterhorn views. Bathrooms have Jacuzzis, and there is a first-rate spa with a sauna. All the bedrooms have recently been refurbished. Families will enjoy the two new apartments in the 2012 annexe; they have kitchens, but breakfast and all hotel facilities are included in the price.

Being in the middle of Zermatt, the hotel can't guarantee total silence. It is, however, right next to the Gornergratbahn.

Ronco

6622 Ronco sopra Ascona

Tel 091 791 5265
e-mail info@hotel-ronco.ch
website www.hotel-ronco.ch

Nearby Lake Maggiore (200 m);
Isole de Brissago (1.5 km); Ascona (4
km); Locarno (5 km); Milan (80 km);
walking; golf.
Location in heart of village, next to
church; ample car parking, some
covered garages
Food breakfast, lunch, dinner,
snacks
Prices FF-FFF
Rooms 20; 14 double, 2 single, 4
suites, all with bath or shower; all
rooms have phone, TV, radio, safe,
wi-fi
Facilities dining room, sitting room,
bar; terrace, garden, swimming pool
Credit cards AE, MC, V
Children welcome
Disabled not suitable
Pets not accepted in hotel (accepted
in restaurant)
Closed mid-Nov to mid-March
Proprietors Casparis family

Albergo Ronco
Village hotel

'Stunning views over Lake Maggiore'
was our reporter's comment on this
former hostel for the neighbouring convent. 'But you have to offer more than a
great view,' insists Guido Casparis, the
fourth generation of this family business.
His father, Willi, a former chef, is in charge
of the kitchen where Leo Piela and his
team prepare house specialities, including
home-made pasta, fresh fish from the Lago
Maggiore and local products such as goats
cheese from the Alpe di Ronco.

Ronco has always attracted artists and
writers: Paulette Goddard was a regular at
lunch, no doubt enjoying the cold *pesce in
carpione* (marinaded lake trout) followed
by *frutta gratinata* (berries with vanilla
sauce), which is still served in season. Our
reporter liked the combination of simplicity and style. While locals sip a beer or coffee at the bar, with tiled floors and wood-
en chairs, upstairs all is quiet. Some of the
bedrooms are modern while others (in
the original building) are traditionally decorated. 'Some guests have been coming
here for a month every summer for over
30 years,' says Guido. 'And we have newer
guests who stay regularly for a weekend at
a time.' Ronco is a great place to explore
the little villages, go walking or even drive
to Milan, as well as a wonderful place to
laze by the pool, taking in that view.

Porto Ronco, Ascona

Via Ronco 61, 6613 Porto Ronco

Tel 091 785 1144
e-mail hotel@la-rocca.ch
website www.la-rocca.ch

Nearby Lake Maggiore; Italian border (5 km); Ascona-Locarno (6 km).
Location hidden from view on twisting road between Ronco (Ronco sopra Ascona) and the lake
Food breakfast, lunch, dinner, snacks
Prices FFF-FFFFF
Rooms 19 double and suites, all with bath or shower; all rooms have phone, TV, radio, minibar, safe, lake view, balcony/terrace
Facilities dining room, sitting room, bar, sauna, gym, heated swimming pool, lift/elevator; terrace, garden, private jetty, free daily shuttlebus to Ascona; golf and riding nearby
Credit cards MC, V
Children welcome
Disabled not suitable
Pets accepted
Closed late Oct to mid-March
Manager Marcel Krähenmann

Boutique-Hotel La Rocca **Lakeside hotel**

Three decades ago this was just a *pensione* with a single shared bathroom. Now, thanks to the hands-on commitment of two generations of the Krähenmann family it's a wonderfully relaxing 19-bedroom lakeside retreat. The biggest asset is surely its view across Lake Maggiore, especially from the terrace where you can lunch or dine in good weather. The only other houses in sight are tiny dots on the far shore. The private jetty, for refreshing dips in the lake, is a bonus too, as is the traditional food, now much more sophisticated than at our last edition, with a mix of local, traditional and Mediterranean dishes.

The bedrooms, all different, and all with the lake view, are thoroughly comfortable, with impressive attention to detail. Service is personal and friendly – the Krähenmanns' aim is to soothe away stress. It would be a shame to just use this place as a stopover: much more worthy of a week's stay, or at least a long weekend.

Taverne

Via Bicentenario 16, 6807 Taverne-Lugano

Tel 091 945 2871
e-mail mottodelgallo@bluewin.ch
website www.mottodelgallo.ch

Nearby Lugano (6 km); Lake Lugano (7 km), Bellinzona (17 km).
Location south of the village of Taverne; ample car parking below hotel
Food breakfast, lunch, dinner
Price FFF
Rooms 4 suites, all with bath or shower; all rooms have fireplace
Facilities 2 dining rooms, sitting room, bar; terrace garden
Credit cards AE, DC, MC, V
Children welcome
Disabled not suitable
Pets accepted
Closed Jan; restaurant only, Sun lunch and dinner, Mon lunch
Proprietors Piero Tenca, Matteo Cereghini and Corrado Parolini

Ristorante Motto del Gallo **Restaurant with rooms**

As our reporter followed signs to this well-known restaurant, she wondered how there could be anything worthy of inclusion in the middle of an industrial zone wedged between the motorway and a main route through the valley. She changed her mind upon seeing the 500-year-old farmhouse on a hill above the road, camouflaged by an apple orchard and a large cherry tree dripping with ripe fruit. Wooden roof tiles cover the wine press and stone fireplace in the former granary, while water trickles from a fountain into a horsetrough. With potted geraniums and strawberry plants, she half expected a menu of rustic food. Instead, she discovered one of the region's most inventive kitchens, where chef Matteo Cereghini delights his guests with Mediterranean and local flavours.

Upstairs, memories of old Ticino are revived with floral-patterned bedspreads brightening the four bedrooms, which have white walls, dark, old beams and decorative wrought iron. 'Not the place for a week's holiday, but a delightful overnight after a gourmet dinner' was her judgement.

Locarno

Via Buetti 11, 6600 Locarno
Muralto

Tel 091 743 0212
e-mail info@piccolo-hotel.ch
website www.piccolo-hotel.ch
Food breakfast
Prices FF-FFF
Closed early Nov to mid-Mar
Proprietor Mario Regusci

Piccolo
Bed and breakfast

This turn-of-the-century villa is a find. Unusually elegant, the Piccolo is powder-blue and white outside and decorated in blues and pinks inside. More than half of the 21 bedrooms have balconies. Floral and butterfly prints cover the curtains; bathrooms are clean and modern.

Locarno centre, the train station and the lake are all less than a ten-minute walk away – guests highly recommend this bed-and-breakfast for those not wanting to rent a car. Recent visitors have said that the bathrooms need reburbishing, but that the owner gave a personal and kind welcome and staff were attentive and friendly.

Locarno at Orselina

Via Al Parco, 6644 Locarno-
Orselina

Tel 091 743 1877
e-mail info@mirafiori.ch
website www.hotelmirafiori.ch
Food breakfast, lunch, dinner,
snacks
Price FFF
Closed mid-Oct to mid-Mar
Proprietors Schmid family

Hotel Mirafiori
Holiday hotel

At first glance, the Mirafiori looks like many other hotels in the Ticino region. What makes it special, however, is the unaffected warmth of the welcome.

Rooms are named for local flora and fauna, but not all are in the main building. Some are in small annexes up the terraced hillside at the back. *Formica* (ant) is large, with a floor-to-ceiling window and its own covered terrace, while *Margherita* (daisy) is a little 'Hansel and Gretel' cottage, all on its own and a favourite with newlyweds. The garden, full of honeysuckle and beds of lilies, has the swimming pool.

Since 1952, the Schmid family has been in charge. Carlo Schmid is the chef and his cooking hits the spot: 'Excellent food here' an English guest tells us.

Lugano

Via Montalbano 5, 6900 Lugano

Tel 091 985 8855
e-mail info@leopoldohotel.com
website www.leopoldohotel.com
Food breakfast, lunch, dinner, snacks
Prices FFFFF
Closed never
Manager Reto Stöckenius

Villa Principe Leopoldo
Luxury villa

Above it all, literally and figuratively. This villa offers 'a prince's seclusion and a prince's view' of Lugano. A hotel only since 1986, the original building has been preserved, with parquet floors, heavy chandeliers and *trompe-l'oeil* paintings. The hillside under the terrace was dug away to build the bedrooms, which are decorated in blues and greens, reflecting the colours of the nearby lake and gardens.

The gourmet restaurant serves imaginative Italian dishes, as well as caviar and lobster, on the terrace in summer. For sporty types, there are two swimming pools and two tennis courts, as well as riding nearby. The Kiso spa offers tailor-made treatments. Luxury without overwhelming formality.

Lugano at Caslano

Via Valle 20, 6987 Caslano, Lugano

Tel 091 611 8211
e-mail info@albergo-gardenia.ch
website www.albergo-gardenia.ch
Food breakfast
Prices FFF-FFFF
Closed Jan, Feb
Manager Andreas Messmer

Albergo Gardenia
Old villa

The appeal of this 160-year-old summer villa is its sense of timeless seclusion, perhaps a throwback to the convent which once stood on the site. Old beams and exposed brickwork throughout contrast with contemporary furnishings.

In good weather, breakfast is served on the terrace in the garden, which is filled with subtropical plants. The villa doesn't have a restaurant, but there are some good restaurants nearby. Some guests drive over the Italian border (1 km away) for dinner.

In the main house, bedrooms are large, with chic Italian furniture. Rooms in the annexe are smaller but have private patios for sunbathing and direct access to the garden; swimming pool.

A fine chunk of the western end of the Alps lies in France, together with famous skiing resorts such as Val d'Isère and Les Trois Vallées. Skiing is a relatively recent development here: much accommodation is organized for big groups, and tends to be functional. We've tried hard to find recommendable places – with some great results.

Italy's share of the Alps is centred on the Aosta Valley in the west and further east on the Dolomites. It's underrated – the Val Tournanche leading up to Breuil-Cervinia, with its neighbouring valleys to the east, a major ski zone. The Dolomites are a beautiful landscape of isolated, rocky hunks separated by broad, pastoral valleys.

Germany's southernmost state of Bavaria has some fine, if low, Alpine terrain. The big Alpine centre here is Garmisch-Partenkirchen, where we have three recommendations. Others are in nearby resort villages such as Bayrischzell and Mayrhofen.

Below are some useful back-up places to try if our main selections are fully booked:

Italy

Auberge de la Maison
Mountain chalet, Entrèves
Tel 0165 869811
www.aubergemaison.it
Boutique hotel with wonderful view of Mont-Blanc.

Dolomiti Wellness
Mountain hotel, San Cassiano
Tel 0471 849470
www.hotelfanes.it
Converted farm with spa and 16thC to 17thC furnishings.

Farm Lüch da Pcëi
Mountain bed-and-breakfast, San Cassiano Tel 0471 849286 www.luchdapcei.it
Apartments and B&B rooms. Serves locally-sourced food.

Garnì Ciasa Roby
Mountain hotel, San Cassiano
Tel 0471 849525
www.ciasaroby.it
Alpine-style rooms close to shops. Large but cosy.

Eggwirt Mountain guesthouse, San Valburga d'Ultimo
Tel 0473 795319
www.eggwirt.it
Family-friendly 14thC inn with superb views; ski deals.

France

Le Cordonant
Mountain chalet, Cordon
Tel 0450 583456
www.lecordonant.fr
Cosy, family-run chalet (1,000 m); walking nearby.

Germany

Postgasthof Rote Wand
Village inn, Bayrischzell
Tel 0802 39050
www.gasthofrotewand.de
No-frills hiker's and skier's hotel with warm welcome.

Garmischer Hof Chalet hotel, Garmisch-Partenkirchen Tel 0882 19110
www.garmischer-hof.de
Ski-resort hotel with mixed reviews, but good views; spa.

Combloux

300 route de la Cry, 74920
Combloux (Haute-Savoie)

Tel 0450 586027
e-mail coin-savoyard@wanadoo.fr
website www.coin-savoyard.com

Nearby Chamonix (30 km); Mont
Blanc; Megève (6 km); Annecy (77
km).
Location in heart of village, N of
Megève; limited car parking
Food breakfast, lunch, dinner
Price €€
Rooms 14; 8 double and twin, 3
triples, 3 mezzanines, all with bath;
all rooms have phone, TV
Facilities dining room, bar, spa; gar-
den, swimming pool
Credit cards AE, MC, V
Children accepted
Disabled not suitable
Pets accepted
Closed mid-Apr to Jun, mid-Sep to
mid-Dec
Proprietors Colette and Philippe
Astay

Coin Savoyard
Mountain hotel

The affluent mountain resort of
Combloux is close to Chamonix but
much quieter, so you have the advantage of
the stunning surroundings without the
crowds. Although it is not right at the foot
of the slopes, there is a little *navette* which
arrives every 15 minutes in season to take
skiers there, so you don't have to walk
with aching limbs at the end of the day.

This is a truly welcoming place to stay.
The house used to be a farm, which
belonged to Colette's grandparents, then
her parents, who opened a few rooms to
guests, and now it is hers. With their
wood-clad walls and ceilings and wooden
furniture, the bedrooms are rustic without
being cloying. A few of them (Nos 3, 5 and
6) look out over the village church with its
pealing bells, and the mezzanine rooms are
perfect for families.

Recommended by Michelin, the food is
based on well-prepared ingredients that
come fresh from the market. Expect plenty of hearty fondues, all served in the
splendid wooden bar and restaurant,
though in summer you can have lunch
beside the swimming pool in the original
orchard. Altogether, an unpretentious,
rewarding find.

Hauteluce

73620 Hauteluce

Tel 04 79 38 18 18
e-mail informations@lafermedu-
chozal.com **website** www.lafermedu-
chozal.com

Nearby St James of Assyria Church;
Albertville (25 km); Megève (30 km).
Location in the heart of Beaufortain
valley
Food breakfast, lunch, dinner
Prices €€-€€€
Rooms 11; 4 double, 2 triple, 4 fam-
ily, 1 suite, all with bath or shower;
all rooms have TV, DVD player,
hairdryer, safe, suite has sitting
room, balcony
Facilities sauna, Jacuzzi, hammam,
massage; terrace, outdoor heated
swimming pool
Credit cards MC, V
Children welcome, cribs available
Disabled one specially adapted
room, lift/elevator to restaurant
Pets accepted (€12 per day)
Closed mid-Apr to early Jun, end
Sep to Dec
Proprietors Anne-Christine and
Frédéric Boulanger

La Ferme du Chozal
Guesthouse

La Ferme du Chozal is a renovated farmhouse with superb facilities and owners
who wish to make your stay in the Alps
special. Refreshingly, Anne-Christine and
Frederic do not simply rely on their prime
position amongst the mountains and ski
slopes to attract or entertain their visitors: service is excellent, too. The staff are
immensely welcoming and eager to cater
to guests' needs. They have been known to
scour resorts for spare cribs, and to pick
up stranded guests who have missed their
last bus. It's well worth knowing that the
house often has a range of discounts.

The rooms are all different and furnished with great attention to detail. The
owners have made imaginative use of a
tiny, low-ceilinged suite in the rafters, turning it into a miniature, tent-like children's-
only room. One guest found the restaurant a 'little gem'; it serves delicious dishes
as well as an excellent selection of wines
from across the Alps. Outside, a heated
pool and a Jacuzzi overlook Mont Blanc,
whilst the living room features a roaring,
open log fire.

Bikes and helmets are free, and there's a
large choice of ski routes. After being bat-
tered on the slopes, guests can book spa
treatments and massages. A real find – one
visitor said, 'this hotel is so good I almost
don't want to tell anyone about it'.

Manigod

Route du Col de la Croix-Fry, 74230
Manigod

Tel 0450 449016
e-mail
contact@hotelchaletcroixfry.com
website
www.hotelchaletcroixfry.com

Nearby Vallée de Manigod; Thônes
(10 km); Annecy (26 km).
Location down the col, 5 km NE of
Manigod, on D16, 6 km S of La
Clusaz; car parking
Food breakfast, lunch, dinner
Price €€€
Rooms 9; 2 double, 7 suites, all with
bath (suites with Jacuzzi bath); all
rooms have phone, TV, terrace or
balcony; rooms in annexe have kitch-
enette
Facilities sitting room, bar, spa; ter-
race, garden, swimming pool
Credit cards AE, MC, V
Children accepted
Disabled no special facilities
Pets accepted
Closed mid-Apr to mid-Jun, mid-
Sep to mid-Dec
Proprietors Guelpa-Veyrat family

Châlet Hôtel de la Croix-Fry **Chalet hotel**

'Absolutely gorgeous' was the verdict of one of our reporters, and our most recent visit confirms the star rating of this wooden mountain chalet at the highest point of an Alpine col, with a ter-race overflowing with flowers. Run with great pride, now by the fourth generation of Veyrats – the chalet was once shared in the summer by the family and their cows – the hotel is cosy and welcoming. A wood fire burns on cool evenings and the sofas and armchairs gathered around the hearth are covered in sheepskin. The bedrooms are attractively rustic – even in the mod-ern annexe-chalets, which provide adapt-able family accommodation with kitch-enettes. But what really impresses us is the evident pride of the family and their end-less efforts to maximize a guest's stay.

The restaurant, serving nourishing mountain food, has spectacular views of peaks and valleys. The *tarte aux myrtilles* from the kitchen can compete with even the best culinary celebrities' dishes. In summer the Veyrats invite their guests to picnic in the pastures with their cows and to swim in the pool; in winter the invita-tion is to ski.

Megève

Photo credit: Au Coin du Feu / F. Ducout, B. Ohayon, C. Arnal & DR

Route du Téléphérique de
Rochebrune, 74120 Megève (Haute-
Savoie)

Tel 0450 210494
e-mail contact@coindufeu.com
website www.coindufeu.com
Food breakfast, lunch, dinner
Price €€
Closed May to Nov
Proprietors Jocelyne and Jean-
Louis Sibuet

Le Coin du Feu
Chalet hotel

It's difficult to know which of the Sibuets'
Megève hotels to highlight, but our
reporter picked out this one, the 'most
authentic'. You could also stay at Les Fermes
de Marie (tel 04 50 93 03 10), Le Mont Blanc
(tel 04 50 21 20 02) or Le Lodge Park (tel
04 50 93 05 03) and experience the same
exclusive sense of rustic sophistication.

Le Coin du Feu has all the right ingredients for a fantasy about living in the mountains: masses of old wood, pretty fabrics,
soft lighting, snug, duvet-covered beds hidden in alcoves behind curtains (as was the
tradition in these chalets), afternoon tea in
front of a crackling fire, friendly, efficient
service, and good honest food served in
the traditional restaurant. A slick interpretation of Alpine charm for the smart set.

St-Gervais

520 route des Communailles, Le
Bettex, 74170 St-Gervais (Haute-
Savoie)

Tel 0450 931185
e-mail chalet.remy@wanadoo.fr
website www.chalet-remy.com
Food breakfast, lunch, dinner
Price €
Closed early Nov to late Dec
Proprietor Mme Micheline Didier

Châlet Remy
Chalet hotel

In sharp contrast to the glossy chalet
hotels of nearby Megève, this chalet is as
simple – and as genuine – as you could hope
to find, with all the associated charm. With
breathtaking views across to Mont Blanc, it's
a traditional stone and log 18thC farmhouse which retains its original woodwork.

Inside, a central staircase leads to a rec-
tangular gallery with bedrooms off it.
These, all wood, are tiny and very simple
but warm, with comfortable beds, and
communal bathrooms. Traditional, satisfying
dishes are served in a candlelit dining
room, and there's a fine terrace with views
overlooking the garden and mountains.

A shuttle bus connects the chalet with
nearby ski lifts, and at the end of the day
you can ski back to the garden.

Barbiano

Trechiese 12, 39040 Barbiano,
Bolzano

Tel 04716 50055
e-mail info@baddreikirchen.it
website www.baddreikirchen.it

Nearby Val Gardena (10 km);
Bressanone (17 km).
Location 21 km NE of Bolzano, exit
from Brennero Autostrada at Chiusa,
head S through Barbiano (6 km);
hotel car park on right (call and the
hotel will send a jeep to collect you
from car park)
Food breakfast, lunch, dinner
Prices €€-€€€
Rooms 26; 16 double and twin, 2
family, 8 single, all with bath or
shower; 1 maisonette
Facilities sitting rooms, library,
games room, restaurant, bar, garden,
terraces, swimming pool, table tennis
Credit cards MC, V
Children
Disabled access difficult
Pets accepted
Closed Nov to May
Proprietors Wodenegg family

Bad Dreikirchen
Mountain hotel

The name of this idyllically situated
hotel, a 14thC chalet owned by the
Wodenegg family for 200 years, derives
from its vicinity to three small churches
which date back to the Middle Ages. The
fact that you can only reach the hotel by
four-wheel-drive taxi also makes for the
perfect escape.

The large old building, with its shingled
roof and dark wood balconies, has wonderful views and is surrounded by meadows, woods, mountains and quantities of
fresh air. There's plenty of space for guests,
both inside and out, and the atmosphere is
comfortably rustic with an abundance of
aromatic pine panelling and carved furniture. A cosy library provides a quiet corner for reading, and simple but satisfying
meals are served in the pleasant dining
room or on the adjacent veranda, from
which the views are superb. The hotel has
had a facelift recently, making it more contemporary, but bedrooms in the original
part of the house are unchanged and still
charming, wood-panelled throughout.

To sum up, the words of a guest in 1908
are still appropriate: 'I stayed for some
days…the weather was continually fine,
the position magnificent, and the food
good.' Recent guests warmly agree: 'I fell in
love with the place. Delightfully relaxed
atmosphere, charming young owners.'

Via Gorret 18, 11021 Breuil-
Cervinia

Tel 01669 49133
e-mail info@hotelgorret.it
website www.hotelgorret.it

Nearby ski lift (50 m); Matterhorn
(400 m); Aosta (50 km).
Location in Cervinia centre, near
pedestrian area; car parking
Food breakfast, half-board arrange-
ment with local restaurants
Price €
Rooms 13; 12 double, 1 suite, all
with bath or shower; all rooms have
phone, satellite TV, hairdryer, safe,
some have balcony, suites have dou-
ble bath
Facilities breakfast/sitting room,
owners can arrange winter sports
equipment rental, ski passes etc
Credit cards not accepted
Children accepted
Disabled not suitable
Pets not accepted
Closed May, Oct
Proprietors Herin family

Hotel Meublé Gorret
Town guesthouse

A guesthouse run hands-on by the Herin family, in the centre of Breuil-Cervinia (a few steps from the Cretaz lift), recommended by a knowledgeable local. It's a low-price alternative to our other (luxurious) recommendations in the resort. In summer you can stay in a simple room here for just 50 euros.

Downstairs there's just a breakfast/sitting room. Upstairs there are chalet style bedrooms at three price levels. The cheaper ones are not spacious, but neither are they cramped, and all are charming, homely and fresh – everything was renovated in 2008. The Gorret doesn't serve food in the evening, but has half-board arrangements with restaurants nearby – you pay a tidy rate for room, breakfast and dinner and only have to take care of lunch.

The Herin family named their house after Abbot Gorret, who, with local guides Carrel, Bich and Meynet, played a part in the first ascent of Monte Cervino (the Matterhorn) in 1865. Gorret was an early Alpinist and writer who observed 'the mountain provides a lonely rest to the minds exhausted by social life and improves the discouraged citizens by contemplation of the nature, sublime work of God' (rough but charming translation provided by the Herins). His spirit still characterizes what they do here.

Stadel Soussun
Mountain hamlet

Località Soussun, 11020 Champoluc

Tel 03486 527 222
e-mail info@stadelsoussun.com
website www.stadelsoussun.com

Nearby Champoluc (2 km); Stafal Tschaval (5 km); Matterhorn (10 km); Estoul (10 km).
Location up mountain from Champoluc
Food breakfast, lunch (book in advance), dinner
Price €€€ (discounts for longer stays or large groups)
Rooms 6 double, all with shower; all rooms have TV, hairdryer, wi-fi
Facilities sitting room, dining room; free transfer to piste, 180 km of skiing in Monte Rosa skiing area (Champoluc and two adjacent valleys)
Credit cards AE, DC, MC, V
Children accepted
Disabled accessible
Pets accepted
Closed Easter to Jun, mid-Sep to early Dec
Proprietor Sergio Fosson

A terrific new find. Many places claim to be mountain hideaways but this really is. You can drive here from Champoluc up very bumpy tracks in summer, but in winter not. When the snow comes, you approach by bubble chair from Champoluc and owner Sergio fetches you on a Sno-Cat. Fifteen minutes later you're in a medieval farming hamlet, perched on a little plateau half way up a mountain.

It's a magical place, restored with skill and imagination. Sergio's grandfather was the last working farmer here, but the settlement dates from the 1400s. At ground-floor level, the cavernous stone-walled eating/drinking area smells of woodsmoke and is charmingly Alpine. Food is homely and superb — we ate the best Alpine cold meat platter in memory, which included delicious honey-coated cooked chestnuts.

Upstairs, the tiny reception area leads to a homely sitting room for guests, with narrow, horizontal windows looking out on to the wonderful scenery. On the top floor, the bedrooms were restored in 2010 using all natural materials. They're snug, unshowy and charming. The service here is complete. Climbing, walking, skiing (and, indeed, heli-skiing)? Sergio arranges it all.

There's more. Rising above this haven is the famous row of taller-than-4,000 m peaks along the Swiss/Italian border.

Champoluc

Via Croues 5, 11020 Champoluc,
Monte Rosa, Aosta

Tel 01253 07128
e-mail hotelannamaria@tiscali.it
website
www.hotelvillaannamaria.com

Nearby Verrès (27 km);
Valtournenche and Gressoney
valleys.
Location off lane to right at end of
village, signposted to hotel; car
parking 50 m away
Food breakfast, lunch, dinner
Price €€ (half board only in high
season)
Rooms 13 double and twin and
family, all with bath or shower; all
rooms have phone, TV, hairdryer
Facilities sitting room, dining room,
terrace, hot tub, garden
Credit cards MC, V
Disabled access difficult
Children
Pets accepted
Closed never
Proprietors Origone family

Villa Anna Maria
Mountain chalet

In a quiet wooded hillside setting close to
the village of Champoluc, the main community in a steep-sided valley beneath the
mighty Monte Rosa, this traditional shuttered chalet is as charming in summer, surrounded by mountain flowers, as it is deep
in winter snow. Its charm lies in the fact
that hardly anything seems to have changed
since the house was built in 1940. In the
rustic dining room, for example, polished
wood covers the floor, ceiling and walls,
red-and-white gingham curtains frame the
windows and bright copper pots gleam
from shelves. Guests sit at tables with crisp
white cloths, and are served simple but
delicious country fare including *fonduta*
with *fontina*, the local cheese fondue.

The cosy bedrooms also have panelled
walls and, whether they look up at the
mountain or down the valley, benefit from
utter peace and quiet, spared from traffic
noise as cars are not allowed up to the
hotel. Guests must park in the private car
park 50 metres or so down the hill, and
then walk up to the chalet through romantic pine woods, while kind staff collect
their luggage. The owners, the Origone
family, extend a warm welcome.

Valnontey, 11012 Cogne, Aosta Valley

Tel 01657 49177
e-mail labarme@tiscali.it
website www.hotellabarme.com

Nearby Cogne (3 km); Aosta (30 km); Turin (135 km).
Location in the heart of Gran Paradiso National Park; garage
Food breakfast, lunch, dinner
Price €€
Rooms 15, all with bathroom, TV and telephone
Facilities sauna, Jacuzzi, massages, ski/mtb rental
Credit cards MC, V
Disabled 2 suitable rooms
Children accepted
Pets by arrangement
Closed Oct to Nov
Manager Stefano Herren

La Barme
Country hotel

La Barme is the only hotel in the village of Valnontey to stay open year round – something of a feat when in winter months you can hardly see it for all the snow, and proof, perhaps, of the hard-working attitude of the Herren family. This former dairy, converted into a hotel by Mr Herren and now run by his sons, is a small, family set up, with 15 bedrooms.

Valnontey lies at the foot of the *Parco Nazionale del Gran Paradiso*, Italy's foremost adventure playground. You won't find luxury here, but, in such a rugged and remote location we think that simplicity strikes a happier note. While the owners will do everything in their power to make your stay comfortable some may find it, well, simple. That said, La Barme's charm is its lack of sophistication. Whitewashed walls and pale pine furniture in the main rooms give the place a simple, Alpine feel. The bright red stove in the breakfast room is one of only a few hints of colour in the main rooms, but none feel remotely drab. Bedrooms are clean, all have a fresh feel, though none are particularly individual.

Mountain photos cover the walls (as if the stunning views from each room weren't enough) making you keen to rent one of the hotel's mountain bikes or a pair of cross country skis and venture out into the great outdoors.

Cortina d'Ampezzo

Via XXIX Maggio 28, 32043
Cortina d'Ampezzo, Belluno

Tel 04368 67344
e-mail info@hotelambracortina.it
website www.hotelambracortina.it

Nearby Corso Italia (150 m);
Faloria cableway (200 m).
Location follow bypass toward
Cortina, after passing former railway
bridge twice, turn immediately left;
car parking
Food breakfast, snacks
Prices €€-€€€€€
Rooms 25; 20 double and single, 5
suites, all with bath; all rooms have
phone, satellite TV, minibar, safe,
wi-fi, some have balcony
Facilities breakfast room, sitting
area, bar; terrace
Credit cards AE, DC, MC, V
Children accepted
Disabled not suitable
Pets not accepted
Closed never
Proprietors Elisabetta Dotto

Ambra
Town bed-and-breakfast

We want to raise the profile of
Cortina and the surrounding area
of the Dolomites, so we have increased
our number of recommendations in and
near the town. Alongside Menardi (page
240) and the Poste (page 241), this is our
other favourite within the town, but for
different reasons – all are great places, only
separated by the fact that they will suit different types of customer.

The Ambra is about small-scale, intimate
charm. It has 25 bedrooms, so can make
you feel very much at home. We noticed
the beautiful flooring, the quotes from Latin
literature on the walls, the pretty, homely
bedrooms, and the attention paid to the
corridors. The new luxury rooms on the
top floor are beautiful and there is a great
loft room, which can house a party of four.
Ambra describes itself as a superior B & B,
but it's more like a small town hotel with
a breakfast room and no dining room. Staff
look after your every need: cocktails at all
hours, winter ski desk, restaurant bookings, information on events in town, and
more. Owner Elisabetta Dotto is obviously a talented hotelier. She has another place
to stay in town, the Panda, with rooms and
two apartments, in the same homely, well
designed, unshowy style and the same fair
prices as Ambra.

Cortina d'Ampezzo

Via Ospitale 1, 32043 Cortina d'Ampezzo

Tel 0436 4585
e-mail info@ristoranteospitale.it
website www.ristoranteospitale.com

Nearby Cortina (12 km).
Location from Cortina center, take SS51 Alemagna road towards Dobbiaco; car parking on site
Food breakfast, dinner
Price €€
Rooms 7 double, twin, triple and quadruple, all with bath or shower; all rooms have satellite TV, safe, internet
Facilities breakfast room, dining rooms, bar; winter and summer sports nearby
Credit cards DC, MC, V
Children accepted
Disabled 1 accessible room
Pets small ones accepted
Closed May
Managers Alverà family

Rifugio Ospitale
Restaurant-with-rooms

Our idea of a perfect restaurant with rooms. True to formula, there is no sitting room; instead, several dining areas, some bistro style, some more formal. A table in a big central area seats up to 20 – singles can slot in here too. The atmosphere is lively and informal and the food is unpretentious, honest and delicious – we ate thick onion soup and green *Spätzle*.

The Ospitale is a venerable local institution, for more than 600 years a stopover on the pilgrim route from the north to Rome. Its new incarnation, after hefty investment in 2012, has done it more than justice. The solid old building has a tasteful green and off-white exterior and copper rainwater gullies. Upstairs, corridors are light, with beautiful timberwork.

You're in among the mountains here, a contrast to the bustle of Cortina (15 minutes' drive) For skiing, we'd seriously consider staying here rather than in town. You can ski cross-country along a disused railway track into Cortina or north towards southern Tyrol. In summer it's ideal for stepping straight out on to endless walks and mountain biking, all well maintained and signposted – the Cortina area is fabulous and sadly overlooked by northern Europeans. It's on a road, which sometimes gets busy, but noise is within reason.

Fié allo Sciliar

Piazza della Chiesa 9, 39050 Fié allo
Sciliar, Bolzano

Tel 0471 725014
e-mail info@hotelturm.it
website www.hotelturm.it

Nearby Castelrotto (10 km); Val
Gardena; Bolzano (16 km).
Location in village, 16 km E of
Bolzano; with garden and
limited car parking
Food breakfast, lunch, dinner; room
service
Prices €€€-€€€€
Rooms 35 double and suites, all with
bath or shower; all rooms have
phone, TV, minibar, safe, hairdryer
Facilities sitting room, dining
rooms, bar, lift, garden, spa and
beauty area, swimming pool, garage
Credit cards MC, V
Disabled access possible
Children accepted
Pets accepted
Closed Nov to mid-Dec
Proprietors Pramstrahler family

Romantik Hotel Turm
Mountain village hotel

A solid former courthouse dating from
the 12th century, with views across
pastures and mountains, Romantik Hotel
Turm offers typical Tyrolean hospitality
with style and warmth. Now run by dash-
ing Stefan Pramstrahler, who is also the talented chef, the hotel has gained a hip edge
in the last couple of years, as well as a
wonderful new 'wellness' suite and a new
wing housing 14 luxurious rooms.

Bedrooms are all different and vary
considerably in size, but even the smallest
has everything you could want for a comfortable stay, including traditional furniture
and somewhere cosy to sit. The suites are
excellent value: one, in a little stone tower,
is decorated as a wood-panelled *Stube*,
with spiral staircase to a double room and
a children's room. The Pramstrahlers' fine
collection of contemporary art is displayed everywhere, including the new
bar/sitting room (with gorgeous sunny terrace) and spills out along the whitewashed
corridor walls.

The main dining room is light and spacious, with low wood ceiling and windows
overlooking the valley; or you can dine in
a romantic little room at the base of the
11thC tower. Either way, the elegant local
food is superb.

Merano

Via Fragsburg 3, 39012 Merano, Bolzano

Tel 0473 244071
e-mail info@fragsburg.com
website www.fragsburg.com

Nearby Schloss Rametz (4 km); Passirio valley; Dolomites.
Location 6 km SE of Merano, in own gardens with ample parking
Food breakfast, lunch, dinner
Prices € –€€€
Rooms 20; 6 double and twin, 12 suites, 2 single, all with bath; all rooms have phone, TV, safe, hairdryer
Facilities sitting rooms, library, smoking room, dining rooms, lift, sauna, wellness spa, terrace, garden, swimming pool
Credit cards MC, V
Children accepted
Disabled one specially adapted room
Pets accepted
Closed Nov to Easter
Proprietors Ortner family

Castel Fragsburg
Converted hunting lodge

A lovely drive along a narrow country lane, through mixed woodland and past Alpine pastures, brings you to the east of Merano where Castel Fragsburg – 300 years old and a hotel for more than 100 years – commands splendid views of the Texel massif.

Externally, Fragsburg still looks very much the hunting lodge, with carved wooden shutters and balconies. A terrace along the front of the house, covered with wistaria, is a wonderful place to eat or drink: you seem to be suspended over the mountainside. The adjoining dining room can be opened up in warm weather, and the food – a seven course dinner prepared by the Michelin-starred chef – is 'superb', says local editor Nicky Swallow, and served in a 'gorgeous dining room with great service'. In cooler weather you can choose from various Tyrolean-style sitting rooms and a congenial little library. Bathrooms are modern and spotless and bedrooms all have balconies, carved pine furniture and colourful country fabrics. A wellness centre has now been added to the sauna.

The wooded gardens provide plenty of space for lazing – as well as a wooden shelter reserved for all-over suntanning. The pool has a stunning view over the valley. Delightful owners.

Ortisei

Bulla, 39046 Ortisei, Bolzano

Tel 0471 797335
e-mail info@uhrerhof.com
website www.uhrerhof.com

Nearby Castelrotto (13 km);
Bolzano (26 km); Val Gardena.
Location in mountainside hamlet,
13 km E of Castelrotto, off
Castelrotto-Ortisei road; garage
parking
Food breakfast, dinner
Price €€€
Rooms 14; 10 double, 4 suites; all
rooms have phone, TV, safe,
hairdryer, some have balcony
Facilities sitting room, dining room,
bar, lift/elevator; garden, health
centre
Credit cards MC, V
Children accepted
Disabled suitable
Pets not accepted
Closed early Apr to early May, 10
days Oct
Proprietors Zemmer family

Uhrerhof Deur
Mountain chalet

The name means 'House of the Clocks', and their ticking and chiming, along with birdsong, are very often the only sounds which break the silence at this traditional chalet set in a tucked-away hamlet 1,600 metres above sea level. Indeed, noise levels hardly rise above a whisper, and Signora Zemmer is at pains to point out that this is a place only for those seeking total peace and quiet. Outside, there is a grassy garden from which to enjoy the wide and wonderful view and a huge rose garden which boasts 200 varieties of rose within its 6,000 plants.

Inside, all the rooms, including the balconied bedrooms, are bright, simple and beautifully kept, with plenty of homely details. The core of the chalet is 400 years old, and includes the all-wood *Stube* with working stove. The three adjoining dining rooms have wooden benches round the walls, Tyrolean fabrics for curtains and cushions, bright rugs on terracotta floors and pewter plates displayed in wall racks. Signor Zemmer is the chef, and his simple yet delicious food is elegantly presented on pewter plates.

Underneath the house is a surprisingly smart health complex, with huge picture windows so that you can relax in the open-plan Turkish bath and soak up the view. The hotel is strictly non-smoking.

38057 Pergine, Valsugana, Trento

Tel 0461 531158
e-mail verena@castelpergine.it
website www.castelpergine.it

Nearby Lake Caldonazzo (3 km); Trento (11 km); Segonzano (13 km).
Location off the SS47 Padua road, 2 km SE of Pergine; in own grounds with ample car parking
Food breakfast, dinner
Prices €-€€
Rooms 20; 13 double and twin, 11 with shower, 4 single, 3 with shower, 3 triple, 3 with shower; all rooms have phone
Facilities sitting room, dining rooms, bar; garden
Credit cards MC, V
Children accepted
Disabled access difficult
Pets accepted
Closed Nov to Easter
Proprietors Verena Neff and Theo Schneider

Castel Pergine
Converted castle

This medieval hilltop fortress is managed with enthusiasm by an energetic and cultured Swiss couple, Verena and Theo. Past and present coexist happily in a rather alternative atmosphere, and the castle has a truly lived-in feel despite its grand dimensions and impressive history. A recent visit confirmed that this is one of the most affordable and distinctive hotels in the region. Though it must be said that it's an aquired taste: one reader comments on the 'daunting approach, strange modern art, refectory-style dining room and Spartan comfort'.

The route from the car park to the hotel leads you under stone arches, up age-worn steps and through vaulted chambers to the airy, round reception hall where breakfast is also served. The two spacious dining rooms have wonderful views, and the cooking is light and innovative. As you would expect from their price, bedrooms are by no means luxurious, and some are very small, but all are furnished in simple good taste; the best have splendid, heavy, carved wooden furniture and wall panelling.

One of the most enchanting features of the castle is the walled garden. Spend an hour reading a book, or simply watching the mountains through the crumbling ramparts, and you may never want to leave.

Pieve d'Alpago

Via Dolada 21, Plois, 32010 Pieve
d'Alpago, Belluno

Tel 0437 479141
e-mail info@dolada.it
website www.dolada.it

Nearby Nevegàl ski area (18 km);
Belluno (20 km).
Location in the hamlet of Plois,
signposted from Pieve d'Alpago;
ample parking
Food breakfast, lunch, dinner
Price €
Rooms 7 double and twin, all with
shower; all rooms have phone, TV
Facilities restaurant; terrace,
garden, cooking courses
Credit cards AE, DC, MC, V
Disabled no special facilities
Children accepted
Pets accepted
Closed never
Proprietors De Prà family

Dolada
Country restaurant-with-rooms

A twisting road leads from the Alpago valley to Pieve, and then corkscrews on up to the little hamlet of Plois. Albergo Dolada turns out to be a handsome building with faded apricot walls and green-shuttered windows with a little garden which looks out over snow-capped mountains and the Santa Croce lake and valley far below (there are wonderful walks straight from the door).

Built in 1923, Dolada has been owned and run as an inn by four generations of the De Prà family. The much vaunted kitchen (one Michelin star, with another in the offing) is overseen by Enzo De Prà, aided by his son Riccardo, while his wife Rossana, a professional *sommelier,* and daughter Benedetta are a cheeful and friendly presence front of house. 'The food' our reporter comments, 'was divine, and the welcome could not have been more friendly'. You can try cooking something divine yourself with a day-long cooking course followed by food tasting and an overnight stay.

The modern bedrooms are named for their colour schemes; the pink one can come as a bit of a shock the morning after an evening of serious over-indulgence in the elegant restaurant, but a long walk in the hills, with wonderful views all around, should sort things out.

San Cassiano

Piz Sorega 15, 39030 San Cassiano

Tel 0471 840138/337 457242
website www.lasvegasonline.it

Nearby Dolomites; pistes.
Location private car parking
Prices €€ €€€€ (half board)
Food breakfast, dinner, snacks
Rooms 6 double, twin and single, all
with bath; all rooms have phone,
Satellite TV, heating, safe, hairdryer,
balcony
Facilities restaurant, sauna on
solarium terrace, shuttle from car
park to lodge, children's play area,
table tennis, table football, toboggan
Credit cards MC, V
Children accepted
Disabled no adapted rooms
Pets not accepted
Closed never
Proprietor Ulli Crazzolara

Las Vegas Lodge
Mountain lodge

Don't let the garish name put you off; Las Vegas Lodge is well away from the bright lights, although it can get quite lively during ski season. Ulli Crazzolara bought this traditional mountain refuge in 2004 and subsequently added a contemporary new wing, making a comfortable, stylish yet relaxed little retreat that fits beautifully into its Alpine surroundings.

Situated at 2,040 metres above sea level at the top of the Piz Sorega ski lift deep in the Alta Badia area of the Dolomites, the lodge is set on a plateau surrounded by jagged mountain peaks. The original building houses a large bar and restaurant (a popular lunch stop for skiers and walkers) while the six spacious bedrooms are in the new part. They are contemporary, done out in blond wood, and have open plan bathrooms, some with tubs overlooking the peaks through French windows.

Delicious meals are served in the resident's dining room where floor-to-ceiling windows make the most of matchless views. Since winter 2012 the hotel has offered 'breakfast on the peak' – guests are taken up the mountain where breakfast is served just before sunrise, then they ski back to the hotel. Wonderful walking and superb skiing are on the doorstep: it's in the middle of the Dolomite Superski area with 1,200 km of interlinked pistes.

San Osvaldo

San Osvaldo 19, 39040 Seis am Schlern, Bolzano

Tel 0471 706013
e-mail info@tschoetscherhof.com
website www.tschoetscherhof.com

Nearby Castelrotto (5 km); Bolzano (17 km); Sciliar Natural Park (10 km).
Location in hamlet, 5 km W of Castelrotto; with parking
Food breakfast, lunch, dinner
Price € (10% extra for stays less than 3 days)
Rooms 8 double, twin and single, all with shower; 2 apartments for up to 4; both have living room, kitchen
Facilities dining rooms, terrace
Credit cards MC, V
Children accepted
Disabled access difficult
Pets accepted
Closed Dec to Mar
Proprietors Jaider family

Gasthof Tschötscherhof
Country guesthouse & apartments

Don't be put off by the unpronounceable name; for lovers of simple, farmhouse accommodation in an unspoiled rural setting, this hostelry could be ideal.

The narrow road from Siusi winds through apple orchards, vineyards and open meadows, eventually arriving at the tiny hamlet of San Osvaldo and this typical 500-year-old farmhouse with its adjacent dark wood barn. The name, painted on the outside of the building, is almost hidden by the clambering vines, and the old wooden balconies are a colourful riot of cascading geraniums. The sun-drenched terrace is a perfect spot for relaxing, as well as for eating.

Inside, we were beguiled by smells from the kitchen at the end of the hall, and were drawn to the warmth of the low-ceilinged old *Stube* with gently ticking clock, rough wood floor and simple white ceramic stove.

A rustic stone stairway leads up to the modest but tidy bedrooms, some of which have balconies. They have no frills, but after a long day in glorious countryside, we were too tired to notice.

Two apartments for two to four people were added in 2008. They are fairly compact, but are available in winter when the hotel and restaurant are closed.

Santa Cristina

Chemun str. 43, Santa Cristina,
39047 Val Gardena

Tel 0471 793215
e-mail info@uridl.it
website www.uridl.it

Nearby Bolzano airport (40 km);
Innsbruck airport (120 km); ski
slopes.
Location in the village of Santa
Cristina, overlooking the slopes
Food breakfast, dinner
Price €€
Rooms 13, all with bath or shower;
all rooms have phone, satellite TV,
radio, hairdryer, safe, some have bal-
cony or private garden
Facilities 2 restaurants (*Stube* for
full-board guests only); garden, hik-
ing, walking, mountain biking, rock
climbing, cooking courses
Credit cards MC, V
Children welcome
Disabled restaurant accessible
Pets not accepted
Closed Apr to May; Oct to Nov
Proprietors Demetz family

Charme Hotel Uridl
Mountain guesthouse

This 'Charme' hotel is certainly charming. It has been passed down from generation to generation of the Demetz family. They are a close-knit bunch, and treat
their guests as though they are part of the
family too.

Built in the 18thC, Uridl is one of the
oldest hotels in the Val Gardena. Its main
feature is a Tyrolean *Stube* with beamed
ceiling, wooden walls and a 19thC wood-
burning stove that still works. Old Italian
president Sandro Pertini once ate there, as
did many Austrian officers during the
building of the Val Gardena railway.

Bedrooms vary. Some are ultra-modern
and relatively minimalist, while in others
some older features remain; all are furnished with pine. Character abounds, with
pretty modern sculptures dotted around
the private garden.

Breakfast is a buffet of cold meats,
cheese, cereals, fruit, yoghurt and boiled
eggs. Dinner is heartier, consisting of several courses – steak, venison and rabbit are
staple mains. It's just as well that the hotel
is a member of Val Gardena Active! – guests
get free access to a host of excursions. For
some, the guided hikes, mountain biking,
nordic walking and rock climbing are what
keeps them returning to Hotel Uridl. For
others, it's the cookery courses and sunrise walks with breakfast at an Alpine hut.

Case Sparse 21, Le Clotes, 10050
Sauze d'Oulx, Torino

Tel 0122 850273
e-mail info@chaletilcapricorno.it
website www.chaletilcapricorno.it

Nearby Susa (28 km); Briançon,
France (28 km).
Location above and 2 km E of town
on Via Lattea ski slopes; car parking
in summer
Food breakfast, lunch, dinner
Price €€
Rooms 10 double and twin with
bath; all rooms have phone, TV,
hairdryer, wi-fi, some have balcony
Facilities restaurant Naskira, dining
room, bar; terrace
Credit cards AE, MC, V
Children accepted
Disabled access difficult
Pets accepted
Closed May, Oct to Nov
Proprietor Giorgio Carezzana

Il Capricorno
Mountain chalet

This typical wooden chalet has a fairy-
tale setting surrounded by pine trees
above the slopes of the busy ski resort of
Via Lattea and can only be reached by a
steep, winding dirt track. In summer you
can drive right up to the hotel, but in winter, you must park in town and be collected by snowmobile. Inside, it is as spick-
and-span and cosy as a chalet should be:
the snug rooms, brightened by fresh flowers, log fires and traditional wooden furniture. The dining room, beyond a tiny bar, is
especially cheerful with its burnished copper pots and kettles, neat pile of logs
beside the hearth and pretty blue-and-
white tablecloths. Naskira, the new restaurant, is open to the public and caters for
children. The ten spotless bedrooms and
bathrooms are named after zodiac signs.
They are furnished with hand-carved wood,
and there are balconies for a select few.

In winter you can ski down the hill from
the front door; in summer there are
mountain hikes that beckon in all directions. After a long day's skiing or walking,
this is the perfect place to return to. And
as more people are beginning to realize
this, you must book early.

Alagna

13021 Alagna, Piemonte

Tel 0163 922822
e-mail
info@hotelcristalloalagna.com
website
www.hotelcristalloalagna.com
Food breakfast, lunch, dinner
Prices €€€-€€€€ (half board)
Closed mid Apr to end Jun, Sep to
end Nov
Proprietor Simona De Simone

Hotel Cristallo
Mountain village hotel

An immaculate, up-to-date mountain village hotel (major recent investment), with a friendly welcome – with less than 20 rooms it's relatively small. Reception and the public sitting room and bar are essentially modern. Alpine architecture raises its head confidently in the attractive restaurant. The bedrooms are particularly impressive, with beautiful, subtle colour schemes and some older integral features and furnishings artfully preserved. On the lower ground floor there is a coolly minimalist indoor pool, gym area and sauna.

Alagna is part of the Monte Rosa ski domain and famed among hard-core skiers worldwide as one of the best places for off-piste skiing.

Breuil-Cervinia

11021 Breuil-Cervinia, Aosta

Tel 0166 948998
e-mail info@hotelhermitage.com
website www.hotelhermitage.com
Food breakfast, lunch, dinner
Price €€€€
Closed May to Jun, Sept to Nov
Proprietors Neyroz family

Hermitage
Mountain chalet

A recent revisit confirmed that this is an aristocrat among mountain hotels, in the best sense – the Neyroz family (third generation in place) don't think they have a right to be at the top, but reinvest and work hard to build on their assets.

Cervinia (2,050 m) is a wonderful place, but this is just too large for a full page. Most rooms have mesmerising views on to the Monte Cervino. Attentions to detail – beautifully designed corridors, a secluded garden with lovely Alpine 'folly' outbuildings – add up to a glossy but sincere operation.

If this place is within your budget, think about ditching French or Swiss skiing and come here. The snow falls early and can melt in May. Great contacts with a small ski school and good mountain guides.

Breuil-Cervinia

Les Neiges d'Antan
Mountain chalet

It is the warmth and generosity of the hands-on owners that make this hotel in the shadow of Monte Cervino (the Matterhorn) a great place. From the outside, you couldn't call the chalet beautiful, but the rustic interior is welcoming, and recent renovation has made staying here a more than comfortable experience: new features include a sauna and a cosy wood burning stove in the living room. Ludovico Bich is the *sommelier*: in addition to a carefully-chosen cellar, he oversees an impressive range of *grappa* in the snug wood-panelled and rough-stone bar. Visitors all say that it is excellent value for money.

Frazione Cret-Perrères, 11021 Breuil-Cervinia, Aosta

Tel 0166 948775
e-mail info@lesneigesdantan.it
website www.lesneigesdantan.it
Food breakfast, lunch, dinner
Price €€
Closed early May to mid-Jun, early Sep to mid-Oct
Proprietors Bich family

Castelrotto

Cavallino d'Oro
Town hotel

Records of this former coaching inn date back to 1326. Located on the central square of postcard-pretty Castelrotto, the hotel has a pleasant, professional and energetic host in Stefan Urthaler, whose family has been in charge for three generations. Parts are ancient and charming, particularly two of the dining rooms and the bar.

The hotel has been recently renovated: a modern fireplace has been added to the bar and there is now a garage for guest use as well as a lift and free wi-fi throughout the hotel. All the rooms and junior suites have Tyrolean furniture; some have four-poster beds and mountain views. The old wine cellars have been converted into a spa area, with a massage room, Finnish sauna, solarium and Roman steam bath.

Piazza Kraus, 39040 Castelrotto, Bolzano

Tel 0471 706337
e-mail cavallino@cavallino.it
website www.cavallino.it
Food breakfast, lunch, dinner
Price €€
Closed last 3 weeks Nov
Proprietor Stefan and Susanne Urthaler

Cogne

Hotel Bellevue & Spa
Mountain chalet

This hotel is aptly named, nestled in a meadow in the heart of a national park on the flat grassy floor of a valley dominated by Gran Paradiso and other peaks. The Bellevue has been owned and run by the same family, with tradition as the keynote, since it was built in the 1920s. The chalet is furnished with local artworks, antiques and *objets d'art*. Open fires blaze in every grate. Home-baked bread is served with the imaginative regional meals by a cheerful staff, who speak French and wear national costume. The new spa has two swimming pools, four saunas, two Turkish baths, salt and ice grottoes and a gym.

The comfortable bedrooms and suites have cosy sitting rooms and fireplaces. The three chalets are ideal for families.

Rue Grand Paradis 22, 11012 Cogne, Aosta

Tel 0165 74825
e-mail info@hotelbellevue.it
website www.hotelbellevue.it
Food breakfast, lunch, dinner
Price €€
Closed early Oct to early Dec
Proprietors Jeantet-Roullet family

Cortina d'Ampezzo

Menardi
Town hotel

This family-run hotel evolved from a coaching inn when its owners, the Menardi family, began hiring out horses. During the First World War, Luigi Menardi began to transform the rustic inn into a proper hotel. Today, the long white building has proliferated carved green wood balconies and tumbling geraniums, plus extra rooms and a separate annexe behind, but the Menardi family can still justifiably proclaim: 'same house, same family, same relaxed atmosphere'. Inside, antique pieces, painted religious statues and old work tools are mixed with local custom-made furnishings which look somewhat dated, but which are nonetheless comfortable. The atmosphere is one of traditional warmth and service is polished.

Via Majon 110, 32043 Cortina d'Ampezzo, Belluno

Tel 0436 2400
e-mail info@hotelmenardi.it
website www.hotelmenardi.it
Food breakfast, lunch, dinner
Price €€
Closed Oct to mid-Dec, Apr to mid-May
Proprietors Menardi family

Cortina d'Ampezzo

Piazza Roma 14, 32043 Cortina
d'Ampezzo

Tel 0436 4271
e-mail info@delaposte.it
website www.delaposte.it
Food breakfast, (lunch and dinner at
Posticino restaurant)
Prices €€-€€€€
Closed end Sep to mid-Dec; usually
after Easter to mid Jun
Proprietors Manaigo family

Hôtel de la Poste
Town hotel

You have to let this Cortina classic get under your skin – it will, which is why we include it in the guide despite its large size. First impressions are good – attractively coloured exterior. Second impressions are good too – loyal, characterful staff. Third impressions – of some rooms – are less so.

The Poste is a historic hotel – health and safety regulations mean huge sums have to be spent making it marginally safer (it's safe already) rather than redesigning. They have our sympathy and travellers should lend support by booking here. It has an honest heart and is reasonably priced. We especially like the timeless panelled bar, the well-sourced produce, the authentic Bellinis, and the smokey spaghetti carbonara, done better here than anywhere. Perfect ski base.

Corvara

Col Alt 105, 39033 Corvara

Tel 0471 831000
e-mail info@hotel-laperla.it
website www.hotel-laperla.it
Food breakfast, lunch dinner
Price €€€€€
Closed early Apr to mid-Jun
Proprietors Costa family

Hotel La Perla
Mountain hotel

This 'glorious family-run mountain hotel', says our local editor Nicky Swallow, is 'luxurious yet full of character'. The bedrooms are decorated in Tyrolean or Biedermeier style with wood-panelled walls, floors and ceilings. Each room looks out to either the peaks of the Dolomites or the quiet village of Corvara.

There is a maze of public rooms decorated with wood panelling: Michelin-starred restaurant La Stüa de Michil; two dining rooms; one bar; the wine cellar – Mahatma Wine; and the spa and relaxation area – Eghes Sanes. One dining room is made up of six eating areas, the tables decorated with red, yellow, green or blue linen – try the desserts. The *après ski* bar, L'Murin, can get busy at times, particularly in winter.

Madonna di Campiglio

Via Castelletto Inferiore 63, 38086
Madonna di Campiglio, Trentino

Tel 0465 441558
e-mail info@biohotelhermitage.it
website www.biohotelhermitage.it
Food breakfast, lunch, dinner
Price €€€
Closed Sep to Dec
Proprietors Maffei family

Bio-Hotel Hermitage
Mountain hotel

We were alerted to this modern 'bio' hotel (it was refurbished in 1999 using only natural materials such as solid wood floors and pure wool carpets, ecological water and electricity supply and so on) by an enthusiastic guest who praised everything, but most of all the relaxed 'at home' family atmosphere and the 'superb' food (home-made pumpkin pasta with black truffle, wild rabbit *alla cacciatore*, sweet chestnut mousse). Also: well equipped rooms ('fantastic mattresses'); a parkland setting; shuttle to the town centre and ski slopes; sun terrace; indoor pool; sauna. 'I'm going back', says a recent visitor, 'this time for the alpine flowers'.

Pinzolo

San Antonio di Mavignola 74, 38086
Madonna di Campiglio, Trento

Tel 0465 502758
e-mail info@masodoss.com
website www.masodoss.com
Food breakfast
Price €€ (minimum 1 week)
Closed spring and autumn
Proprietors Caola family

Chalet Maso Doss
Mountain chalet

Here's the real thing: a simple, heart-warming 17thC chalet in the Brenta Valley, set amidst the spectacular landscape of the Adamello-Dolomiti di Brenta National Park.

In winter you can explore on cross-country skis, in summer on mountain bikes provided by the chalet. On your return: wood panelling and simple furniture, check tablecloths and lace curtains, a warm fire, an excellent dinner, a Finnish sauna, and one of six cosy bedrooms with warm duvets and hand-embroidered sheets. The atmosphere is very much that of a welcoming private house.

Redagno di Sopra

39040 Redagno di Sopra, Bolzano

Tel 0471 887215
e-mail info@zirmerhof.com
website www.zirmerhof.com
Food breakfast, lunch, dinner
Price €€
Closed mid-Nov to Christmas Day,
early Jan to Apr
Proprietor Sepp Perwanger

Zirmerhof
Mountain hotel

Situated just outside the tiny hamlet of Redagno di Sopra, this 12thC *mas* has been in the Perwanger family since 1890. Views are of mountains, green pastures and forests – 'idyllic', a contented guest tells us.

The dim, low-ceilinged hall with its intricate wood carving immediately plunges you into the atmosphere of an old family home. There's a tiny library, a sitting-cum-breakfast room and a rustic bar with a grassy terrace. The large wood-panelled dining room is a fine setting in which to enjoy the local dishes and sophisticated wines on offer.

The comfortable bedrooms vary enormously in size, but all have traditional carved furniture and pretty fabrics; the largest rooms are on the top floor. For the energetic there's ice-skating, curling and skiing.

San Cassiano in Badia

Strada Micura de Ru 20, 1-39030
San Cassiano in Badia

Tel 0471 849500
e-mail info@rosalpina.it
website www.rosalpina.it
Food breakfast, lunch, dinner
Prices €€-€€€
Closed end Apr to mid-Jun, end
Sept to end Nov
Proprietors Pizzinini family

Rosa Alpina
Country villa

We tend to shy away from Relais and Chateaux branding, but this hotel has been in the Pizzinini family for three generations. Current owners, Paolo and his son Hugo, run it as if it were a small hotel catering to their guests' every whim. There are more than 50 bedrooms, making it too large for a full page, but care has been taken to furnish each in an individual style. Decoration throughout is rustic but chic, and furniture has been lovingly collected over the years – each room feels as though care has been taken over its decoration.

Breakfast is renowned, and simple food made with fresh, local ingredients is served in four restaurants, each offering something different. A range of facilities, including a luxurious spa, make this hotel worth a detour.

Sesto

Moso, 39030 Sesto, Bolzano

Tel 0474 710386
e-mail info@berghotel.com
website www.berghotel.com
Food breakfast, lunch, dinner
Price €€€
Closed Easter to mid-May, Oct to
Christmas
Proprietors Holzer family

Berghotel – Sexten
Mountain hotel and apartments

The little town of Sesto (or Sexten) is one of the prettiest in the region, and the surrounding area must be one of the most beautiful parts of the Dolomites. The Berghotel is a recently constructed chalet, with dark wood balconies overlooking classic Alpine scenery: a gentle valley dotted with chalets, a church spire in the foreground and, in the distance, the jagged peaks which are so characteristic of the area. In summer, there are walking trails; in winter you can ski. The comfortable, pine-furnished hotel is run with great hospitality and efficiency by the Holzer family. It has 45 bedrooms with white walls and modern wood fittings, or, for self-caterers, there is an apartment-house next door. Plus three swimming pools and an eight-sauna spa.

Siusi allo Sciliar

Ratzesweg 29, 39040 Seis am
Schlern

Tel 0471 706131
e-mail info@badratzes.it
website www.badratzes.it
Food breakfast, lunch, afternoon
tea, dinner
Price €€
Closed end Mar to end May, early
Oct to weekend before Christmas
Proprietors Scherlin family

Bad Ratzes
Mountain hotel

Situated in a clearing in an old forest where Hansel and Gretel would have felt at home, the hotel is large and modern, but the warmth and enthusiasm of the Scherlin family will put you immediately at ease. Inside, the decoration is traditional southern Tyrolean, with modern comforts. Public areas are extensive. Spotless bedrooms are spacious and all have balconies.

Food is important at Bad Ratzes: local dishes are carefully prepared and pasta is home-made. The breakfast buffet is generous, lunch is light, and evening meals include Italian and South Tyrolean specialities.

There's varied walking – guides Martina and Roman are on hand, or pick up a guidebook from reception (walking sticks and baby carriers also available). Free ski bus.

Ettal

Kaiser-Ludwig-Platz 18, 82488 Ettal

Tel 08822 3596
e-mail info@posthotel-ettal.de
website www.posthotel-ettal.de

Nearby scenic drive west along
D314 over mountains to Schloss
Linderhof (10 km).
Location centre of village, beside
monastery; free car parking
Food breakfast
Prices €-€€
Rooms 21; 3 single with shower, 18
double, 3 with bath, 15 with shower;
all rooms have TV, clock/radio,
hairdryer
Facilities breakfast room, restau-
rant, fitness room, steam room,
sauna, solarium, *Stube*; terrace, gar-
den
Credit cards MC, V
Children welcome
Disabled no special facilities
Pets accepted (extra charge)
Closed Nov to mid-Dec
Proprietors Fischer family

Posthotel Ettal
Village inn

Herr Fischer was appalled at the idea
that there might be telephones in his
guest rooms, 'Our guests come here to
relax'. Most are on holiday and Herr Fischer
offers them plenty of relaxation opportunities. The bedrooms ooze space and comfort, encouraging long lie-ins after a day in
the clear Ammergau mountain air. The modern bedroom decoration may be somewhat
ordinary, but half the rooms in this old
chalet have a balcony, and those in the new
wing at the back open on to a terrace. You
can contemplate Ettal's grand Benedictine
abbey church (famous for its ceiling paintings by the Baroque painter Zeiller) and the
surrounding mountains, from all of them.
There is a sauna, a steam room and a solarium to chill out in, a *Stube*, and, for sightseeing, Oberammergau and King Ludwig's
fairy-tale castles are an easy drive.

The Zur Post has close associations with
skiing, starting with the cross-country ski
route 50 m behind the hotel, and nearby
downhill skiing. Herr Fischer cooks for the
German Olympic ski team, so expect
breakfast to transform your energy levels.
But you may prefer to eat in your room
rather than endure the music that is sometimes piped into the dining rooms.

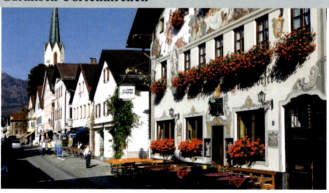

82467 Garmisch-Partenkirchen,
Ludwigstrasse 24

Tel 08821 9270
e-mail info@gasthof-fraundorfer.de
website www.gasthof-fraundorfer.de

Nearby Partnachklamm gorges (2
km).
Location Partenkirchen centre close
to church; 5 km from end autobahn
A95/E533; free car parking
Food breakfast, lunch, dinner
Prices €-€€
Rooms 25; 19 double, 3 single, 3
suites, all with shower; all rooms
have phone, TV, radio; some have
hairdryer, safe; 5 apartments, 1 with
bath, 4 with shower
Facilities breakfast room,
restaurant, sauna, steam room;
terrace, garden with sandpit
Credit cards MC, V
Children welcome
Disabled some special facilities
Pets accepted (extra charge)
Closed 3 weeks Nov; restaurant
only, Tue
Proprietor Barbara Fraundorfer

Gasthof Fraundorfer
Chalet hotel and apartments

Book here for the full Bavarian experience. We love this eccentric chalet
hotel, its white façade cheerfully fes-
tooned, Bayerischer style, with colourful
murals and summer window boxes. It is
easy to spot in Partenkirchen's old centre.

The Bavarian Fraundorfer family have
run this hostelry for generations and love
to display their traditions. Lederhosen and
dirndl skirts are *de rigueur* among the
entertainers at the jolly Bavarian evenings,
when accordion music, yodelling and folk-
dancing are part of the entertainment. The
restaurant is appropriately wood-panelled
and clutter with knick-knacks; the food is
richly traditional and served with regional
beers. The humour extends to the beds,
some carved to resemble cars and ships,
others with carved posts and canopies or
white curtains, perfect for honeymoons.

The whole extended family runs this
hotel, making it an ideal environment for
the families, many from Italy and America,
who book in August. There are family
apartments in an annexe, high chairs, a
children's menu, toys to play with in the
restaurant, and a sandpit in the garden.
And since the Fraundorfer father has
retired to a wheelchair, there are special
facilities for guests with restricted mobility
in Gästhaus Barbara, just behind the chalet.

Maierhöfen bei Isny

Schanz 2, 88167 Maierhöfen bei Isny

Tel 07562 975510
e-mail info@landhotel-zur-grenze.de
website www.landhotel-zur-grenze.de

Nearby Paradies mountain view-
point near Obserstaufen (30 km).
Location on hill outside Maierhöfen
village; autobahn A96/E54 (exit
Leutkirch Süd/Isny) 30 min; garage
Food breakfast, lunch, dinner,
snacks
Prices €-€€
Rooms 14; 9 double, 5 single, all
with bath or shower; all rooms have
phone, satellite TV, hairdryer, wi-fi,
some have balcony
Facilities sitting room, restaurant
with bar, sauna; terraces, garden
Credit cards MC, V
Children welcome
Disabled not suitable
Pets accepted (extra charge)
Closed never; restaurant only, Mon
Proprietors Georg and Hannelore
Rainer

Zur Grenze
Country hotel

This holiday chalet in the Allgäu marks
the beginning of a ski run from mid-
November when the first snows usually
fall. After a day in the snow, this long, low
chalet with wood-lined interior and kindly
family atmosphere is a welcoming shelter.

The restaurant benefits from Georg
Rainer's award-winning cuisine, which is
highly rated all over Germany. There is a
warm tiled stove to sit in front of while
you fuel up on his baked *Ziegenkästascherl*
(goat's cheese pasties), or veal steak with
Rahmsteinpilzen (mushroom cream sauce),
which taste best when accompanied by
wines from a well-stocked list. On Saturday
evenings the restaurant serves a candle-lit
three- to five-course dinner.

In winter, you can see the snow etched
with cross-country ski routes from the
south-facing terrace. In spring, tables are
set on the west-facing terrace and guests
enjoy the setting sun for hours in the
evenings, Maierhöfen's farmlands turn green
and sunlight streams into the rustic bedrooms, which are decorated in wood and
red patterned upholstry. The ones with
balconies face wooded hills on the west
and Alpine foothills on the east. Summer
here is no excuse for inactivity. The rolling
terrain is right for hiking and cycling –
routes pass right by the hotel – and you
can swim in a nearby lake.

Frasdorf

Nussbaumstr 6, Frasdorf, 83112

Tel 08052 4071
e-mail info@karneronline.de
website www.karneronline.de
Food breakfast, lunch, dinner
Prices €€-€€€
Closed never
Proprietors Christl and Gunter Karner

Karner Hotel
Country hotel

Only a stone's throw from the motorway to Austria, this is a popular weekend retreat for high-powered city types who want to get away from it all – but not too far away. The Karner is not your run of the mill Alpine chalet – the old whitewash exterior at the front of the hotel is now covered by wood panelling, but inside, it is still impressive. The dining room is stylish, with old panelling and simple, beautifully made curtains. Bedrooms have rustic furniture, though the good-quality rugs have been replaced with beige or red carpet.

The food certainly draws the crowds – especially on a sunny afternoon in high season, when the lovely terrace can be filled to bursting. A pleasant base for walkers who enjoy creature comforts.

Garmisch-Partenkirchen

Höllentalstrasse 48, 82467 Garmisch-Partenkirchen

Tel 08821 9290
e-mail info@staudacherhof.de
website www.staudacherhof.de
Food breakfast, lunch, dinner
Prices €-€€
Closed never
Proprietors Staudacher family

Staudacherhof
Chalet hotel

This hotel has been in the same family for more than 500 years, but the Staudachers keep it up-to-date. When Peter Staudacher and his wife took over the family business, they expanded the spa (whirlpool, swimming pools and five saunas, including one in the garden). They describe their hotel as 'true Staudacher style, from wellness and romance to natural cuisine.'

Public rooms are decorated with natural stone and woods; bedrooms have red carpets and plain walls. In the restaurant, chef Peter Dazert satisfies all tastes and there are vegetarian and low fat healthy-eating menus. There's plenty to do outside; mountain exercise programs; golf courses; cycling and hiking in summer; skiing (both piste and cross-country) and snowboarding in winter.

Index – hotel names

In this index, hotels are arranged in order of the first distinctive part of their name; other parts of the name are also given, except that very common prefixes such as 'Hotel', 'Gasthof', 'Landhaus', and 'Pension' are omitted. More descriptive words such as 'Schlosshotel', 'Seehof' and 'Villa' are included.

Index – hotel names

Index – hotel names

Index – hotel names

Index – hotel names

Index – hotel names

In this index, hotels are arranged in order of the names of the cities, towns or villages they are in or near. Hotels located in a very small village may be indexed under a larger place nearby. An index by hotel name precedes this one.

Index – hotel locations

Index – hotel locations

Index – hotel locations

Index – hotel locations

Index – hotel locations